Source Magic

"*Source Magic* heralds what legions of countercultural readers have known (and sometimes jealously guarded) for years: Carl Abrahamsson is not only among today's leading occult writers and artists but is, in fact, one of this generation's most vital public intellectuals. From *The Prisoner* to Ezra Pound, no single descriptor captures how Carl has pried apart the floorboards of postmodernity—and done so as few are able: with laser-like precision, joie de vivre, and the literary power of an exploding sun. Carl is our magical Moses hoisting a fiery serpent in the cultural wilderness. I will be returning to *Source Magic* for a lifetime."

MITCH HOROWITZ, PEN AWARD–WINNING AUTHOR OF
OCCULT AMERICA AND *UNCERTAIN PLACES*

"Carl Abrahamsson is a rare voice of lucidity in the complex world of magic. He explains the most profound and esoteric knowledge in a way that just keeps the pages turning and the ideas flowing. Reading Abrahamsson is like starting a fire deep within the imagination that continues to warm the spirit long after reading."

KENDELL GEERS, SOUTH AFRICAN ARTIST

"Carl's work always brings you to the edge of reality, asking you to peer through the veil and question if said reality even exists. In *Source Magic,* Carl stretches this further, inviting one to view life as a study in magic, in causal effect, in shapeshifting. By embracing life as a vessel for occulture and magico-anthropology and using this as his framework for his studies and explorations, Carl guides a new generation of thinkers into a future that asks *what if* and gets even more strange, surreal, beautiful, and mystical than one can dream. This book will change what you thought you knew about the possibilities of life and spirituality."

GABRIELA HERSTIK, AUTHOR OF
INNER WITCH: A MODERN GUIDE TO THE ANCIENT CRAFT
AND *SACRED SEX: THE MAGICK AND
PATH OF THE DIVINE EROTIC*

Source Magic

THE ORIGIN OF
ART, SCIENCE, AND CULTURE

Carl Abrahamsson

Park Street Press
Rochester, Vermont

Park Street Press
One Park Street
Rochester, Vermont 05767
www.ParkStPress.com

SUSTAINABLE Certified Sourcing
FORESTRY
INITIATIVE www.sfiprogram.org
SFI-00854

Text stock is SFI certified

Park Street Press is a division of Inner Traditions International

Cataloging-in-Publication Data for this title is available from the Library of Congress

ISBN 978-1-64411-501-5 (print)
ISBN 978-1-64411-502-2 (ebook)

Printed and bound in The United States by Lake Book Manufacturing, LLC
The text stock is SFI certified. The Sustainable Forestry Initiative® program
promotes sustainable forest management.

10 9 8 7 6 5 4 3 2 1
Text design and layout by Kenleigh Manseau
This book was typeset in Garamond Premier Pro with Nexa and Trajan Sans Pro
used as the display typeface.

To send correspondence to the author of this book, mail a first-class letter to the
author c/o Inner Traditions • Bear & Company, One Park Street, Rochester, VT
05767, and we will forward the communication, or contact the author directly at
www.carlabrahamsson.com.

For Vanessa, with love.

Contents

☼

Acknowledgments

I would like to thank the following individuals for being part of this particular project in some way or another: Nicholaj de Mattos Frisvold, Hans-Peter Söder, Michael and Annabel Moynihan, Morgan Russell, Wilhelmina von Auersperg von Keyserling, Angela Edwards, Jarrett Earnest, OTO Österreich, Rudolf Berger of the Thoth Hermes Academy, Erik Davis, Daniel Schulke, Laetitia Barbier and Joanna Ebenstein of Morbid Anatomy, Frank Rynne, the Master Musicians of Joujouka, Blanche Barton, the #psychartcult cabal, Ugo Dossi, Mary Pound and Siegfried de Rachewiltz, the Society of Sentience, Iris, Matthew Samways, Flesh Prison Records, Genesis and Genesse and Caresse P-Orridge, Ryan Martin, Graham Hancock, Gabriel McCaughry, Henrik Møll, Michael Matton, Guido Zeccola, Jon Graham and the Inner Traditions team, Sofia Lindström-Abrahamsson, and Vanessa Sinclair, to whom this book is lovingly dedicated.

Foreword

Nicholaj de Mattos Frisvold

In *Occulture: The Unseen Forces That Drive Culture Forward* (2018) Carl Abrahamsson took the stance of an involved observer analyzing the world, culture, and magic through binoculars of a somewhat Reichian diffraction. In this new volume Abrahamsson has moved to the center of events and invites the reader to delve into the magic of being his passenger. This sentiment is largely supported by several of the articles and essays in this collection that are both personal and intimate, whether they are contemplations on the temporality of life itself or the influence that departed magicians and artists hold on our contemporary world. At the root of all of these articles and essays we find the importance of magic and the persistent admonition of rooting our experience of the world in a magical and shamanic awareness, yet the backdrop here is drawn up by death.

The articles "Into a Time and Space of Wordship" (honoring the memory of Genesis P-Orridge) and the meditative piece "Memento Mori Forever" are personal musings on the temporality of life, both as symbol and meaning as it crawls toward its inevitable death. Death, apocalypse, corruption, and renewal is the theme of the chapter entitled "Lux Per Nox," where the importance of destruction for renewal signified by Ragnarok is presented as something necessary and wonderful. These articles lead to further contemplations on death through Vesalius's *Anatomy,* and the art of Albrecht Dürer and Hans Holbein, in a refrain of "Remember that you will die! Remember to live!"

This tangent, touching on the temporality of our existence, doesn't stop there. Carl's essay recounting a trip to the home of the German philosopher Ernst Jünger becomes a meditation on timelessness; about the ghostly interspaces where the past and the present merge and meet. It is in this realm of existential reverence that Abrahamsson develops the main ideas of his "magico-anthropology," which he describes in the following way:

> The basis of human behavior stems from shamanism. It's inherent in the advanced human mind to constantly pose self-reflective questions. It is only natural that these then spill over and take on proxy forms (the tribal shaman, priest, magician, healer, et al.). But the need to ask existential questions is a unique trait of all human individuals, and this is very much the key to the constant development of human intelligence . . . But it is only by reappraising and reappreciating magic as the core activity/mind frame of human existence that we can fully change things in a more life-affirming and life-enhancing way.

In the chapter "The Imaginary Is a Real Thing" Abrahamsson stresses the importance of shamanism as the fountainhead of human knowledge, and in this he speaks of the importance of acting upon life in its totality; both its inner and outer planes as much as the visible and invisible dimensions. In this he echoes a significant passage in Thee Temple ov Psychick Youth's (TOPY) main text *Thee Grey Book:* "As things are, so must they change. So we are all socially and biologically conditioned to put away our fear ov death yet in a real paradox we becoum too efficiently oblivious to this fear in our conscious life. Thee Temple tries to reconcile all our consciousness. To do this embraces thee knowledge ov our own inevitable death with courage and uses it to justify action and thee proper use ov time."[1]

In this work, for Abrahamsson, the proper use of time appears to have become a search for spiritual peace and a sense of harmony and completeness in all dimensions of the human being. In several of these essays we can find a certain frustration with mankind's somnambulist state, and also a call to open our eyes in the midst of magic precipices (to paraphrase French poet Louis Aragon). Our eyes are opened by applying a shamanic stance to our experience of the world, and this also entails viewing the work of people who inspired us from a magical point of view. This allows the subtle streams that shape reality to become *occulture*. Occulture is that fascinating realm of hidden or obscure building blocks that are beneath society and within subcultures that are guarded in mysterious ways, awaiting greater integration in the larger societal web. For this to happen on an individual level, we need to have antennae to detect waves and pulses and tendencies, seeing what patterns in the past might have caused the contemporary designs and forms we try to make sense of today. In this context Abrahamsson brings up Ezra Pound, and in particular his epos *Cantos:* a spiritual exercise where Pound, over the course of five decades, built a magical and poetical model of his consciousness. This model exemplifies the potential grandeur of the work of perception undertaken by a magician or an artist in such a way that the artist *becomes* magic and the magician *becomes* the artist.

The artist-magician is exemplified by adopting a shamanic stance to one's self and the world, as exemplified by people like Brion Gysin, André Breton, Genesis P-Orridge, William S. Burroughs, Ornette Coleman, Pierre Molinier, and many others who managed to "belong to themselves" in such unique and inspiring ways that it is possible to see the shape of legacy and succession taking form long after they left their earthly shell. To belong to yourself, to become a conscient and self-aware individual, is crucial for establishing the shamanic state of the artist-magician, as Abrahamsson writes in "The Magic of Individuation."

"It's important to be self-critical as well as critical. How else can we progress? If a ritual or a system doesn't bring real, tangible insights about yourself, then they are merely pleasant psychodrama, at most . . . Eventually, it's as important to acquire your own tools and language in magic, as it is within the individuation process. You are who you are, and that's who you should be—once you have found that out. And your magic is exactly what you make of it—once you have found that out."

At the heart of this collection, we find a deep concern with how we can develop the shamanic sensibility that generates a sound and truthful artist-magician. This pursuit finds some sort of apex in the chapter titled "Embracing Magical Realism." Here Abrahamsson suggests magical realism as a method, a way of approaching the world and the human existence. The magical realism of Marquez, Aragon, Borges, and others does owe great parts of its inspiration to the Dadaist and surrealist movement that surged during the upheavals and transformations in Europe during World War I. It was the creative force beneath the paradoxes and absurdities taking place on a linear factual line; very much its own occulture taking gradual form into becoming socially accepted and integrated through the art of Max Ernst and Salvador Dalí. Abrahamsson writes about this as follows: "Magical Realism is a discernible bridge between the two extreme realities that our specific culture consists of: Fact and Fiction, or, if we allow us some logically speculative slack, Truth and Un-Truth . . . We can see then that Magical Realism is not merely a literary technique or tradition: it is very much an attitude to life itself. Enhance a little, and experience a lot!"

Using magical realism as an approach to life, as a method of living life as an artist-magician, will at some point become a shamanic exercise in itself as it will open up our minds for the great paradoxes. In this we realize that it is in-between all possibilities we can see our self reflected in all things and realize the truth of who we are and how we should act upon the world so we can finally belong to our self. This is the great achievement in this collection of articles and essays—showing a way of becoming our magical self in a world of paradox, fragmentation, memory, death, beauty, and nature—and showing how necessary this chaotic world is for us to generate meaning and a sense of self. This is a meaning forged in the subtle force resounding quietly beneath the bouquet of articles and essays in this collection . . . "Remember that you will die! Remember to live!"

NICHOLAJ DE MATTOS FRISVOLD

NICHOLAJ DE MATTOS FRISVOLD studied and graduated in the fields of psychology, anthropology/science of religion, and cinema studies at the University of Oslo, and the Norwegian University of Science and Technology (NTNU), in Trondheim, Norway. In addition to a long academic career, he has traveled extensively in pursuit of personal and academic knowledge of African- and Afro-derived cults and forms of spirituality as well as traditional forms of spirituality on a more global scale. He is a native of Norway who migrated in 2003 to Brazil, where he still lives. Frisvold is the author of numerous acclaimed books discussing magical and spiritual traditions of the world such as *Arts of the Night* (Chadezoad Publishing, 2008), *Invisible Fire: Inner Dimensions of Western Gnostic and Theurgic Tradition* (Capall Bann, 2010), *Palo Mayombe* (Scarlet Imprint, 2010), *Pomba Gira* (Scarlet Imprint, 2011), *Exu* (Scarlet Imprint, 2012), *Ifá: A Forest of Mystery* (Scarlet Imprint, 2016), *Trollrun* (Hadean Press, 2021), and *The Canticles of Lilith* (Troy Books, 2011).

PREFACE
Come Join the Garden Party!

When contemplating nature, whether in great things or small, I have constantly asked the question: is it the object which is here declaring itself, or is it you yourself?

JOHANN WOLFGANG VON GOETHE,
MAXIMS AND REFLECTIONS

Looking through these essays and lectures from the most recent years, I find themes and recurring ideas that I'm usually not consciously aware of on a day-to-day basis. But for some reason or other they always seem to press on until they're duly formulated. That makes me happy.

There's the general occulture, there's the ever-beloved magico-anthropology (and its ties to a "protoshamanism"), and there's also a fairly recent focus on the individuation process itself. Of course I'm aware of these, my fascinations, but it has undoubtedly been interesting to see how they overflow and merge with each other when tossed into the same cauldron.

It all seems to be consistent with what it is I'm actually eventually writing about, which is that there's a pressing need for magic to reemerge. A huge chunk of that mystery lies in the human individuation process itself—as well as an integration of shamanic consciousness in some form or other.

All of that inevitably creates an accessible occulture, which in turn awakens and morphs all of the previous instigations . . . A wonderful synergetic and symbiotic force field emerges; a field, I would argue (and often do), that is quintessentially necessary for human survival. So it seems to me, anyway.

My outlook or perspective is not that of an academic; nor is it entirely fanciful, fabulating, and fictional. I guess my own life experience so far, and my trusting my own intuition enough when it comes to choosing directions in life, has accumulated enough malleable nodes of wide-eyed amazement to secure a constant influx of literally wonderfull stimuli. It could be an expedition to Tibet, editing a new issue of *The Fenris Wolf,* or realizing that even a trashy Mondo film can contain more substantial signal than what first meets the eye . . . Every little experience matters in my big picture, and everywhere I look I see an occulture that is totally necessary for the times we're in. It's high time to look back, forward, upward, downward; to reevaluate what has been discarded, mocked, tossed out, ostracized, perhaps even criminalized, and also to seek this information and these frames of reference in new (sorry, that should be: *timeless*) ways.

Most of what we desperately seek on existential levels we already have within us. It's very easy to access, too. The seeds are in place within us, in our own nature. These we should nurture and refine as we see fit and are able to, until they bloom and generate new seeds anew. The dominant cultures in most parts of the world have put a lid on this kind of human ingenuity and freedom for a long, long time.

A great way to begin your own individuation process is of course simply to ask: "Why are they still doing that?" What could be so threatening to the rigid, complacent status quo about you making choices that are yours and yours alone?

Please don't expect an answer from me because I'm quite busy with my own process! However, I have successfully pushed on so far (at least according to myself), and find it much easier to navigate as time goes by. Method? Begin with the toughest nuts, and then everything will gradually run more smoothly. Honestly, I do think that looking at culture as such helps a lot in this nutcracking. Sometimes we don't really need complex models or academic abstractions to see what makes us humans function. What's your position in life? What's good and bad? Who makes you feel good? Bad? If you consistently stick with the negative nodes, you can only really blame yourself for not feeling great.

To a certain extent we are inspired not only by the real live human beings around us, but to an increasing degree by the culture we exist in—as in news, blogs, podcasts, movies, TV, books, music, sports, and so on. But . . . when did you last *seriously, consciously* curate your cultural input? Do you see it as equal in importance to food and nutrition?

You should.

In my life, all along I have actively immersed myself in materials and input that I know will bring the inspiration I need to continue exploring myself. These small choices of stratification and preference each and every day have helped me become a person I'm very happy to be. I get depressed when I see how passively most of the world seems to swallow whatever is given—whether in fiction, politics, relationships, or technology itself. There is really no need for such a subservient attitude. Consciously making small choices that at first may seem banal could in fact be life-changing . . . Don't underestimate who you really are!

I am someone who thinks and writes about such things, and it makes me supremely happy that a lot of other people find my work interesting, too. This work includes anthologies of essays and lectures like the one you're now holding in your hands—or the previous ones: *Reasonances* (2014) and *Occulture* (2018). There is also *The Devil's Footprint* (2020), or my documentary films about Genesis P-Orridge, Kenneth Anger, and Anton LaVey. Regardless, for me the adventure is always the same: gathering up illuminated pebbles and plants for my own garden of delights. And to this garden you're always welcome, provided you are a genuine and committed fellow gardener (of whatever kind!). Whether you bring exotic seed from far away or simply your own manure, it will all find its place somewhere!

So I say, "Welcome, and let's begin!"

1
Occulture and Beyond

Back in 2016 I was amassing an increasing number of essays and lectures of an occultural nature, and a friend remarked I was becoming like the "Umberto Eco of the underground" in my eclectic approaches. This made me happy and even more inspired to carry on, as I had always appreciated (and still do) Eco's open-mindedness and curiosity a great deal. And his concept of "Librido" is nothing but an expression of book-loving genius! In the true Librido spirit, I regard everything I write to be chapters of a book yet to exist rather than whatever it may appear to be in the moment.

Synchronicity or not, at about this same time I was offered the opportunity to assemble the chapters of the period into a proper book, and this is what eventually became *Occulture: The Unseen Forces That Drive Culture Forward* (Park Street Press, 2018). Not only did it give me a chance to look back at the most recent years' lectures and essays, it also presented a unique opportunity to (re)evaluate my own thinking about this most fascinating subject. And not forgetting, this at a time when the very concept of occulture seems to be expanding quaquaversally all over the world: in academia, major exhibitions, and popular culture. I was wholly immersed in all things occultural, inside my own sphere and outside of it, and now I could finally put it all together in a book.

"Occulture and Beyond" was originally written for Graham Hancock's website, coinciding with a conversation we had on his podcast, 2018.

I quickly found some red threads or unexpected consistencies. I had written about historical phenomena and people but also allowed myself the creative slack to speculate under the umbrella of something that could be called "magical philosophy." I realized that this was very much my background, a formulation of my own identity if you will. I looked at people like Aleister Crowley, Rudolf Steiner, Carl Jung—and even unexpected people like the American author Paul Bowles. I merged that historical perspective with one of looking at questions like, "Why are people attracted to phenomena like magic and occultism?" And "Is there more than meets the merely historical eye to these phenomena?" Well, there certainly is, because whatever humans do there is a magical thought or desire that drives it forward.

What happened then was a result of decades' worth of pondering and thinking. I realized that my youthful creation of the term *magico-anthropology* (in the early 1990s) contained much more than youthful and zestful hubris. Magico-anthropology actually contains everything! Putting the book *Occulture* together made me see that all of human history can—and perhaps even should—be looked at through magico-anthropological goggles. Without them only fragments or facets can be seen. Without a full understanding of the magical perspective, one can only scrape the surface of *anything* in human culture. To actively negate or distance oneself from it is to consciously not see the big picture.

Regardless if we choose the natural sciences, arts and letters, or any other aspect of human endeavor, the creative spark always stems from a magical place. Even the fairly recent phenomenon of "empiricism" is rooted in creative speculation and desire. That's one piece of this fascinating puzzle: wherever we look, we see a distinctly metaphysical origin. Chemistry has roots in alchemy; astronomy in astrology; clinical medicine in herbal, "natural" medicine; theater in ritual; art in talismanic manufacture; writing in spell work; psychology in healing; religion in magic; and so on and so forth. This realization made me think that perhaps one should subordinate all these disciplines (perhaps even *all* academic disciplines) under the banner of magico-anthropology.

Whatever we do in life has motivations that are usually far deeper than the expressed, rational version. The further in ourselves we backtrack, the more clearly we see that there are deep-rooted issues such as "survival" and "power" at hand. The instinctual morphs into the intuitive, which in turn morphs into the rational. It is on these same deep-rooted, instinctual levels that the "magic" exists. I choose to put the word in quotation marks but not to denigrate or diminish its value—quite the contrary. The fact is that it's a phenomenon so ingrained in the human psyche that our contemporary, colloquial use of the term (so often imbued with banality or even ridicule) simply can't do it justice. When we talk about magic today, people associate it freely with fairy tales and movie franchises, or even the stage variants. "Mentalism" sounds like a disease but is just essentially a clever appropriation and development of the rabbit in the hat. Magic proper lies much deeper than that.

Magic is a perceptive mind frame, a multifaceted filtering of information, and an expressed, intuitive will churned through an optimized and quite often aestheticized understanding of the importance of the irrational, emotional psyche. That magic is so dear to all human individuals has to do with the fact that just like breathing and eating, this mind frame is essential in the true sense of the word; it is needed for survival.

What do we need for survival? On a strictly individual level we need to satisfy our biological needs. But we also need to temper the panic of handling the threatening chaos outside of our corporeal sphere. This requires rational action but also constantly an evaluation based on both sensual and mental impressions.

On a group level it's basically the same but with an endlessly fascinating factor added: group dynamics. We absolutely realize that we can survive better together but one's own power within this dynamic or structure is even more important than the group one. From this perspective we have not evolved far at all since the early cave days. The king of the hill rules supreme and gets the foxiest ladies. That is, until there's a new king! All of the *dramatis personae*—the king, the ladies, and the new king—use aspects of magic to enforce whatever is best for them. Staged manipulation, sensuality, sexuality, and violence are just blunt euphemisms for ritual, perception, seduction, and catharsis. Or vice versa. At the same time, the players integrate an active use of intuition and reliance on "cosmic proxies" (such as calling on gods, forces, spirits, ancestors, et al.). Whether it's reflected from fire on a cave wall filled with primordial paintings, or a steady flow of social media posts on a "smart" phone, the messages all convey the same thing: the struggle to be in the best position for one's own survival and, in extension, for those one sides with (usually the ones who help one survive).

The primordial dog-eat-dog scenarios didn't really get any better when humans banded together, got the agricultural train rolling, and created BIG religions to alleviate the daily grind by simplified, moral(istic) proxy. In fact, that distancing from the uniquely individual or tribal perspective (which some would call "gnostic") may have been very detrimental to holistic health. This is because one should never assume that those who *claim* good *are* good. They are as involved in their own magical thinking and power dynamics as you are, or wish to be. That this proxy power was developed parallel to feudalism and its integration of serfdom is not a random occurrence.

The occultural waves that are splashing on our impoverished shores these days do so because we need them. These important reminders of deeper layers within ourselves, preferably untainted by religious layers of control, are necessary for us to reevaluate what's going on. Did someone miss that the planet we're inhabiting is in dire straits? We could fix so many of its life-threatening problems, but that won't happen with further distancing from the primordial appreciation of life. We need an active reintegration of that deeper understanding that we are all connected. Holistic bliss. An empirical scientist can claim that it's beneficial to breathe on a plant because it gets stimulated by our carbon dioxide, and through the overall process of photosynthesis gives us oxygen back. A magical scientist would go further (and often does) and say that it's not just the breath but also what's being said that makes the plant say something back. Magico-anthropology always takes a deeper look at any facet of human life and culture, and it's in that depth that we find the magic we need now more than ever.

On a recent trip to Egypt many of these perspectives literally came alive for me. While traveling down/up the Nile and seeing all the beautiful temples and sites (some of which have survived for five thousand years!), I was struck (again) by the need for magico-anthropological filters. The Egyptian pharaonic culture was one steeped in magical sensibilities, credibilities, and ample abilities. The reason we know this is because of the occultural enlargement of the historical scenario. The pharaonic culture would not have been available for us to study and be inspired by had its amazing, creative prescience (and, yes, pre-science too) not constructed so many magnificent buildings and artworks. The Egyptian magic still affects us—simply because there's something there to reflect it.

The ancient Egyptian system allowed the pharaohs to become godlike travelers in between life and death. That is, until they were taken out of their sleeping mummified beauty scenarios and put on display in museums. The curses that originally protected them had an effect on those who literally unearthed the sleepers. Whether humorously and disrespecting or not, the curses are real enough to spawn an endless array of bad movies and other cheap fictional thrills. However, the pharaonic culture undoubtedly lives on because it was a genuine culture, and a very well-made one, too.

The same could be said for many sites and buildings even within the spiritually more impoverished monotheistic religions. Beautiful cathedrals and mosques over a thousand years old still radiate human ingenuity and inspiration, and definitely with an occultural sensibility. But the present-day representatives of these faiths would never accept such an analysis or association although it's the easiest thing to fathom. They are too immersed in their earthly power to go beyond any mechanical, physical limits. Their ancestors understood considerably more though, when they were erecting these edifices. They were aware and, to an extent, also respectful of previous powers. Holy sites were very holy for the local people, and for the new imposed symbols to become holy too, they needed to be placed literally on top of the previous and pagan ones.

This ultramagical phenomenon of "constructive desecration" was also very clear to see in Egypt. In many temples and tombs, early Coptic

Christians had sought refuge from an assortment of enemies. But they just couldn't remain grateful and respectful of the magical surroundings that kept them safe and alive. These early Christians had to ritually desecrate these places with graffiti and carvings of primitive crosses. Today some Copts are trying to pay penance by integrating Egyptian wisdom and symbolism in their monastic life and works (such as the interesting and totally magico-anthropologically sensitive Bishop Thomas at the Anafora Monastery, just outside of Cairo). Today, as if by some strange twist of karmic fate (or pharaonic curse), the Copts are more persecuted in Egypt than ever—although by Muslims, not by people of the old Egyptian religion. What goes around comes around in whatever shape, I guess.

What I'm saying is that not even the major religions can eradicate the individual's need to relate to the world magically. "Magical thinking" is usually looked upon as being something negative, but on a deeper level everyone knows that each empirical or tangible success stems from the same source or sphere as the child playing. The components of this are the inner spheres of fantasy and desire; of empathy and imagination; of individual will and creativity. How we actually deal with the findings of those processes is what constitutes our individual identities in life. When we are aware of what we desire beyond the most primordial state of yearning, and apply our own creativity (no matter how primitive it may be), together with a formulated will, we have a timeless formula for human greatness and success.

This brings us back to my *Occulture* book. I realize that perhaps it's not just a smart overview of things and people past, albeit inspiring, with some attempts at philosophy thrown in between the lines. It may actually be my own desperate attempt to make people realize that it's time to wake up to a scenario that can no longer be avoided by primitive escapisms. The situation needs to be addressed by looking at the past. We need to question why some cultures and attitudes manage to live on while others are as fickle and fated to be forgotten as a tweet from last week. There are distinct keys to survival. One is magic in and of itself and the other is its integration in culture. Hence "occulture." Hence "magico-anthropology."

That said, I wish us all the best of luck.

2
We're on the Road to Somewhere

The greatest thing in the world is to know how to belong to oneself.

MICHEL DE MONTAIGNE, "OF SOLITUDE"

In the summer of 2009 I decided to go on a pilgrimage, together with friends who temporarily lived in Vienna. We all wanted to enjoy a short vacation in the Tyrolean region, and our main object of pilgrimage was the home of German author Ernst Jünger (1895–1998).

From Vienna we drove a few hours westward, sometimes hugging the scenic Donau. The cultivated slopes and landscapes were overflowing with vitality, beauty, and produce, including peaches—a real treat in the Tyrolean heat!

At St. Koloman we trekked by foot up to the lake Seewald See—an almost unbelievably beautiful scenery with mountains, valleys, rolling hills, forests, meadows, grazing cows (complete with cowbells echoing in the distance), barking dogs, twittering birds, and waving people. And then . . . the lake itself—a pastoral paradise pool. Swimming in that ice-cold water was refreshing to say the least.

Moving on at a leisurely pace we traveled through Hallein, once the home of the founder of the German fraternity Ordo Templi Orientis (OTO), Karl Kellner. Then we continued onward toward Salzburg, a town overflowing with history. Specifically, we enthusiastically wanted to see protomagician and (al)chemist Paracelsus's cemetery, St. Sebastian. Although he was so infused with God-fearing (or should that be "church-fearing"?) language, no one can deny the radical intersectional power he wielded. Steady and strong at the crossroads of religion, the natural sciences, alchemy, magic, and medicine, Paracelsus formulated a zeitgeist increasingly innovative and open-minded, and in defiance of blind religious authority.

Always returning to nature itself—and our personal interaction with nature—as the fundament of *any* scientific understanding, Paracelsus was, in quite a few ways, a source of German thought and art for many centuries. Perhaps he is even still a vital and influential force for lingering esoteric romantics? Quoting Paracelsus, "The magus can transfer many meadows of heaven into a small pebble which we call *gamaheu, imago,* or character. For these are boxes in which the magus keeps sidereal forces and virtues. Just as the physician can give his remedy to a patient and cure his disease, so the magus can transfer such virtues to man, after he has extracted them from the stars."[1]

Our next goal for that day was the village of Matrei am Brenner and its castle: Schloss Auersperg. We arrived in the late afternoon, driving up serpentine dirt roads until we reached our destination.

My friends knew the old princess still in residence, Wilhelmina "Willie" von Auersperg von Keyserling (1921–2010), and she greeted us with generosity and hospitality. For me our visit with her wasn't merely something royally exotic. Together with her husband, Arnold, Count von Keyserling (1922–2005), Willie had brought Indian philosophy, yoga, and shamanic awareness to Europe from the early 1960s onward. Also, Arnold's father had been the prominent philosopher Hermann, Count von Keyserling (1880–1946), whose travel stories and philosophical ruminations I greatly enjoyed in my youth. When the Bolsheviks stole the Keyserling estate in Livonia (current Estonia), Hermann was forced to build a new life in Darmstadt, Germany. Here he developed the Gesellschaft für Freie Philosophie (Society for Free Philosophy), later known as the School of Wisdom. After Hermann's death, this organization was kept up by Arnold and Willie, who infused it all with a strong dose of teachings from Gurdjieff, who was a friend of theirs.

Willie was eighty-eight years old at the time of our visit, and quite infirm. Frail and petite, she had soft, finely wrinkled skin and clear blue eyes. She upheld not only appearances but also genuinely a sense of friendliness and noblesse oblige. The castle as such was very much an extension of her—or vice versa. It had been bombed by the Allies in frequent air raids during World War II, yet its remains were enough to evoke the grandeur of greater—even medieval—times. White-haired Wilhelmina likewise remained alive, defying setbacks and illness with her aristocratic aloofness. When she showed us around, it felt like our experience was literally connected to history in the best possible way: taking part in a journey that stretched from medieval times to present day; guided by a delicate human body as protected by stone, wood, aesthetics, and attitude—like the very castle itself. The interior was adorned with a schematic poster displaying the School of Wisdom's "Der Rad" (circle) spiritual system, African sculptures, family portraits, stones on the windowsills, and dried pieces of wood. Looking out from on top of a majestic cupboard were striking photos of Arnold and Hermann.

At dinner we talked about the place itself, about yoga, Sweden, gardening and what grew in the neighborhood, and much more. In the evening I got to sleep in an office that housed Willie's desk. Before I fell asleep, I sat at this desk writing in my diary, at the same time fantasizing (or evoking?) Arnold sitting in the very same place, working away. And perhaps the desk had even at some point been used by Hermann, too? Maybe this explained my ensuing night, which was filled to the brim with magical dream experiences.

After breakfasting and talking some more with our delightful princess hostess, and visiting the village cemetery where her father, Karl Hieronymus von Auersperg, lies buried, we drove on toward the medieval town of Laufenburg. It's quite a unique crossroads kind of place, as the border between Switzerland and Germany runs right through the town in the form of the Rhine River. None other than Napoleon himself gave this order of arbitrary division, and it has simply stuck since then. Having arrived on the German side we met up with the local troubadour Roland Kroell and his wonderful partner Claudia.

Kroell is a specialist in preserving and performing medieval music on old instruments, and we were lucky (or prescient enough) to be able to attend one of his concerts. Like our recent visit to the old castle—in which life undeniably lingered on—listening to Kroell's performance was a bizarre journey in time. When I closed my eyes and let the music take hold, I found myself in a completely timeless zone that could equally well have been 1309 as 2009.

On the following day we drove together with Roland and Claudia over Hohenfels, Tiefenstein, and St. Blasien to the town of Ibach, where we parked the cars and headed straight into the Black Forest on foot.

I now find it hard to describe the majestic beauty of the Schwarzwald, as is the case for me with other overwhelming natural places, too. It's of a serene beauty and immense strength; lush and dense yet with patches of open meadows overflowing with a delicate wealth of flowers. The forest engulfs you and won't let go until you're thoroughly rejuvenated in inexplicable ways.

After hiking for some hours, Roland and Claudia suggested we all remove our boots. The ground was grassy, mossy, and delightfully soft. To put down our "civilized" feet on moss-clothed soil was a genuinely sensual delight for our poor little feet that just keep on walking day after day . . . Here was truly some natural therapy for sole and soul alike.

We then also put our happy feet in the cold water of a brook and sat down like amazed children; splashing gently, moving our toes while feeling the feet grow number and number. When they eventually were back in their snug hiking boots my feet walked on; happier than I've ever known them to be.

Roland and Claudia encouraged us to look for fairies and other beings in the forest. But as we all know, we seldom see when we look too hard. However, later in the evening, as I was going through some photos of my friend bathing in a stream, I was very happy to notice that there was indeed something right in front of her that in my mind was nothing less than curious fairies. I have looked at this photographic image many times since then, and any rationalization—it being mosquitos, it being mayflies or dragonflies, it being whatever—simply cannot compete with the joyful acceptance that it was a group of fairies excitedly checking my friend out! As the early Roman poet and philosopher Lucretius said, "Whoever thinks that we know nothing does not know whether we know enough to say that this is so."[2]

Exhausted but very happy we said farewell to our precious guides and stayed at Tittisee overnight before we set out toward the true goal of our journey: the Ernst Jünger Haus in Wilflingen. Today, the residence of the German author houses a museum dedicated to his life and work. It is literally a time and space capsule, overflowing with his vibrant mind and spirit. Stepping into that zone definitely affected me right away—as each genuine pilgrimage destination should. To be inside someone's former living and working quarters is in many ways an intrusion, but I felt I entered respectfully and in awe almost. It immediately felt like a remarkable privilege to be there.

An impressive totality is naturally made up of various parts, and this wonderful place had parts galore. First of all, Jünger's house was the home of someone who genuinely loved books; not only writing them but also reading them. Books were neatly (and sometimes not so neatly) shelved all over the house and revealed a curious mind entranced since youth by the power of language and stories; by formulations in the service of myth.

Then we have the reverence for nature itself. Jünger was a keen entomologist who also studied zoology early on. His meticulously ordered displays of thousands of insects likewise revealed a mind obsessed with the wealth of small creatures—like words and sentences—all working to assemble a sense of meaning in the greater scheme of things. There was in Jünger's mind always a grey area between the natural sciences, myth, and an intelligent form of religiosity, and they contributed considerably to his own narrative strengths. Seeing all those bugs made me think of them as very literally housing stories.

The building itself was an eighteenth-century forester's house on the grounds of Stauffenberg Castle—the center of the tiny village of Wilflingen. It was filled with Biedermeier furniture, bookshelves, collections not only of insects but also of stones, crystals, shells, and walking sticks, along with paraphernalia from his experiences as a soldier in both world wars (including photographs of fallen comrades). The house vibrated with a sense of awareness that history was very much a part of the present—perhaps the most important building block there is.

But for it to become active and alive one needs of course the insight into and awareness of what history actually is: a *continual, continuing* story. Revisions and restructuring are going on all the time. No one is more susceptible to these kinds of postmortem changes than artists in general, onto whom surviving successors, friends, and enemies alike project their own emotions and views.

It struck me as interesting that in Jünger's house a genuine sense of timelessness ruled supreme. Securing the space and maintaining it as it had been at the time of the author's death also affected our own sense of time while being in the space, and not only causally, as in "being there at a specific time." The intersection itself tells a story of what is actually possible for someone who knows what they're doing: taking refuge and creating a sacred space based not only on one's own time of life but—more importantly—one's own *preferred* time and its related aesthetics.

Most people seem to enjoy being stuffed with immediate waste in the belief that it carries nutrition and culture. However, once the immediate evanescent experience is gone, nothing remains. Building

one's own world then becomes a resistance against the soulless acceptance of the contemporary mechanical times. If this world consists of
more than merely accumulating material pieces that feel resonant with
one's soul or existential vision, and also houses objects or other traces of
one's very own creativity, the chances are that one will find oneself in
a very satisfying space-time continuum that will also have the power to
affect others. It is a kind of three-dimensional, magical manipulation of
perception and apprehension that doesn't need to have been consciously
constructed. It can equally well be formulated in very intuitive ways
(such as creating art in various forms, including interior decoration).

I found myself mesmerized by the end of a table in the living room.
It was obviously a place where Jünger sat and wrote. An old chair was at
the very end of it, covered by a sheepskin. Orchids were on the window-
sill and on the table was a big notebook filled with his cursive writing, along with a fountain pen, ink, a Swiss Army pocketknife, and a
small glass containing fresh flowers from the garden. This was the exact
spot where the magic happened; where the nib met the paper texture;
where the formulations materialized. I thought of the Keyserling desk I
had sat at a few days earlier, and about how material objects can indeed
somehow talismanically perhaps not *transmit* but most certainly *emit*
an energy or a spirit (better expressed in German as *geist*) that affects
those in the spatial proximity. This is much the same way that great art
continues to radiate and emit beauty and/or messages hundreds of years
after it has been created.

If one walks around in Jünger's house with knowledge of and respect
for the man and his mind, one will naturally get more out of the visit
than if one is merely an unwitting visitor. But the careful preservation
of a slice of curated history will of course affect everyone regardless of
whether they understand it or not. Hence the importance of schooling children in museums . . . They will very likely find it boring and
tedious in the moment, but it will contribute to a fundament that exists
beyond the merely intellectual, and which reaches resolutely into their
adult selves.

There are many things one could write about the creative and philosophical work of Ernst Jünger, but one of the key concepts from a philosophical point of view is his definition of the anarch as someone who exists on the outside while still on the inside. More specifically, the position of quiet resistance to stupidity, totalitarianism, oppression, and general negativity. Taking a cue from the thoughts of Max Stirner, this could be seen as a survival mechanism, and increasingly so in dire times such as war and state-based oppression.

Jünger contrasts this to the position of anarchist, who is someone always attached to authority, albeit in opposition. The anarchist will always be a prisoner of his own position and will be terminated either by the force of the enemy or by his own design.

The anarch, on the other hand, can exist under the most horrible of circumstances because he experiences freedom on the inside; a freedom that no one can see, hear, or touch, and hence can never take away.

A metaphor that Jünger often used both in literature and in his philosophical writings is "Der Waldgang"—the walking in the forest. (It is also the title of one of his books.) Of course, this could be a literal activity too—to be immersed in nature and solitary speculation. The willed isolation, if even for a minute or less, of the mind or soul from the overwhelming saturation of stupidity and primitive cruelty of *la comedie humaine* can help us deal with daily challenges and inspire us to manage our lives better. Der Waldgang is a strengthening meditation in exterior or interior praxis that can literally become a lifesaver.

Jünger's home was very much an externalization of his inner spheres and attitudes; of his own walking in the forest. The house was filled with his history; material objects in resonance and conversation with each other. The many books he read tell an inspiring story—not necessarily of *their* writing but rather of *his* reading—the accumulation of spirits from near and far in time and space. The insects, ditto. They existed on their own. However, he collected them very literally. He restructured them not only to create a *Linnaean* order for its own sake, but to display them—if to no one else, then at least to himself in his religious admiration of the natural universe. The space as well as time is imbued with a talismanic sense of awe in which even the smallest part accessible by one's proximity tells the whole story. This whole story consists of an appreciation of the smallest common denominators—whether they be genomes, bugs, or the letters of an alphabet—because of their inherent power to create entirely new scenes and scenarios, given the chance through an intelligent authorship.

The Jünger Haus garden was kept up beautifully, eleven years after his demise. And in the garden, as this was a summer trip, we could find Jünger's pet turtle slowly moving around. It was checking out the lay of the land quite literally, and occasionally was lifted to higher ground when some curious human being lifted it to inspect and express admiration that it was still alive.

This made me think very much of a similar scenario in which Jünger himself had been the actual turtle. As such, he eagerly and actively inspected nature close-up, busying himself with joining the dots of soil and roots and fellow animals, but occasionally he would be lifted to the realms of the gods. This was not only so that they themselves could inspect this remarkable animal so diligently and eloquently admiring life itself, but also so that they could allow *him* a bird's-eye perspective of the garden in question. This would permit a more substantial joining of the dots through deep associations and references that simply don't exist on the ground level.

Jünger's experiences in both world wars brought insights that he used in his literary and philosophical work. In the field of battle, he had been a keenly observing protagonist and a decorated soldier wallowing through mechanical death and a great number of life-threatening situations. All of these scenarios provoked not only bravery but also an immediate transcendence in him in order that he shouldn't succumb to despair and demise. Further insights were gleaned through Jünger's experimentation with psychedelic drugs, which took place throughout his life (and which included tripping on LSD with the Swiss chemist and admiring friend of his who developed this magic potion, Albert Hofmann).

The temporary glances given at what Jünger described as "toll-booths" allowed him to enrich his thinking and descriptive powers; to concoct something truly unique in form and content based on transcendental moments. To further displace expectations and indulge in the timeless, Jünger used classic metaphors and referenced gods stemming from antiquity rather than the flat commercialized surfaces of the contemporary. As well, he employed the natural agents of flora, fauna, and geological forces that also defy time and space by their mere existence—through their submission to the totality.

Jünger was definitely a Nietzschean in outlook—or perhaps more of a Schopenhauerian—advocating free will for those who are capable. Yet there was in him an almost religious humility in the relationship between human affairs and greater historical movements. Looking at this, as well as at nature, Jünger claimed one needed a "stereoscopic" vision in order to fully grasp any context or bigger picture. We see what we see or perceive with our senses, but there's also the aspect of *meaning* based on *inherent capacity*. This has to be taken into account as much as what we causally perceive, and preferably at the same time. It's why history can be shifted by very small cogs in the machinery, given the right opportunity or insight. Although we are taught that history is written and edited by the winning side, it may not always be that simple. There is undoubtedly a causal and material movement that pushes humanity and culture forward, but to the individual this doesn't essentially carry greater value than one's own perceptions. This is why humans can survive under horrible circumstances such as war and totalitarianism. They have their own inner vision and process—something that can only be threatened if it's voiced or expressed unwisely.

The stereoscopic regard is one of insight and honesty; one which brings epiphanic potential and poetic rather than logical deductions. It is of great use to authors like Jünger, of course, but equally to any thinking human who has the audacity to look beyond the given parameters. In each offering of solace and comfort—whether it be religious, political, or any other system of faith—there is always a seduction to accept one's place in a given power dynamic. Usually this is not a seduction or outcome conducive to a full blooming of the individual soul and its potential. Where most people do seem to find comfort in the safety of numbers and collective rigidity there are always individuals who simply cannot accept it for themselves. In publicly expressed opposition these become the anarchists; in silence, the anarchs. For Jünger the choice had already been presented early on. Although a prolific writer and celebrated thinker, his stance—almost paradoxically—as a visible and audible anarch helped push an attitude of resolute inner strength and radiating spirituality that could definitely be seen as religious but never "sectaristic." In this he was similar to other thinkers and authors from the German-speaking sphere at the time, such as Hermann Hesse, Rudolf Steiner, Ludwig Klages, and Carl Jung.

Of course one can always delve even further back in time if one wants to understand Jünger; to Goethe of course, but also to Alexander von Humboldt, whose scientific expeditions in the outer world brought much poetic fodder to his inner work. In many cases, von Humboldt's characterizations and statements sound like pure "programming" or an establishment of the man who was to become Ernst Jünger: "He who seeks spiritual peace amidst the unresolved strife between peoples therefore gladly lowers his gaze to the quiet life of plants and into the inner workings of the sacred force of Nature, or, surrendering to the instinctive drive that has glowed for millennia in the breast of humanity, he looks upward with awe to the high celestial bodies, which, in undisturbed harmony, complete their ancient, eternal course."[3]

And to quote Humboldt again, "But nature is the domain of liberty; and to give a lively picture of those ideas and those delights which a true and profound feeling in her contemplations inspires, it is needful that thought should clothe itself freely and without constraint in such forms and with such elevation of language, as may be least unworthy of the grandeur and majesty of creation."[4]

Before leaving Wilflingen we also visited Jünger's grave and had lunch at the restaurant Vier Löwe (Four Lions). I munched away at my schnitzel with fried potatoes, sipping some beer, talking to my friends. Looking at my friend across the table and then upward, I noticed a photo of Jünger right above him. Jünger must have eaten here many times during almost fifty years of residence down the street. And although there was certainly no "milking" of any touristic Jünger aspects, you could certainly feel the pride among the remaining villagers and guests. In the end, it's not really the fame that matters locally but rather the real living memories of those who actually met him, and the stories that will remain after those people are gone.

Stories are always retold in slightly different ways, but in Wilflingen one can at least always go straight to the horse's mouth (or at least the horse's stable!) and *feel* what Jünger was really about. To have a beautiful and inspiring home is one thing; to have it continue to inspire future generations requires tender loving care more than anything else.

As we left the little village, we were amazed at the power of not only a unique author's mind, but also of his particular intersection in time and space that we had just been graced by.

As we drove on toward Switzerland, we stopped over at the "flower island" of Mainau in Lake Constance. Developed by Prince Lennart (1909–2004) of the Swedish royal family the Bernadottes, the castle as well as the island was a huge celebration of nature in general, and of flowers in particular. Although this was a relatively grey day, the radiance and colors overwhelmed us as we strolled the paths and gardens. Jünger must surely have visited Mainau many times. He seemed to have appreciated the order of gardens in general, and perhaps especially when they were as well-ordered as they were there at Mainau.

However, and this is the real philosophical insight of any gardener or naturalist, as humans we can only very temporarily take care of the land and make of it what we desire. Although much beauty can be made in harmony with the inherent potential of plants and produce, it is very much an ambitious vanity project. The beauty we partake of and the vegetables and fruits we ingest definitely keep us alive. But if the upkeep and (illusory) sense of order is removed then other interests immediately take over and the harnessing stemming from raw force rules supreme (again). Although we can accept a temporary stewardship we should be aware of our insignificance in the big picture. Depending on which cultural position one has adopted, it could either be "Nature is Satan's church" (Lars von Trier) or "The Lord works in mysterious ways." If we don't tend to our allotment, it will be quickly overgrown. Voltaire perhaps expressed it best of all with his *"Il faut cultiver son jardin."*

Jünger's garden of books, ideas, and attitudes will hopefully last a long time. But interestingly, he himself believed that his longevity would more have to do with the fact that he has a few insects named after him—provided the Linnean system lives on. Although most often casual and detached on the surface, it seems that Jünger had given this dilemma a great deal of thought. "Yet that is my principle: writing has to have a timeless element. Every work ultimately perishes, even Homer will disappear. As the Greeks said, the universe periodically goes up in flames so that it may be resurrected. However, there is something in Homer that has no distinct relationship to society: that is what I look for in an author."[5]

As we finally drove into Zürich in the evening, we were genuinely exhausted after a weeklong journey that had taken us through so many inspiring experiences. When a pilgrimage is over, it is always with a sense of sadness one evaluates even the beautiful things one has experienced. Memories need to be planted in one's own system so that everything can grow and bloom in new ways. An in-spiration is literally a "breathing in" that will vitalize one's system with existential oxygen. On the most ephemeral levels, it could be diary entries or photographs that remind us of what actually happened. But on a deeper level it's always the emotions and memories themselves that must be allowed their own life and growth within us.

With great tending, new flowers will grow. I am certain Ernst Jünger would agree.

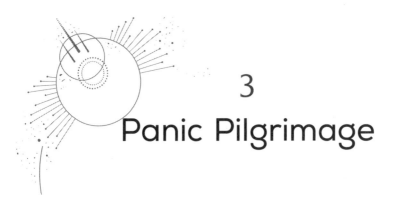

3
Panic Pilgrimage

When we are young and impressionable we are formatted by strong experiences that instill imprints. These stay with us throughout our lives, sometimes as solid behavioral programs and sometimes as mere romantic guides of preference. Our sexual crystallizations, tastes, habits, quirks, traumas, and mannerisms all have a source. As we grow and develop, some of these crystallizations change and morph with new epiphanies along the way. But some remain deep inside, affecting us in invisible and inaudible spheres of body and mind.

Getting to the source of these imprints is indeed a mixed bouquet and an ambiguous challenge. This is evident in the process of psychoanalysis: if one is doing well and being honest in talking about one's memories, dreams, and emotions, there will come a moment when the clarity seems almost threatening, overturning. The dots are connected on a game board that suddenly lights up brightly. But you don't want to lose your position on that board and what it means for you in terms of comfort, habits, and safe routines. But still, these sources *will* call out to you to revisit and discover more about yourself. It's in their nature as it is in yours, and in many ways this process is a duty or obligation to yourself.

In my work as a writer and journalist I have actually done very little else *but* explore avenues to find out more about what once inspired me.

"Panic Pilgrimage" was originally written for the Canadian journal *Pillars,* 2021.

I do this not because they no longer inspire me, but because they—for enigmatic reasons—still do. I have traveled far and wide all over the world to reconnect to creative minds and magical places. This has been in order to come to terms with my own interests, and quite possibly to replenish the inspiration. The more I think about it, the more I realize that my entire life has actually been some kind of indulgent pilgrimage; a self-sustaining "echo system" perhaps.

One of the most powerful experiences of my life so far was visiting the mountain village of Joujouka in Morocco with my wife, Vanessa Sinclair, in the summer of 2019. The Master Musicians of Joujouka had arranged a summer solstice festival for three days (and nights), and we didn't hesitate one second when we saw the invitation. Instant affirmation! It was a trip so thoroughly meaningful and beautiful to me that it is still visceral in so many ways. It also made me think about what had actually led up to it.

Where to even begin? Psychoanalytically, we should probably go to my own childhood, and probably even further back. My father was a beatnik kind of a guy. In the late 1950s, when he was in his late teens, he worked his way from Stockholm to New York as a kitchen assistant on a ship. The goal was to experience the jazz music he loved so much "live and direct," and indulge in the culture that permeated the scene. This also meant traveling to Morocco and partaking of its delights and many temptations. One of my big regrets in life was not discussing these experiences of my father's with him in greater detail before he died. He was certainly aware of William S. Burroughs, Brion Gysin, and the other beats who were in Tangier at the same time.

Who knows what actually happened there? One thing is certain (in my mind, at least!): his experiences were recorded in his own genetic mass, and then passed on to me. We may not have talked about it much, but the recording mechanisms of DNA itself never lie or stay silent— DNA simply records and moves onward.

What happened a few years later was that my father's love of jazz bloomed into a club in Stockholm called The Golden Circle. Many world-famous musicians came, played, and enjoyed Stockholm in general and the club in particular. These musicians included the likes of Dexter Gordon, Ben Webster, George Russell, Dollar Brand, Charles Lloyd, Archie Shepp, Don Cherry, Ernestine Anderson, Keith Jarrett, Sonny Stitt, Bud Powell, Bill Evans, Krzysztof Komeda, and Ornette Coleman (to mention but a few).

I had just been born in January of 1966 when there was a buzz at the door of my parents' apartment. It was Ornette Coleman, who was in town to play, and who had bought me a cradle. I still have the little wooden trinket that he signed: "To Aake and Family, Many Happy Years. Ornette." It was only decades later that I acknowledged how cool this was. It was a magical imprint beyond conscious apprehension.

Zoom forward to my twenties, in the mid-1980s, and I was now deeply involved with Thee Temple Ov Psychick Youth (TOPY), to the extent of setting up a Scandinavian branch and later administering the European goings-on of this magical order cum occultural think tank network. I was knee-deep in the TOPY mythology of Crowley and Spare of course, but also of Burroughs, Gysin, and North African magical thinking. TOPY's "Godstar" project included elevating Brian Jones as a gnostic saint who also integrated his own very trippy recordings of the Master Musicians of Joujouka from 1968. It was basically a quaquaversal beat magic romance 24/7 in my mind, with the Brian Jones LP often spinning on repeat in my own spaceship apartment. It was a great soundtrack for rituals and meditations, as well as for psychonautic explorations into the spheres of romance and contemporary myth.

And wait . . . Ornette Coleman had recorded with the Master Musicians, too, for his 1973 album *Dancing in Your Head!* It was indeed a small world full of golden circles, reawakenings, epiphanic results of greasing the glitch, and spraying synaptic love juice all over the 23rd mind. Historically and holistically speaking, it was very much still rocking in Coleman's cradle amidst the swirling flutes and pipes of ecstasy, the incessant rhythms, the psychic psyncopations, the collective labor of psychedelic enlightenment for each and every one. All of it was a celebration of the purely pagan Pan as a living symbol and sculpture of life-affirmation and enhancement, sexual force and expression, the all-embracing and all-penetrating libido, the sensuality, the short-circuiting of rational blocking attempts . . . And so on and so forth. What wasn't to like? Actually, what wasn't to *love?*

In the summer of 2019, Vanessa and I traveled around Morocco, and ended up in Tangier (as one is apt to do). This entailed another kind of pilgrimage. At the American Legation in the Petit Socco there is a wonderful museum preserving the life and work of Paul Bowles. In many ways Bowles was the actual instigator and introducer of most things Moroccan to the hungry beat beasts. Bowles had fallen in love with Moroccan music on his own first trips there in the 1930s. He discovered many gems all over the country and relayed these findings—often together with Joujouka-born poet/author Hamri—to Brion Gysin. Gysin, having become entranced himself, then passed these findings on to William S. Burroughs (and others), who in turn became entranced as well.

And so on . . .

The documentation has indeed been quintessential to the mythology. In the early 1950s Bowles had become obsessed with recording and preserving the folk music that was threatened by looming modernity and political chaos. In a letter to his fellow composer Peggy Glanville-Hicks in New York, Bowles wrote: "A month ago I lent my tape-recorder to Brion for a while, and taught him how to run it, so that between us we have got a good deal of beautiful material preserved on tape. Your assurances as to the possibilities of getting it into more permanent form, on records, are very encouraging."[1]

Eventually Paul Bowles secured a grant from the Rockefeller Foundation, which made it possible for him to travel on four different six-week trips in 1959 all over Morocco to record his beloved music. These recordings were issued on two LPs in 1972, and in a lavish CD box in 2016. His own liner notes read: "The neolithic Berbers have always had their own music, a highly percussive art with complex juxtapositions of rhythms, limited scalar range (often no more than three adjacent tones), and a unique manner of vocalizing. Like other Africans, they developed a music of mass participation, which frequently aimed at the psychological effect of hypnosis. When the Arabs invaded the land, they brought with them music of a very different sort, addressed to the individual, music that existed only to embellish the word, with the property of inducing a state of philosophical speculativeness."[2]

It was Brion Gysin who then took the main Joujouka baton and ran with it. He hired the Master Musicians to work at his legendary beat mythos Tangier restaurant A Thousand and One Nights, and tried to protect them from whatever temptations there were in the big city:

> When these musicians from Joujouka worked with me in a place that I found for them in Tangier, I forbade them to have a radio in the house. I didn't have one, I forbade them, anybody, to own one. Because I didn't want them listening to that slush that came over Radio Cairo, which was already "Hollywood-ized." I did hear that, because I couldn't resist listening to some things that I liked. I was amazed to see that Hadj, the oldest man—the leader of the group—was putting a few little Jazz riffs in through his Oboe . . . [*laughter*] . . . dancing away on the top of the line . . .[3]

Gysin's protective attitude increased as Tangier became more and more of a hotspot for creatives looking for kicks (as it had been since the 1940s, basically). Initially Gysin was even hesitant to bring the Rolling Stones to the remote mountain village, and to assist Brian Jones in recording the Master Musicians:

> Brian was the best musician of the lot, obviously the most inventive musician, and part of the thing was that coming to Morocco like that, particularly the second time, after he'd split with Anita, who'd gone off with Keith, he came back again and spent quite a lot of time in Tangier. Got up into the mountains and recorded

that music in Joujouka. Whatever he really intended is hard to say. I knew nothing about the record business at all. I didn't particularly want him to go up there in the first place. And I was discussing it with William . . . like, would it be wise? "Can Pan survive the attack of Allen Klein?". . . is about the way we were putting it to each other, and the musicians were saying, "What are you talking about, WE NEED THE MONEY! OF COURSE bring him up!" Hamri was involved. Hamri was very keen because there was money involved, naturally, in taking Brian up there.[4]

The Brian Jones Joujouka LP was successful, selling tens of thousands of copies, which brought more attention to the ensemble, the village, and its self-imposed custodians like Bowles, Gysin, and Burroughs. The attraction to this Rif hotspot was stronger than ever before. In 1973, when Ornette Coleman wanted to renew and redefine himself as a musician, he went to Joujouka, bringing Burroughs with him (or was it the other way around?). Coleman made his album *Dancing in Your Head* while "Uncle Bill" also recorded straight performances by the Master Musicians at the same time. These recordings eventually ended up on the album *William S. Burroughs: Break Through in Grey Room*.[5]

But it is (always?) to Paul Bowles that we have to return in our own pilgrimage sourcery. Bowles was the original pathfinder and interpreter, and one that has certainly affected me more than the more proper beatniks of the late 1950s and 1960s.

For this very reason, I was completely "buzzed" at the American Legation when we entered the Paul Bowles sanctuary. I charged one of my magical pens on Bowles's Olivetti typewriter and then touched it. I also touched the keys of the Ensoniq keyboard he used for composing music. I just immersed myself in the spirit of this literary giant and explorer. It was a moment when mere conscious existence and immersion became a powerful ritual in its own right regardless of any "intentions" I may also have had.

This was indeed a blissful time, but the real focus of our trip was to leave Tangier and get up in the Rif Mountains. We took a taxi to the town of Ksar el-Kebir, where we met up with a few others who were on the same pilgrimage. After a few hours of sipping the inevitable mint tea at a café by the train station, we were picked up by minibuses and driven up a dusty road to the little village of Joujouka.

It's a serene place, with dogs moving around freely and curiously. The women are mostly indoors taking care of their homes and the children. The low white-walled buildings are spread out, and one narrow asphalt road passes through it all like a jugular vein of imposed necessity. There is a school, a house that keeps the shrine of their own Sufi saint, a tiny-hole-in-the-wall store or kiosk, and then a compound where the Master Musicians rehearse, work, and perform. It consists of a house with a kitchen, a garden, and a big tent, with carpets straight on the ground. The staggering view is of mountains, valleys, and more of the same basically wherever one looks. The Moroccan flag (a solid red background with a green pentagram!) proudly moves in gusts of dry, hot wind.

We were welcomed into the compound where everyone got acquainted and we sat serenely looking out and chatting with the friendly musicians and the other guests. A large contingent of that year's visitors had come all the way from Japan, including a Japanese Brian Jones look-alike who had brought his own sitar to jam with the Master Musicians. We also met some Australians who we already knew but hadn't known were going to be there . . . Confluences on a completely different (in many ways!) continent.

Vanessa and I stayed in a house that belonged to a village elder and his hospitable family: a very tough old man with a great sense of humor. What he lacked in terms of knowledge of the English language he compensated for in great smiles and telepathic bravado. It turned out that this man was in fact Bou Jeloud, the very magical center figure of the ancient rituals; a real, modern-day Pan gestalt of mythical proportions. Bou Jeloud is nothing less than a personification of the great god Pan, and the annual ritual that we were about to witness has been going on since Roman times.*

The first afternoon in the village was calm and welcoming, with music and delicious couscous. Later, during the starlit evening, the Master Musicians revved up, and we eventually fell asleep enwrapped in a very visceral shroud of pilgrimage.

The next day a nine-man-strong version of the ensemble played drums, string instruments, and flutes while the approximately fifty guests were settling into this new—or should I say timeless?—zone of entrancing over- and undertones. The day passed by in bliss. After a communal midnight meal (Chicken Tagine!) the full, fourteen-member ensemble, who were dressed up in brown djellabas and yellow head-pieces, brought out their drums, pipes, and flutes. As the first sounds and rhythms blasted out into the chilly Moroccan night, sending echoes far, far away in the valleys, the assembled throng basically went crazy.

Enthusiastically people got up and danced on the carpets in front of the encouraging music makers. Vanessa swirled, I danced my own slightly hesitant, Swedish old-guy dance, and everyone was swept away in something that has been going on since time immemorial.

In the night there was no more romance involved; no thoughts, no concepts, no experiencing via earlier psychonauts and explorers. In the night, and in the music, one was on one's own and completely immersed. Any intellectual references were swept away and one was quite simply a human being experiencing the same kind of vibrant ecstasy as an indefinite—perhaps infinite—number of people have done throughout the millennia.

We were lulled into our own movements and transcendental emotions, swaying to the loud music, or sitting down and "spacing out." There were blissful smiles on everyone's faces. And then, out of the dark, he suddenly popped up: Bou Jeloud! Our wonderful and serene

---

*Speculative and perhaps beat-infused etymology claims that *Bou Jeloud* is the origin of the words *bogaloo,* the *bogeyman,* and *boogie-woogie,* for example. These words have African origins and are connected with dancing and ecstatic parties, and, as in the case of the bogeyman, a related fear.

old host had turned himself into a terrifying, raving beast, dressed in goatskin. He danced and moved spastically through the crowds; a source of laughter and fear at the same time.

On the next day, June 23, 2019 (incidentally TOPY's thirty-eighth birthday!), Bou Jeloud (back in the shape of our old host) took us for a trek through hills and shrubs to the special Bou Jeloud cave. It's a space inside a rock where the Master Musicians have rehearsed together for a long, long time—no one could tell how long. The old Moroccan man simply climbed up the steep rock—exactly like a goat—and talked about its history. It was another timeless space, for I could well envision musicians up there in the seventeenth, eighteenth, and ninenteenth centuries . . . Playing basically the same music and smoking the same kind of kif, spreading fragrances of pagan majesty from their secret dwelling.

We also visited the house in the village that contained the shrine of the patron Sufi saint Sidi Ahmed Scheich, who founded the village in the ninth century CE. The Sufi connection is still alive and very vital here. The gnostic connection to higher states of being is neither demagogic nor religious in the monotheistic fashion; it is visceral and comes via physical motion and vibrations. Although the Master Musicians are officially Muslim, they are more devoutly Sufi. The obvious worship of Pan connects to the celebrations of Lupercalia in the Roman Empire that existed long before Islam was dreamed up in the seventh century. This frenzied Lupercalia ritual was well-known and looked forward to for the very same reasons that it still exists in the Moroccan mountains: fertility and life force were its object—*not* existential enslavement by religious dogma.

After lunch and more music from the smaller troupe we were pleasantly relaxed in this pastoral haven, waiting for the big midsummer celebration that very same evening. Many visitors and locals, including musicians, hung out at the minuscule "Café Bou Jeloud" in our host's house, sipping lukewarm Coca-Cola or having a cup of tea or instant coffee. The walls were filled with postcards, press clippings, and various kinds of memorabilia pertaining to the Master Musicians, indicating their success. Some people in the little room smoked the local spice ambitiously, and even the contact high made everyone smile and feel completely at home.

The midnight meal was goat meat and vegetables; a goat sacrificed for this very special occasion. After the full ensemble had begun playing again after midnight, a bonfire was lit in the garden. And then out of the darkness he suddenly appeared again: Bou Jeloud! This time he was dressed not only in skins but also adorned with the head of the very goat we had just eaten together. With even more frenzy, this "father of fear" ran around with a bundle of leafy branches and whipped musicians, some guests, and the local women (present but sticking to themselves), who started laughing when the old man threatened to give them a good whipping. This blessing has, according to the myth, always ensured fertility and happiness. (This is not at all unlike our own Swedish midsummer celebration, which is all about communally building a big phallus and adorning it with flowers, before it's ceremonially stuck in the ground and danced around to the tones of traditional folk music played on violins. To take part in these life-affirming and life-enhancing rituals is a real, solid key to understanding life itself—a chthonic force spiraling upward to the starry and endless sky.)

The fourteen musicians drove everyone to an absolute frenzy, dancing and acknowledging Bou Jeloud with laughter and shouts. When they were really rocking, the entire place turned into a timeless rave of sorts. People got up and danced, including those from the entourage of the musicians, and just basically spaced out. Sometimes there was a whiff of kif or hash in the air, but the rhythms and sounds in and of themselves were enough to make one high. Even if I was just sitting down and trying to suck in the totality on some far-fetched and ridiculous intellectual level, I soon found myself moving around—I simply couldn't help it. It was an overpowering sensation that revealed what proper religious rituals are really all about: communion, community, and communication. No priest or imam was needed here; this was the real religion of the land, and of the world. In rhythm and ecstatic emotions we joined forces with mighty nature herself.

One of my favorite descriptions/interpretations of this very moment was written in 1973 by Burroughs.

> This was Bou Jeloud in his role as the Goat God, God of Panic, Master of Fear. There were three dancers in the circle two with bare feet, one with his face covered by a cloth the other two bare faced. One boy in green shirt slacks and moccasins was riding the current like a surfboard. He stands a few feet in front of the musicians his body vibrating as if in contact with a high-tension wire . . . a whiff of ozone and sea air and horses. He spins away thrown by the music around the circle whipping at the women possessed by but possessing and controlling the force of the music. I saw him aim a kick at the face of a young child on the women's side who had stepped out of line and stop his foot an inch from the child's face. Magnetic spirals spun through the room like clusters of electronic bees that meet and explode in the air releasing the divine perfume, a musty purple smell of ozone and spice and raw goatskins, a perfume you can smell and see.[6]

When we were about to leave the village the following day—exhausted but very happy—the Irish organizer of the event, the wonderful Frank Rynne, gave Vanessa and me Bou Jeloud's bundle of branches from the ecstatic night before. It still resides in a special place in our home. It's not only a memento of an amazing trip, but also a reminder of the timelessness and spacelessness that humans yearn for more than anything else. It is in those moments of "disconnected connectivity" that we may ascertain what it really means to be human—to be free of the shackles of the petty rational mind and its self-loathing, death-driven culture.

Any experience—flaunted or secret—of these moments is an essential replenishment and reminder that in itself serves as a magical pilgrimage. If, however, these experiences take place (and transpire) in a spot where tradition rules and still inspires, there is really no limit to what can be boosted—both in the moment and in its delightful aftermath.

4
Into a Time and Space of Wordship

Where to even begin? How to even express all the emotions evoked by this one single yet highly complex being?

Well, why don't we begin with the end? Genesis Breyer P-Orridge died on March 14, 2020. Although it was expected (a battle against leukemia that lasted for several years), the actual moment one hears of the demise—that definitive, irreversible insight of mortality—is always downright horrible.

BAM! That's it. It's over. No more hugs, looks, conversations, dinners, drinks, spontaneous decisions, telepathic jokes, or any of the millions of other types of interactions that make human communication so endlessly fascinating. Gen was now gone, leaving behind a sense of very acute loss.

We'd been scheduled to host an evening together at the wonderful NYC bookstore Mast on March 19, celebrating the release of *Sacred Intent,* a book that anthologizes all of our interview-conversations between 1986 and 2019. On March 11, my wife and I decided not to go to the United States (we live in Sweden) because of the increasing

"Into a Time and Space of Wordship" was originally written for *The Brooklyn Rail,* 2020.

coronavirus panic. I wrote to Gen that we should postpone the evening so that there would be no risk of him getting infected, and he agreed. The next day, Thursday, our decision was (re)enforced by the official ban on traveling to America. So, a done deal! Then, on the morning of March 14, Gen died.

On the very last page of *Sacred Intent* (which featured a conversation from November 2019), Gen asked what I thought a world without him would be like.[1] Hesitantly, I answered:

> I'm trying not to think of it too much. But if I do, I'm just thinking of how blessed I've been. You know, we've worked together since 1986; we've never really had a disruption except for normal disruptions of time. It's just been extremely valuable. We've made these three beautiful albums, and this book, and many other things, and it's just a blessing. I don't think I will have emotional problems with it. It's just a matter of carrying on the work, like you did; you carried on the work. I will carry on the work, and then other people will carry on the work. It feels like a blessing to me.

This is what psychoanalysts call "rationalization." I very rationally moved a potentially threatening emotional cluster to a sphere of thinking. This does not work out so well in reality, however, and that is where I'm at as I write these words.

This remarkable artist changed things—thinking, people, movements, art, memories, perceptions, culture in general, and so many other things. I can't think of any other punch-packer of similar stature in the Western world of art and esotericism.

Neil Andrew Megson was born in 1950 in northern England, and gradually morphed into the new identity of Genesis P-Orridge in the late 1960s. Inspired by a beatnik approach in which a casual and carefree attitude ruled supreme, the young poet P-Orridge developed an uncompromising attitude both alone and together with others of like mind. What started as communal psychedelic art experimentation transformed into an art collective with a radical and ultracreative view of performance art: the infamous "C.O.U.M. Transmissions." P-Orridge's ideas then grew further inside the conceptualization of "industrial" music via Throbbing Gristle (TG), and were carried on in the development of the magical and occultural network Thee Temple Ov Psychick Youth (TOPY) and the ever-shape-shifting sounds and gestalts of the music and video group Psychic TV.

Radical transformation took on new meaning in the much written about Pandrogeny Project, undertaken with Gen's wife, Jackie "Lady Jaye" Breyer. In the early 2000s the couple morphed together into an artistic, alchemical *pandrogyne* simply called "Breyer P-Orridge." Together they created gender-dissolving art and philosophy in theory and practice, while a new constellation of Psychic TV, called PTV3, traveled the world as psychedelic renegades of love and colorful illumination.

P-Orridge was always writing, always talking and giving interviews about ideas and projects. The P-Orridgean eloquence gave birth to not only the "industrial" culture of the mid-1970s (and onward) but also to a new way of looking at occultism and its inevitable result: "occulture" (a term Gen coined early on). These inherently essential areas of human culture were now suddenly no longer compartmentalized, arcane, and dusty, garbed in pseudo-religious symbols and ensuing patriarchal power struggles.

As Throbbing Gristle changed the way music was perceived, so Psychic TV and TOPY changed the magical spectrum and catapulted it into a distinctly contemporary scenario. In this, individual liberation became a highly charged weapon against the draconian forces of "control" (a concept inherited from Gen's friend and mentor William S. Burroughs).

Pandrogeny then did the same thing in and for the decidedly dysphorian identity culture of the 2010s. As new reactive positions were also on the verge of becoming too rigidly dualistic, suddenly here came the magical pandrogyne, saying that you don't have to be either-or—

either male or female—and you also don't have to change into the other "either-or" either. There are always more options, and they're never definite or eternal. Identity, like everything else, is completely malleable.

Working in music, writing, performance, collage, sculpture, and many other expressive forms, Gen amplified this malleability and unpredictability of given solutions, and even developed it into a solid artistic method: "If you want to do something creative and new, you have to step away from what's expected and destroy the expected; find what is around you that could make a sound, look at what people expect, and do the opposite."[2]

This is not mere head-on "contrarianism," but rather an application of the proven insight that there's potentially real impact in constructive transgression, and especially if the time is right, which it always seemed to be for Gen as the celebrated "cultural engineer". . . Throbbing Gristle wasn't just against the prog rock or heavy metal or pop music of the mid-1970s, however. The project also distanced itself from the punk scene by leaving any kind of three-chord proletarianism (or the romanticizing of it) far behind, through weaving in real intellectual ideas and new sounds (including primitive "protosampling" via cassette recorders).

This was then totally topsy-turvied with Psychic TV's first album (*Force the Hand of Chance,* 1982) integrating lighter pop sounds and more ambitious orchestrations. It was sort of one hundred eighty degrees from the harsh existentialist experimentalism that TG was known for. It would be amplified further in mid-to late 1980s rock 'n' roll PTV and, again, in PTV3's psychedelic rock-cum-spaceship music.

The cut-up technique, as developed by mentors William S. Burroughs and Brion Gysin, was quintessential in both theory and practice—not only in writing and collage work, but also in life in general. Cutting up the given, and trusting the "random" process when reassembling the new parts often reveals hidden aspects of meaning that can guide one onward. This was more than mere intellectual Dada wordplay; for Gen the cut-up method was very literally a way of life.

The year 2019 saw/heard the release of what was to be not only our final joint album, but also Gen's: *Loyalty Does Not End with Death,* put out by Ideal Recordings. It contained beautiful, spoken-word recordings of poems, cut-ups, and texts that I had set to ambient, electronic music. This would hopefully amplify the potency and emotional reverberations inherent not only in the words themselves but also in the absolutely flawless delivery from Gen. He was, of course, in every way not only a poet par excellence but also a master vocal seducer.

It turned out we had made an album together every fourteen years. In 1990 there was *At Stockholm* (by Psychic TV and White Stains). In 2004 there was *Wordship* (by Thee Majesty and Cotton Ferox). In 2018 (when we recorded the *Loyalty* album) we had divested ourselves of monikers and project names, which felt very good. We stripped away superfluous layers to reveal what was underneath the surface: a creative "third mind" friendship, this time described simply as Genesis Breyer P-Orridge and Carl Abrahamsson.

In 2016 I made the documentary *Change Itself* about Gen's work. He was overjoyed that it deliberately transcended the musical projects and instead focused mainly on the art and poetry: "We thought art has to be about your life; your life has to be about art and the act of creation. Comprehension by others is the least important aspect. You do things that touch you and that feel symbolically powerful to you. You look for potency and the reclamation of your right to create and dream and reassess and adjust and rebuild consensus reality as you see fit. It is your absolute right."[3]

This altruistic-demagogic side of Gen's permeated a lot of the output, regardless of media or form. In this sense I think Gen genuinely carried on a torch from the 1960s that most others let slip and slide and fade away as an entire generation left the psychedelic states of mind behind. It is never mere loose "hippy" philosophy, though. Gen's multifaceted ideas and concepts were tried and tried again (in praxis as much as theoretically), and over the decades he wove in ideas from many different times and cultures. The red thread was always the "sacred intent . . ." Even if one does things strictly for oneself, they should be altruistically anchored. And if one does beneficial things for others, one can rest assured it will be of gain for oneself as an individual, too.

The P-Orridgean philosophy is basically a holistic approach that could be shamanic, Buddhist, Santeria, vodun, or stemming from Western magicians like Aleister Crowley and Austin Osman Spare. Arguing that it was all essentially the same, Gen integrated ingredients of infinite intelligence and cooked up a masterful and tasty dish for others as much as for himself.

Working with Gen back in the TOPY days was extremely exhilarating. (As mentioned earlier, I was administrator of the Scandinavian "branch" called TOPYSCAN, and later on TOPY EUROPE between 1986 and 1991.) With Gen there was this constant sense that we were breaking new ground—probably because we were. There were no other magical orders like TOPY. There was no other network of free-flowing, radical information (often disseminated by Xeroxes or cassette tapes of rare archival material) like TOPY, and certainly no Internet to help out . . . There was no other "movement" that encouraged its members to explore magic and individuation by actively making talismanic art—including a ritualized use of sex. There was no other similar think tank that endeavored to apply wisdom from the 1960s without falling into the traps of wishy-washy (re)sloganeering—at least not as far as I know.

And that was what brought me into the *gesamtkunstwerk** that the sphere of Genesis P-Orridge actually was. My interest in magic and pop culture, and how they could potentially merge, led me to become a subscriber to TOPY's newsletters. This boosted me so powerfully in terms of inspiration that I immediately wanted to become involved. I had watched the mind-bending and soulful video experiments of Psychic TV at an art college in Stockholm in 1984. That

---

*Gesamtkunstwerk: An artwork that is assembled by many different kinds of artistic expressions: music, painting, film, poetry, photography, conceptual art, performance, for instance. One clear example of a gesamtkunstwerk would be an opera.

made me realize that this unique mix of theory and practice was not only extremely creative and magical, it was also (still) of multipurpose use and relevance for and in the future.

In 1986 I visited the TOPY headquarters in London for the first time. Gen and I had already been in touch via letters, but this first personal meeting was definitely life-changing for me. It was beyond mere Psychic TV fanboy-ism, as that first interview also touched upon quintessential, philosophical P-Orridgean concepts in the making.

> Some of the people are part of what we call "Thee Sex Tribe." They follow us around and tend to do what they call "sexual terrorism." They strip off and dance and do all kinds of things. The sexual tribe is growing considerably. What's interesting is that the girls don't act as heterosexual girls or lesbian girls. They just act in a sexual way. Boys who otherwise would never kiss a boy might kiss a boy and not feel embarrassed or inhibited at that moment. That's the healthiest part of all. They feel free from any inhibitions at that period of time. There is a temporary, yet very strong, suspension of any Either/Or, male/female definitions. It's a zone of new sexuality.[4]

There was already then also the "staple" attitude that never changed for Gen, and which inspired me greatly in terms of self-discipline and productivity: "I don't think that just because I'm Genesis P-Orridge I have to do all the exciting work. I'm happy to sweep the floor and knock down a wall and make a cup of tea as well. Everyone should feel like that. There is no more important or less important job. There's just, 'What has to get done? Who can do it? Let's get it done as quickly as we can and let's do more and more and more . . .'"[5]

That constructive workaholism has helped shape my own life for the better, and I'm very grateful for that. Gen proved time and time again that one has to walk the talk. To have highfalutin, cosmic ideas is not enough. You have to reinforce your vision by hard work, and, yes, why not amplify it all by some ritual magic as well?

So I guess that was the beginning: November 1986. I left Gen's house with a goody bag full of Xeroxes, cassette tapes, pamphlets, and magazines, and with life-altering impressions of this weird, soft-spoken little sorcerer with sad, tired eyes and a relentlessly rewarding work ethic.

It will take time and effort to process the huge loss of Gen's death, and I'm certainly not going to be alone in this. Together we'll sadly also have to wallow through disgruntled ghosts' recollections of injustices here or abuses there; of angry moments here, and sad conflicts there. Yes, Genesis P-Orridge was human like the rest of us, and a human life is always filled with downs as well as ups, and with people who will hate us when relationships are over. There's nothing new there. But there is one aspect that brings solace, justice, and protection to our memory in these bitter little rain showers that sprinkle down upon us. Without Genesis P-Orridge it is highly unlikely that these tepid hang-arounds would have had any artistic careers at all.

As for those of us who do remain genuinely grateful to this enigmatic and generous humane being, all we can do is carry on the work. And rest assured, we absolutely will.

5
Temporarily Eternal

Some Thoughts on the Psychic Anarcho-Sartorialism of Genesis P-Orridge

We reveal our private nature by the décor of our fantasies.
GENESIS BREYER P-ORRIDGE,
"THE DARK ROOM OF DESIRE"

The book *Genesis P-Orridge: Temporarily Eternal—Photographs 1986–2018* both is and is not a satellite to *Genesis Breyer P-Orridge: Sacred Intent—Conversations with Carl Abrahamsson 1986–2019* (Trapart Books, 2020).* It is, in the sense that the present book also focuses on shared moments during the same period of time. It is not, in the sense that it's not an intellectual trip into concepts and thoughts expressed via language, in conversation.

Instead, the book contains photographic portraits: some are staged, considered, thought through, and some are pure snapshots of auspicious and fleeting moments. And some are definitely somewhere in-between: juggling immediate form with desired content. The focus

---

*"Temporarily Eternal: Some Thoughts on the Psychic Anarcho-Sartorialism of Genesis P-Orridge" was originally written for the book *Genesis P-Orridge: Temporarily Eternal—Photographs 1986–2018,* which was published by Trapart Books in 2021.

of *Sacred Intent* was the actual conversations, in which Gen could lay out thoughts on spirituality, magic, existentialism, pandrogeny, and many other things. The photos chosen for that book were from the time of the conversation in question—somewhat like illustrations for a magazine. But given that we didn't meet over the decades to only have these talks, there were plenty of other photographic moments, too. Many if not most of these are included in *Temporarily Eternal*.

Why the title? Well, one drive or motivation that I could perceive in Gen was the transient nature of human life and existence. We do what we can and then it's over (or perhaps not). The uncertainty about what happens next became for Gen both a depressant and a motivation to take one's life more seriously. Often, he* would share a magical piece of wisdom: "You should look at life and the present day as if it were your last. At the end of the day, are you happy with the day and how you spent it?"

This attitude became not only an incentive for an existential efficiency on mundane and tangible levels. It also gave a nod in respect to the overwhelming, awe-inspiring finality of individual human time/life.

That said, and with ample analyses of art history and its many colorful destinies, Gen realized that although we can never be fully certain about longevity, we can at least secure our work for the future—whether that be short- or long-term. What do we leave behind, and what does it transmit?

I have argued before that although there is no major difference between an artist and a magician (or shouldn't be), Gen was a magician

---

*Genesis P-Orridge early on referred to himself as "we," "us," and "they," suggesting and exploring the fluidity of personalities we all carry inside. Later on, as the Pandrogeny Project matured, this also included a transcendence of fixed gender identities. The new role or identity was *not* suddenly being a "woman" after having been a "man." The pandrogyne overrode the classical binary mode, and words like *s/he* and *he/r* became more prevalent in Gen's discourse. Over the years some people referred to Gen as "her," others as "him." I respect all explorations into the malleable aspects of identity, sexual or otherwise, but have chosen to stick with the masculine denominations as that has, in this case, been my own personal experience in our thirty-four years of interactions and dialogue.

first and foremost, and an artist second. This means that there was a conscious approach to work, and to how it all was based in and on an invocation of the desired. The work itself (in performance, concerts, visual art, etc.) could certainly be irrational, intuitive, and emotional. However, the handling of the work as such was integrated in rational and intellectual contexts—strategic, even—as parts of one single yet multidimensional magical operation.

Growing up and maturing in an artistic zeitgeist that supported both ideas of malleability and (literally) unselfish traits (as in C.O.U.M. Transmissions) *and* the Warholean notion of "protobranding" through stark iconography (for distinctly selfish reasons, and having begun already with Throbbing Gristle), Gen was aware of the dichotomy and paradox, but also of the power involved in *contradiction*.

Genesis P-Orridge is temporarily eternal in the sense that there is very likely an end for our culture as such, and what we leave behind now will simply one day be gone forever—especially considering the ephemeral quality of digital culture. But until that day we do have a large body of his work that continues to attract and inspire. One acquaintance in the art world told me shortly after Gen died (again, on March 14, 2020) that during the last year of life, Gen had transitioned from what's called a "major minor" to a "minor major." What this means is that a new degree of acclaim—a euphemism for increased financial worth—within the art world had taken place over a decade's time.

I feel that this was very much according to Gen's own plans. There was an increase in work, although health was failing (or perhaps for that specific reason?). There was an increase in interviews in more mainstream types of media (*New York Times,* etc.), exhibitions in bigger venues (The Warhol Museum in Pittsburgh, The Rubin in New York, several solo shows at respected galleries, etc.). There were three documentaries made (including my own *Change Itself* in 2016), the PTV3 concerts and records were many, and so on.

There was an intuitive and skillfully utilized understanding of the causal mechanics of Andy Warhol's crass worldview, as well as an attitude of "change itself" and "sacred intent" as being philosophical, spiritual filters.

There is one term that has stuck in my mind as signifying this apparent contradiction (if not in terms, then at times certainly in spirit): the title of the Velvet Underground song, "I'll Be Your Mirror," (which is also the title of a great volume of interviews with Warhol).[1]

One looks at things around one, filters them, and then expresses what one has filtered, embraced by emotion rooted in one's own ideals. This is a mirroring process that pretty much sums up the task of any artist. But for Gen there was also an *amplification* in the mirroring. It was not only a shard or a fractured piece of the cultural or societal mirror, wielded by an underdog renegade. It was a powerful, amplified mirror of a human soul that at times took on the shape of funhouse distortions and at other times reflected the literally bare necessities. All of this was based in existentially apt and painful realizations of what needed to be fixed—whether in the human individual or within the greater culture. As he said, "Just as we were adjusting to the gossamer fragility of nonsensus reality and absorbing the thought that what we all see is an age old, often useful, often discouraging social agreement and cultural construct, we were deliriously creative."[2]

Gen adopted the occupation of "cultural engineer" and undeniably brought an impact on many levels. Some of the phenomena that he was involved in as cultural engineer were the development of a Fluxus/mail art network mentality with the art world; "industrial" music/culture and its creative "cottage industry" sensibilities; "modern primitivism;" Acid House music; cyberculture; pandrogeny; and the conscious "invocation/evocation" of earlier kindred spirits (to keep them alive in the zeitgeist): Brion Gysin, William S. Burroughs, Pierre Molinier, Austin Osman Spare, Timothy Leary, to name but a few. Some of these phenomena and people may have been in the zeitgeist already, but no one can deny the amplification feats of the Genesis P-Orridge molecular media machine. It helped make these terms, concepts, and minds more readily available and palatable to the general culture.

Repetition of names is a mirroring. Talking about current affairs is a mirroring. Producing art that contains thoughts, feelings, and will is a mirroring. Weaving in the desired in an aestheticized discourse is a mirroring. Changing your own appearance is certainly a mirroring—transtemporal and transdimensional. Gen articulated this very well, as the following passage reveals.

> The psyche, in its deepest reaches, seems well able to participate in an existence beyond the web of space and time. This dimension is often dubbed "eternity" or "infinity," yet it actually seems to behave—if we for the moment take Spare's art as representative and, more vitally, functional and in no way symbolic—as either a one-way or two-way mirror, dependent for its operation upon a translation of the unconscious into a communicable image that bonds the actual atomic structures of the graphic image with its driving forces, unlocked from the unconscious into a fixed or mobile source of power dependent on previous viewers and, more critically, with our own individual abilities to interface directly with it.[3]

Gen was a mirror of the times, but one that peppered the reflection with concepts. By disseminating attractive and seductive words, and outrageous (for the most part) looks and appearances, the curious flocked and were presented with fodder for mind and senses alike. Many people found the dishes distasteful and foul—mere provocation for its own sake—whereas many others found that there was real nutrition there.

Another contradiction, perhaps: concepts were mirrored and spread, but the real key was not always *what* was spread but the fact that it *was* spread; that someone like Gen had the eloquent audacity to face counterforce and ridicule, and with no apparent "personal" ulterior motives.

A lighter term than *cultural engineer* would be *trendsetter*. Today something even lighter (and considerably more problematic) would be the term *influencer*. Gen was all of these things at once; using the same platforms—any platforms basically—to get the message out there.

His radical outrageousness in physical appearance as well as in the relayed messages became a magical method that very few have fully mastered. And these people have certainly been more magically aware than artistically so; knowing that one's own appearance is a necessary feature for the appearance of those who would/should transmit the message further.

The McLuhanesque in P-Orridge was always more multifaceted than a strict, causal equation. The medium itself may very well be the message, but the message is clearly defining and reflecting the medium, too—and beyond the strictly personal sphere, and beyond the present times.

Gen appreciated the concept of "quaquaversal," meaning something moving from a center in all directions at the same time. But just as those ideas and concepts did move out in attractive forms, there was also input coming in, "retro-quaquaversally." Gen was always interested in things going on, in popular culture as well as in scientific findings. One could apply both a spiritual/magical and a psychedelic filter when looking at this phenomenon (eventually these filters may be the same). Gen apparently made no real (or "moral") difference between high and low. Instead all input was equally percolated to see if perhaps some bits and pieces could be used in artworks, writings, and/or just plain unplain thoughts. Substantial fodder for the imagination often comes from beyond our own curating: we cannot fully decide what we take in on all levels. But what does come in also ends up somewhere.

This is where I find that Gen was a master. He assigned meaning to the initially apparently meaning*less,* and then assigned new positions for this within new constructions that carried some kind of thought-form or ideal. This thereby created an optimal fluidity in the prerogative of interpretation. Who has the right to interpret what, if basically anything can actually turn out to be absolutely filled with signal or meaning?

A few examples: championing the cut-up method of Gysin and Burroughs, and crossbreeding it with a tradition of magic and occult philosophy; championing the "third being" of pandrogeny as a transcending position, and the multiplicity of self, instead of being zeitgeistishly trapped in the "binary" or "nonbinary" pseudo-politicized demagogia; mastering the art of collage-making in which meaning is assigned to a new totality of previously meaningless pieces/fragments; turning intimate body piercings and alterations into political/philosophical symbols/memes/statements.

These are all mirroring processes that not only require a personal submission to an experiment, but also, given the flamboyant extroversion of Gen's psychological makeup, a desire to do this publicly. It is an externalization, an offering, a mirroring. (Strangely though, Gen often said that the collage work, which I would claim is the most inherently magical, was something that was made as a soul-searching kind of private work.[4])

The influence of French artist Pierre Molinier on P-Orridge cannot be overvalued in this regard. Molinier's pandrogyne, imaginary spheres, and exquisitely psychedelic collage work opened Gen up to what was possible, both existentially and in terms of art as an aid in personal, psychosexual development. As Gen so eloquently said, "The irreversible compulsion of Molinier's montages, where men become women, become clones of themselves, become animalistic, become erotic, become gross, become romantic, generates a maelstrom of fluid possibilities. We are in the eye of his tornado, red slippers flash past, a witch, a dildo, a mask, always a mask. Pierre Molinier insists we face the impenetrable fact of our obliteration. Yet simultaneously he describes a frolicking masqued ball, a carnival of interchangeable characters. All of who can be him and equally therefore all can be ourselves as well."[5]

Adornment, embellishment, and symbolic empowerment were concepts that transcended the mere look or the desire to visually shock. In the overall magical *weltanschauung* (worldview) of Genesis P-Orridge, the integration of symbols and sartorial externalizations became parts of a talismanic totality. The design of latter-day PTV3's denim uniforms, invoking outlaw bikers, can be traced back to the formation of specific intent, post-C.O.U.M. When the pure lysergic anarchy of C.O.U.M. fizzled out into a Thatcherian frying pan, the integration of (para)militaria was sizzling in another pot entirely: the camouflage TG uniforms designed by Laurence Dupré, the inclusion of SS insignia and other totalitarian talismans, and the bleak "famished" look in general. This then drifted on into the further paramilitary styles of Thee Temple Ov Psychick Youth (TOPY) and first-generation Psychic TV, with grey felt trousers, Dr. Martens boots, shaven heads, priest's shirts and collars, and stern talismans like skulls and daggers. For some the costume included the integration of a tuft of hair and a little braid à la Hare Krishna. This perhaps signified the next wave of psychic sartorialism: going full circle back into the safety of multicolored saturation ("Godstar," the emergence of Acid House, etc.).

As we were working together on setting up TOPYSCAN (again, the Scandinavian branch of TOPY), Gen donated four volumes to our library, called *Uniforms, Organization and History of the Waffen SS*.[6] These books had served as inspiration in the early TG days, Gen explained, when the collecting of cherry-picked dark symbols and insignia had begun in earnest. He inscribed one of the volumes, "Here it all is! For thee archives ov TOPYSCAN and Carl, all L-OV-E, Genesis 23."

And in many ways, it *was* already all there. The construction of a look can be intuitive and immediately aesthetic, or it can be thought-out and sought-out, with conscious effects in mind. Even toward the end of Gen's life, when physical energy was dwindling and health was failing, there was still a sense of uniform expression, even in the comfortable monotone pants and T-shirts he wore—which very often contained a didactic or provocative slogan or message.

Let's also return to the word(s) *makeup*. Gen's fascination with using makeup was included all along, even in the sterner and more masculine looks of his TG persona (eyebrows, and at times full facial makeup, with mascara and lipstick, etc.). In a sense I think this was to an equal degree a legacy from the flamboyant theatrics of C.O.U.M. as one dealing with strict gender perspectives.

The other main meaning of the word is useful, too: *makeup* as a creation of something fictitious. "He made it up," "he made himself up," and so on. This is extremely important when addressing the "psychic anarcho-sartorialism" of Genesis P-Orridge.

The outer changes in appearance were indicative of similar processes on the inside. Gen was making himself up as he went along, and truly adhering to the mottos of "Change Itself" and "Sacred Intent." This could swing both ways in terms of reception. It's easier to disbelieve someone far removed in your own affinity circle of references. It's easier to believe someone who you immediately trust as "being like me because the person looks like me." It's a very simple mechanism, and one that Gen used all his life. He created a surface that was most often in full accordance with inner thoughts and feelings. The sense of uncanny eeriness that many people felt certainly had to do with their own rejection of the immediate visual response. And yet it also definitely had to do with the clash—the apparent contradiction—between this immediate response and what was actually being presented (which was always pretty attractive, eloquent, and interesting).

Makeup was part of the makeup here: creating another layer of the controlled prerogative to control. It ranged from the subtle eyebrows of TG times, to the full-on palette overdrive of lysergic, late 1980s PTV, to early pandrogeny mimicking experiments together with partner Lady Jaye. It also included all-in surgical procedures and enhancements, and led to eventually enhancing and cheering up daily life in illness as an aging pandrogyne via vitalizing, colorful cosmetics.

It's hard to say what came first in these quite distinct phases: chemically induced awareness and enlightenment leading to more colorful clothing and radical makeup styles, or vice versa? Was it a case of altering one's physical body in theory and practice because of actual sexual inclinations, or vice versa? Perhaps it was indicative of coming to terms with one's own emotional need to be acknowledged because of/through a willingness to create wild looks to achieve that attention, or vice versa?

I believe it was very much a parallel kind of development—perhaps even quaquaversal. Gen lived in a psychedelic, magical bubble in which things happen. Whatever happens is to some degree controllable (by one's own makeup and design) and to some degree absolutely not. Even the most skilled magician cannot fully foresee the future and its reactions.

Taking on roles and personas via the outer mirror is always as much a protective shield as it is a signboard or megaphone. We define ourselves by what we're not as much as by what we are. Flaunting outrageous and sometimes even surreal looks is both saying, "Hey, look at me, I have something to say!" and *"Noli Me Tangere!"* The psychic anarcho-sartorialism is a defense mechanism as much as it is demagogia in potentia. I am absolutely *this,* but also absolutely not *that!*

Here it is also interesting to bring out the old P-Orridge slogan/motto, "When in doubt, be extreme!" It was certainly a well-tested modus operandi for Gen, rather than, "When in doubt, be silent," or "cautious," or whatever else. When conveying this wisdom in writing he often spelled *extreme* as *ex-dream.* This is an example of a further piece of the puzzle that goes beyond mere punning. To be "ex-dream" is of course *to have come from a dream;* a psychic sphere in which you can, either by happenstance or your own design, be completely malleable and also completely symbolic. When in doubt, retract or move forward to the magical bubble of creation and recreation, of definition and redefinition. Then boldly step out into the sphere of quaquaversal reflection and present/represent your self.

I can't foresee what effect photographs like the ones in *Temporarily Eternal* will have on the overall Genesis P-Orridge imprint or legacy. It's interesting because the book displays so many faces and phases over a long period of time—more or less half of Gen's life. And also because even those who've never heard of Gen or the ideas will quickly realize that this was a person who was genuinely committed to change as an existential principle. This in turn, of course, raises questions like, What was this person about?

Making oneself attractive for photographs (as well as interviews) is in many ways an indication that one knows how these things work. One will be interesting even beyond death if people only look at one's pictures or read one's words. And then that can—hopefully!—lead to some kind of integration or appreciation of those words (or art, or whatever the person's done in life).

Let's not forget another cornerstone of identity . . . What's in a name? The answer? A whole lot. Perhaps even more so than in a mere reflection or externalized aesthetics. When Neil Megson changed his name to Genesis P-Orridge in 1971, he created a literally "nominal" symbol, onto which people could project whatever they felt. This could be scandalous attacks and reprieves or admiring art-world servilities. This "brand" was created early on, during C.O.U.M. times, and lasted a whole lifetime (and apparently beyond).

But even that wasn't fully static. Gen's relationship with Jacqueline Breyer (who was born in 1969 and died in 2007) from 1993 on led to the development of another moniker. Now it was Breyer P-Orridge who was not only the new artist brand but also signified the living, breathing pandrogyne.

Even in the subtle shifts of the name were integrated deep thoughts and concepts. Letters and e-mails were signed, for instance, "Gen 23" (often with an added "psychick cross"). Or they would be signed "Gen," "Genny," "Djinn," or "Djinny." This showed not only the malleability of identity and gender but also included magical symbols and personae (a djinn is a supernatural creature/spirit in Arab/Muslim mythology). Gen also graciously assigned nicknames to many key people and collaborators over the decades. Peter Christopherson was "Sleazy," Christine Newby was "Cosey Fanni Tutti," David Bunting was "David Tibet," and Jacqueline Breyer was "Lady Jaye." Many of these nicknames stuck for life and would become personal career brands.

The will (or perhaps psychological need) to not only define and create but also continually redefine and recreate is the mark of the magician. What you make up becomes a tangible reality, which then becomes part of your own makeup and toolbox. And so on . . . The Pandrogeny Project together with Lady Jaye was undoubtedly the peak of this lifelong examination of the magically malleable. From the late '90s onward, Gen and Jaye began centralizing a look that would unite them and carry forth a distinct physical force field for the third mind concept of Burroughs and Gysin (in which two transcend and become something else: the *third* mind). Experimenting not only with makeup and clothes, sharing as much as was possible, they, as hinted at earlier, also began integrating cosmetic surgery, including breast implants and enhancements. In this they were not only reflecting themselves, each other, the inner and the outer, but also the third mind being of the pandrogyne. That this entity or psychic cluster also "fed back" to them seems highly likely.

As things and appearances changed pandrogynically, it was interesting to see how the outside world reacted. Most of Gen's already existing fans seemed to love it. The unexpected was always expected and appreciated. But it was also something that opened the doors to an international art world that had previously placed Gen in a fairly tight corner of 1970s British Fluxus and performance art. The feats of musical provocation didn't really count here, but the early collages and postcards, as well as documentation from C.O.U.M. performances, did. The pandrogyne was interesting not only because it was radical and visually appealing, it also connected with decades of actual theories and postmodern "justifications" in the zeitgeist. There was a thread of experimentation that had now come to fruition by merging intellectual theory with magical practice, as well as the "reality" of the body. This was done not only by cross-*dressing* but also cross-*fertilizing* two human bodies and minds.

In this regard, I would like to mention a book far more ambitious than the present one. In 2013, First Third Books published *S/he Is (Still)*

Her/e, which is a massive tome of photographs of Genesis P-Orridge. It is a wonderful book, covering basically a lifetime of experimentation and making up new reflection surfaces. Featured in the book is one particular photograph of Breyer P-Orridge, seated together in a car, adorned with surgical bandages yet dressed as if headed out for a fun night on the town. The text (by Gen) for this image references another source of key influence in our anarcho-sartorial perspective: Australian (performance) artist Leigh Bowery. " . . . a genius, thee Pablo Picasso of fashion. He changed everybody's view of clothing, how it works, why it functions. And there were absolutely no boundaries. Nothing was impossible to wear. He was inspired by anybody and created something for nobody. His approach was mystical and shamanic in a very profound way."[7] Does this in some way sound like Gen describing himself? He goes on as follows.

"Obviously, identity is a key concept. Who creates it? Who tries to shape and control it? The search for possible techniques to change it, mutate it and ultimately SELF re-design it is a constant theme. CHANGE. Sincere hunger for change for its own sake, see a cliff . . . JUMP OFF! When in doubt . . . BE EXTREME . . . or EX-DREAM. CHANGE THE WAY TO PERCEIVE AND CHANGE ALL MEMORY."[8]

All media and expressions became "victims" of the P-Orridgean approach, and all contributed to the multifaceted *gesamt* reflection. Essentially no distinction was being made between one thing and another thing—a concept in itself also heavily anchored in magical practice, and one that Gen was aware of.* There was apparently only one single distinction: the realization of mortality. No matter how we choose to look at this, it certainly is a great incentive to be active and creative. If we can see a connection, correlation, or even an equation between degree of this realization and creative output, Genesis P-Orridge's massive body

---

*This can be found, for instance, in Aleister Crowley's *The Book of the Law,* or in the practices of the Indian Aghori Babas.

of work is not at all surprising. The realization was present on so many levels and constituted the original impetus of expression and reflection; and one that just kept on ticking until the clock eventually stopped.

As time relentlessly moves onward, we have to do the same. Gen provided many useful approaches that were not cultic (as some would argue) but essentially individualistic and inspiring. "Dress as you wish" does not in any way mean that you have to dress (or act) outrageously. We all have our own psychic makeup to deal with (and deal with it we must). The key is to find one's own limits and boundaries, and then . . . to transcend them. Whether someone else notices it or not is another matter entirely.

Gen certainly transcended, over and over again. He placed his own being outside the mechanical apprehensions and comprehensions of time and space, and by doing so (and reporting back), left behind a multitude of clues and information for others. That in itself touches upon the bodhisattvan ideals of Buddhism. It also touches upon the role of the shaman and magician and courageous enlightened artist—all sharing the qualities and traits of the temporarily eternal.

6
Tripping the Dark Light Fantastic

Some Notes on Derek Jarman and His Influence

The imaginatio is to be understood here as the real and literal power to create images (Einbildungskraft = imagination)—the classical use of the word in contrast to phantasia, which means a mere "conceit" in the sense of insubstantial thought. In the Satyricon this connotation is more pointed still: phantasia means something ridiculous. Imaginatio is the active evocation of (inner) images secundum naturam, an authentic feat of thought or ideation, which does not spin aimless and groundless fantasies "into the blue"—does not, that is to say, just play with its objects, but tries to grasp the inner facts and portray them in images true to their nature. This activity is an opus, a work.

CARL JUNG, *JUNG ON ALCHEMY*

Sometimes I find it very hard to answer questions like, Which is your favorite film? They are numerous and they come in so many shapes and sizes. But it's intriguing how some films never go out of style or lose their impact. One keeps on returning to them time and time again, always finding some little detail or nuance one hadn't perceived before. This rare quality of continually unfolding and inspiring of course exists in other media, too, but I find it especially true for film, as the "dissemination" is such a strange and powerful mix of passive and active intake.

I think we all have those films in our lives; the ones that provide some kind of spiritual or intellectual service that is more or less inexplicable. They lie hidden in the dark and occasionally shine a literal light that one needs at that given moment.

One such film has for me always been *In the Shadow of the Sun* by British filmmaker and artist Derek Jarman (1942–1994). Its influence has been massive for me; much more so than Jarman himself. Sometimes the reverse relationship is true—a creator becomes more influential than the actual work. However, in this case his film has been ever present in my life, and in ways I can only describe as "occult." What I mean by this is that the film itself as a unique artwork that contains considerably more than merely meets the eye. There are substantial and exciting things underneath the surface. It has been a gateway to more information and inspiration—to more emotion and empowerment than I could ever have envisioned.

The film was completed in 1973, and came to some kind of definitive finished status in 1980 when a soundtrack by Throbbing Gristle was added. Although Jarman had worked on big movie productions like Ken Russell's *The Devils* (1971, as set designer) Jarman was always a manic Super 8 aficionado. With his small and handy Nizo camera, Jarman shot material with friends, at outings, and on journeys. He also staged performances that included scenography, choreography, and costumes. Using the Super 8 format's advantages (inexpensive film and processing and very easy to use, being "point and shoot"), as well as disadvantages (limited control over exposure, complicated editing),

Jarman refined his technical craft as stemming from or belonging to his cinematic vision.

I believe that his frantic immersion also affected his vision as it progressed. In other words, he conceptualized new images and scenes as he had seen similar material before on Super 8: a kind of creative feedback loop in which form and content merged with his creative mind. This was, I suspect, to a degree helped by his knowing his own technology so well, and using it as much as he could. An example of this was the Nizo camera's intervalometer, which allowed the user to expose the film at variable speeds—thereby altering the normality of perception when the film was projected/shown. "The re-filming and original shooting speed allowed Jarman control over the imagery which produced a strong painterly texture and pulsating rhythm. The grainy streaked colour effect is like a strong broad brush-stroke, and assisted by the degeneration effect of re-filming, the colours are often softened and suffused. The rhythm is one which Jarman describes, aptly, as like a 'heart-beat'—sensual, dream-like and erotic."[1]

When people talk of Jarman's work from the 1970s (mainly), the first association will always be that it's slow-motion and grainy. *In the Shadow of the Sun* is exactly that: slow and grainy. It's a vision that evokes dream states, in which we have a hard time hanging onto (or understanding) what the people in the film are actually doing. It lingers, meanders, and flows on, and we get caught up in a meditative beauty rather than any kind of linear narrative or traditional understanding. There are layers superimposed on each other, the colors are muted and saturated at the same time, and the soundtrack further amplifies a general and most uncanny eeriness.

It's undoubtedly a work of beauty, however, one that attracts not by mere aestheticized eye candy but rather by the evocation of curiosity, intrigue, and secret references. Jarman himself described the film as ". . . related to John Dee and alchemy where the distinction between words and things is obscured by the identification of symbols with things."[2]

The film is quite simply a masterpiece of understated impact. I assume that most people will immediately dismiss or discard it as experimental or pretentious. For me it has always been a manifestation of a very precise kind of poetry; one that uses color, movement, chance, and playfulness, yet in a decidedly minor key, so to speak. As Jarman himself said, "This is the way the Super-8s are structured from writing: the buried word-signs emphasise the fact that they convey a language. There is the image and the word, and the image of the word. The 'poetry of fire' relies on a treatment of word and object as equivalent: both are signs; both are luminous and opaque. The pleasure of Super-8 is the pleasure of seeing language put through the magic lantern."[3]

When I first saw Jarman's film in the early 1980s, it wasn't easy to come by rare experimental films, or cult films, or the extreme horror films that I knew I loved before I'd even seen them. If one was lucky, one could possibly catch some screenings abroad at independent cinemas or cinematheques. But it was mostly the stuff of fantasy and imagination, with seed coming from fanzines and books that wrote about early surrealist experiments from Europe or the "new American cinema"—or similar currents that flowed and ebbed.

Then something very magical happened in the early 1980s: video appeared. Suddenly films were available on VHS cassettes to buy and play in the comfort of one's own home. It was expensive as hell, which of course created a booming market for second- or even third-generation VHS copies. If one was a diligent networker (which I was) one could soon see grainy, blurry copies—with distorted colors—of the films that one had—until then—only read about. It was truly magical.

As VCRs (videocassette recorders) spread quickly, the market for all kinds of films grew—highbrow, lowbrow, and in-between, and even for small and arty films. Several video labels put out music and films by contemporary avant-garde artists, and suddenly a new world opened itself to unsuspecting yet curious teenagers like me.

One of the first films I bought was the aforementioned *In the Shadow of the Sun*. (I still have that original VHS cassette, just in case all other technologies should one day fail . . .) I more or less immediately understood or sensed that there was more to this film than what met the eye. The otherworldly soundtrack had been created for the 1980 version of the film by Throbbing Gristle, one of my favorite bands. As with many bands at the time, TG was immersed in art, philosophy, culture, and occulture, and it widely disseminated references to authors, filmmakers, magicians, and other powerful protagonists of hidden histories. The merging of Jarman and Throbbing Gristle for me became a rabbit hole into which I gladly threw myself headfirst. There was an occultural hot spot or intersection right there and then, which already in 1981 spilled over into Jarman's work with Psychic TV (PTV, which was Genesis P-Orridge's band after TG), Coil (Peter Christopherson's band after TG, together with John Balance), and the communal effort of them all with Thee Temple Ov Psychick Youth (TOPY, the infamous magical order/think tank/occultural network).

I started collecting information, books, and music, as well as relevant films on VHS video. The first and quite controversial Psychic TV videos included a short piece of propaganda called "Message from The Temple" in which TOPY's focus on sexuality and sexual magic as a resistance was poetically stated against soft and alluring music by PTV. In the film, a man is sitting at a desk, and then standing at a pulpit of sorts (but deliberately out of synch with the eloquent and seductive declamation that is heard)* and holding a large psychick cross (the emblem/symbol/talisman of TOPY). I soon found out that this man was Derek Jarman, which just made this collective of artist-magicians even more attractive to me.

The art and information that was produced by these people was philosophically based, psychedelic, magical, alchemical, sexual, occultural, liberating, and very inspiring. I delved into it all more and more,

---

*Delivered by another TOPY collaborator, Alan Oversby, aka Mr. Sebastian, a famous tattooer and piercer in the London underground scene at this time.

to the point of becoming actively involved and working with TOPY and PTV, as well as initiating a friendship with P-Orridge that went on to span more than thirty years.

At about the same time I got involved with TOPY, Christopherson and Balance left to focus more on their own musical project: Coil. They continued working with Jarman on many projects, including his 1985 film, *The Angelic Conversation*. As in many, if not most, of Jarman's films, the theme had some kind of occult origins. Curator and British Film Institute archivist William Fowler had some interesting commentary on this point.

> He was always actively interested in the occult and, among other esoteric volumes, he acquired an original copy of Heinrich Cornelius Agrippa's sixteenth-century work *Three Books of Occult Philosophy*. He was also very taken with the Elizabethan occultist and alchemist Dr John Dee, a figure evoked in Shakespeare's *The Tempest*— hence Jarman's adaptation of the play. Dee claimed to speak with angels and used a black obsidian mirror to make contact with them. Jarman thought of the film camera as a modern equivalent, an occult technology through which to gain insight into the less visible aspects of existence and explore ideas about magic. "Film is the wedding of light and matter—an alchemical conjunction," he wrote in his memoir, *Dancing Ledge*.[4]

As a thank-you for Throbbing Gristle's delightful soundtrack for *In the Shadow of the Sun* Jarman made the short film *TG: Psychic Rally in Heaven* in 1981. It contains his signature style of multiple layers in saturated Super 8 footage that was filmed at a TG concert at the club Heaven, with music from their album "The Second Annual Report."

Slightly later, in 1982, Jarman ambitiously documented the event The Final Academy in London, which brought together sources of inspiration like William S. Burroughs and Brion Gysin with younger artists like P-Orridge, Christopherson, and Jarman. Of this material, only the 1982 film *The Pirate Tape* remains, showing Burroughs and acolytes hanging around on a pavement in London; signing books and chitchatting.

In 1984, Jarman made the film *Catalan* together with P-Orridge and Catalan surrealist Jordi Valls. It was shot on 16mm in Catalonia and has a slightly different aesthetic based in strict montage/editing rather than Jarman's usual meandering pace. The eerie music of Psychic TV fits well into this homage to surrealism in general, and perhaps to the early work of Buñuel in particular.

The same year, Jarman worked together with Coil as well, on *The Angelic Conversation,* which was released in 1985. Renowned musician Peter Christopherson captured some of Jarman's magic in the words that follow.[5]

> It was impossible not to be buoyed by his passion and energy. Soon footage and beautiful calligraphic notes started dropping into our letterbox. Of course, the images were wonderful. When the film was assembled, we all went to a studio on Camden to record the soundtrack. One or two "set pieces" were from existing Coil albums, but most was improvised directly to picture, John and I constantly trying out new things on cutting-edge sampling equipment, and Derek bouncing around, burning sulphur-bright, as always: "Yes, that's good . . . well, perhaps not that . . . but what about the sound of rowing here? Yes, wonderful, marvellous!"

Jarman's Super 8 work, and *In the Shadow of the Sun* in particular, quite simply left a dent in my aesthetic and magical formatting, and it all still keeps on spinning. In the 2010s I was increasingly receiving offers to teach at art schools and universities, and my distinctly occultural focus in the classroom had (and still has) deep roots in this formatted soil.

On a more distinctly creative level, most of the personal art films I've made over the decades carry the same kind of *verfremdung* (alienating) effect that Super 8 in slow-motion so elegantly provides. This same effect is also felt in the superimpositions and applications of the more or less random potency of cut-ups.*

At an art college in Cali, Colombia, in 2018, I let the film *Lunacy* be the springboard for a discussion about talismanic films and how to upheave the narrative structures and expectations in the most efficient way. For instance, Vanessa and I filmed the students one and one (head-shots) expressing their desires, but edited together the specific sound with someone else's headshot. I have also tried the same approach with students at a workshop in Skopje, Macedonia, and at the Royal College of Art in Stockholm.

An important thing for me in all of this was to tie everything in with art history, and to see how distinctly it also tied in with occultural history and experimentation. Meaning, what you are creating is not "only" art, but also a talismanic platform through which desires may or may not be processed. This is a living and thriving tradition, not just an odd intellectual occurrence in our contemporary times. As Jarman said, "In 1974, I bought copies of Jung's *Alchemical Studies* and *Seven Songs to the Dead,* and these provided the key to imagery that I had created quite unconsciously in the preceding months, and also gave me the confidence to allow the dream-images to drift and collide at random."[6]

As in magical practice, the key to this artistic process is the upheaval of the rational mind and its attempts to structure everything to the degree that no room for the imagination or play exists. As in magical practice, one uses one's creative tools and abilities to change (the percep-tion of) time and space. This thereby opens the door not of certainties but of uncertainties and all their potential—albeit temporarily.

Today we're indoctrinated with fast-paced, causal, and perfectly CGI-maneuvered epics, either in commercial entertainment or more artistic approaches. Technology rules, for good and bad. More often than not, the tempo is high—or what could be called normal. This is

---

*These films include, for instance, *Lunacy,* made in 2017 with my wife, Vanessa Sinclair; *Mementeros,* which was made in 2019 also with Vanessa; and *Reseduction,* made in 2022.

of course a zeitgeist phenomenon. If things are moving in any one direction, it's in the direction of higher speed. The fragmented culture that nurtures us (or the younger generations specifically) leads to an incapacity to grasp the irrational, erratic, slow, or nonlinear. What cannot immediately be interpreted is discarded as quickly as it appears.

Yet it's only when the linear, rational cinematic curse is upheaved that things get interesting. Today, to reach truly emotional or psychic states when watching a film, we have to go beyond someone *visually* shedding a tear or someone *telling* us what they feel. The cinematic language as such has been depleted by a tsunami of normality, media-based mediocrity, and visual technicalities. The American slogan often used by people like David Mamet—"The story is in the cut"—no doubt stemming from writers like Stephen King and his massacre of adjectives—is counterproductive when it comes to showing or conveying deep psychic or emotional states of mind. Upheaval is needed.

One contemporary curse is that technology enables such a multitude of enchanting possibilities, which I think can be quite negative. An analogous situation exists within music technology. Does having so many user-friendly digital building blocks to choose from stifle or encourage inner vision and ideas?

Of course, this is not an absolute equation. But what signified many pioneering filmmakers was that they made the absolute most of the little they had. Their work was very often conveyed through a cinematic language that was based on intuitive vision rather than preformulated statements or ready-to-use filters. I would argue: ergo, a most magical approach! Jarman weighs in on painting versus filmmaking when he says: "Painting is obsolete in a sense; it's no longer dealing with the world outside. What I discovered in film was community. I discovered my world in film. I wasn't the director of those Super-8 films in that sense. I merely directed the camera."[7]

The surrealists were ahead in many ways. The early films of Buñuel, Hans Richter, Man Ray, and many others consciously approached the subconscious by violent yet poetic upheaval. Some artists like Cocteau even managed to weave in dream logic and visual poetry in films that were more or less commercial. Kenneth Anger and Maya Deren used it too, slightly later, and also integrated distinctly magical elements and themes into their films. Although Anger often claimed to be mainly inspired by the very structured montages of Eisenstein, there is still a strong element of subconscious logic in there.

Derek Jarman always strived for poetry, even in his more structured feature films. Sometimes it worked, sometimes it didn't. But the main thing is that he tried to retain and develop a cinematic language of his own. And in this he succeeded. *In the Shadow of the Sun* evokes something magical that doesn't need an explanation about how or why Jarman was actually interested in magic and occultism. The postmodern information/explanation approach is irrelevant, redundant. The work forcefully transmits through its own language. The film opens up a vista that is not necessarily filtered through will or concrete agendas. It's enough that it just *is,* in a similar way to how Brian Eno once defined "ambient" music. In his view, there is no real end or beginning, because there is no traditional narrative. According to Jarman, "We might need those dreams and they might really be part of us, and that's what interests me about John Dee. Alchemy is about turning matter to gold, about dross and being. About dark dross being pure gold. And for pure gold don't read capitalism, read gold in its spiritual sense—metal that doesn't corrupt. Of course, gold is the ultimate corruption . . ."[8]

Many of my favorite films are intensely psychedelic, in part probably because the filmmakers were interested in mind-expansion and intuitive explorations of form and color. This is interesting because it creates an aesthetic loop over time. With this, people get turned on to or by certain films and their languages while in an elevated state of mind, and the experience seeps into their own creative expressions, even in other fields or disciplines. This then goes on to affect others in a similar yet new way. And so on and so forth.

When talking about experimental or poetic film, this seems to imply mainly an aesthetic perspective. It's easier to drift into the film form if there's not a distinct narrative function and if it evokes a "dreamy" feeling. But that's not an absolute statement of course. The early Jodorowsky films managed to do both: merge form and narrative content for a turned-on generation. Conrad Rooks did this with his film *Chappaqua,* as did Dennis Hopper with *Easy Rider.* Even early David Lynch films reflected this composite. And, of course, there are many others.

I suspect that the reason we like films like this is the immediate resonance that comes from narrative upheaval. It doesn't have to be form-based. It can also be content-based, and perhaps it's even best when it's a mix of both? I think it's totally possible to try and explain what Bela Tarr's *Werckmeister Harmonies* or *Satantango* is about, but why would one? Why should one? The enjoyment comes from letting go and just being part of something that is not predictable, yet may be totally full of meaning. In films such as these, the story is strange, the storytelling perhaps ultraslow, and the audiovisual impact so compelling that one has to either reject or, preferably, immerse oneself in it.

The feeling that one is part of something unpredictable leaves one temporarily open. The cinematic language becomes a door-opener in itself. Now the question appears: Can this be used for something creative, or possibly magical? Can it be used on a personal level? We know that the opposite is painfully true: the predictability of commercial advertising and commercial television exists to close the door of critical thinking and creative behavior by seductive repetition. So the opposite must surely be true, too?

And indeed it is. It is totally possible to use the open state of mind to sow seeds stemming from one's personal will rather than harvest from someone else (and also pay for it).

Basically one makes a film based on genuine expression and vision, in one's own aestheticized way, and one consciously plants something in there, in form or content or both, which will then be allowed to manifest via the viewers. I'm not talking about propaganda or exploitation of the audience, which has more to do with the psychology of commercial advertising. What I mean is something more personal, something that doesn't need to be obvious or blatant. It can be a poetic trace of what one desires in a visual frame, a line or sentence of speech, or a contrapuntal use of audio in relation to the visuals. It could be anything that one decides and conceptualizes. It's essentially the difference that lies in whispering "I desire" rather than loudly demanding "I want."

In 2014, I decided I wanted to make a tribute to this very special "cinemamour" of mine. I wanted my film to be a tribute to Jarman's masterpiece, but of course for it to stand on its own two feet. Whereas the aesthetic grid is there (and hopefully always will be), this film needed to be my own—how else could one pay tribute to such a strong "auteur" as Jarman?

Having filmed a lot of material on Super 8 ever since my own glorious 1980s days of experimentation, I have accumulated a pretty vast archive. I have also collected other people's films, and basically anything Super 8 whenever I've come across it.

I used this archival Super 8 material, shot some new ditto, and made it all synaptically sensuous; slow, saturated, and superimposed. The soundtrack was performed live by my musical project at the time: Cotton Ferox. We improvised and recorded it in my band member Thomas Tibert's apartment in Stockholm. We were joined by Joakim Karlsson Kurén, and together we immediately entered an almost mystical state of mind. We had all loved TG so much since early on. (Incidentally, when I first met my longtime musical partner Tibert at a party in Stockholm in the mid-1980s, my spontaneous question to him was, "Do you like TG?").

In the film I was making I wanted to retain method rather than "sound." We just improvised attentively, and without watching the film. The magic of the moment would simply decide what the music would sound like, and how well it would fit the film. And I'm happy to say, it did! When I felt the film was perfect, I simply added the music, and wham-bam . . . there it was: my own little miasmic epos, encapsulating a spirit or gestalt I had lived and worked with for thirty years. I decided to call my Derek Jarman tribute *Sub Umbra Alarum Luna* (Latin for "In the Shadow of the Moon").

When it was released in early 2015, Genesis loved my *Sub Umbra* film, and wrote the following blurb for the DVD cover: "It's amazing. It truly captures the precise vibe of Derek's SHADOW in a way so perfect it could BE a Derek film!" For me, it was one of those beautiful and synchronistic moments that meant a perfect circle had been drawn as well as lived.

Incidentally, in 2016 and 2017, PTV3 (as the incarnation was called then) performed and recorded new music to screenings in New York and London of Jarman's slo-mo masterpiece. It seems the attraction never really fades away, but rather just seeps into impressionable and impressed minds; new and old alike.

7
Mondo Transcripto!

In the late 1980s I traveled around Europe with a film program called *Visions of Occulture*. It contained some Jodorowsky classics, Benjamin Christensen's *Häxan* (in the "Witchcraft through the Ages" version from 1968, narrated by William S. Burroughs), and other films. Also included was the classic 1975 Italian Mondo film *Mondo Magic*.

This highly entertaining "shockumentary" takes us into a world of strange rites and weird customs of indigenous people in Africa, Asia, and Latin America. It features manual surgery in the Philippines, drug use and duels in the Amazon, Moslem magical spells, Christian self-torture, fertility rites, and a whole lot more. The film is literally a colorful trip through a world of remarkable and sometimes disturbing phenomena.

I loved all the documentary footage (and still do). Also, the juxtaposition between images of wonder and fascination and a narration that swings between deadpan observation and casually condescending comments—yet always under some kind of umbrella of tolerance and understanding—immediately made me love these kinds of Mondo films. An example of this narration is as follows. "Much like the days when Stanley cut through the jungle in search of Livingstone, there are still places on the outskirts of our global village where calloused hands pounding on tom toms announced the intrusion of the white man."[1]

One might assume that the weirdly poetic tone used would come from some hack writer's desk, quickly penned down as bizarre scenes flickered on the editing table monitor. But no, *Mondo Magic* was written by Alberto Moravia, esteemed Italian author of highbrow books such as *Il Disprezzo*, written in 1954. That book was made into the celebrated Godard movie *Le Mépris* in 1963, and starred not only Brigitte Bardot but Fritz Lang as well. Moravia was also friends with other contemporary intellectuals like Pier Paolo Pasolini.

When watching Mondo films, one feels uncannily uneasy because the discrepant relationship between what's being seen and heard (through the narration) is often sizzling in temperature—even to the degree of causing what I will henceforth call Spontaneous Synaptic Combustion (SSC). This is the moment of experiencing astounding disbelief that is still somehow accepted by the assaulted senses and the mind. It's a common occurrence when watching good "exploitation" films, and/or derivatives such as "sexploitation" or "blaxploitation," or "psychotronic" films.

In other words, one may experience surprising reactions to films that are not entirely what they claim or seem to be. This is undoubtedly a direct heritage stemming from hyperbolic, competitive marketing campaigns where "more is always a whole lot more." These are films that set out ambitiously but most often fail to deliver. They contain an artistic vision incomprehensible to anyone but the artist, and exploit whatever's in the zeitgeist but perhaps a little bit over the top. Their limited budgets provoke hysteric overcompensations in their shortcut-driven ingenuity.

These films carry those "Wait? What?" and "Wow!" moments that produce laughter as a kind of defense mechanism rather than as an amplification of the pleasantly familiar (as in sitcoms or rom-coms). The best Mondo films are filled with these Spontaneous Synaptic Combustion moments. One could even argue that most often they *are* SSC experiences from beginning to end—at least the good ones.

Someone who was genuinely affected by the groundbreaking and pioneering 1962 film *Mondo Cane* and its subsequent copycats was British author J. G. Ballard. Ballard's dystopian fictional (?) oeuvre stretched from science fiction to meditations on machine culture and a fetishizing of humanity's ever-present death drive. His absolutely classic experimental novel, *The Atrocity Exhibition,* was published for the first time in 1970. It contains scenes that are presented as almost culled from a sensationalistic "shockumentary," and there's even a character/presence called Jacopetti (the name of the infamous Italian author/director of *Mondo Cane*).

"The Six-Second Epic. Travers waited on the mezzanine terrace for the audience to leave the gallery floor. The Jacopetti retrospective had been a success. As the crowd cleared, he recognized the organizer, a now familiar figure in his shabby flying jacket, standing by a display of Biafra atrocity photographs."[2]

In an interview from 2004, Ballard speculated about the impact of these transgressive films. "What the *Mondo Cane* audiences wanted was the horrors of peace, yes, but they also wanted to be reminded of their own complicity in the slightly dubious process of documenting these wayward examples of human misbehaviour. I may be wrong, but I think that the early *Mondo Cane* films concentrated on bizarre customs rather than horrors, though the gruesome content grew fairly rapidly, certainly in the imitators' films."[3] Ballard's musings continue: "We needed violence and violent imagery to drive the social (and political) revolution that was taking place in the 1960s—violence and sensation, more or less openly embraced, were pulling down the old temples. We needed our tastes to be corrupted—Jacopetti's films were part of an elective psychopathy that would change the world (so we hoped, naively)."[4]

Whether they were titillated by shots of indigenous women's breasts in slow-motion (or their fellow tribesmen's penises), or outraged by the fact that people in other cultures eat dogs and other pets, or nauseated by gruesome burial customs, international audiences were adjusted to a new level of desensitizing that perhaps eased and suited, like hand in glove, the ever-present TV footage from Vietnam, student revolts, political terrorism, and other 1960s and 1970s crisis hotspots of the time.

The Mondo film took on the form of a "serious" documentary; a form that people recognized from TV and therefore assumed trustworthy. But the showing of considerably more than was allowed on TV, and the snide, quasi-philosophic narrations on top—and not forgetting the often cheesy soundtracks—created a new cinematic form in which the real collided with the (almost) unbelievable in a gently surreal fashion.

One can of course always argue about what's cause and what's effect, and still not really come up with any distinct answer. Film historian and academic Mark Goodall sums up this Mondo ambivalence and ambiguity well in his great book about the genre, *Sweet and Savage:*

"Such films were often not conceived to 'exploit' audiences—although many mondo films later did this; they were not made to 'break the taboos' of societies or agitate for any meaningful socio-cultural or political change, but some did this too; they were not intended to be pornographic, although many exhibited and encouraged voyeuristic tendencies. These films were created as cinematic, poetic and useful commentaries on human behaviour in some of its wildest and weirdest formations."[5]

Film historian and author Bill Landis (together with his partner Michelle Clifford) wrote extensively about the genre in his influential fanzine *Sleazoid Express.* He also shares this ambiguous outlook: "Stunning pre-mod era color photography adds to an already potent mixture. It delivers the exploitation movie requisites of shock value, violence, sex, and grotesque comedy, and continues to fascinate almost four decades later, personifying the misanthropy it ostensibly criticises, morally implicating the viewer by default. *Mondo Cane* is ultimately more symptomatic of man's foibles than a wry commentary on them."[6]

Some would argue that these films were full of cheap shock tactics and were exploitative, and some would argue that they heralded a groundbreaking new documentary attitude, yet perhaps filtered via distinctly Italian hysterics. Gualtiero Jacopetti, who authored *Mondo Cane* and many other controversial films, believed in the filmmaker as a kind of superman with a vision, rather than merely as a casual observer. This of course leads to a great deal of subjectivity and a conscious experimentation with (desired) effects vis-à-vis the audience: "For me, a documentary is a film to be narrated exactly like a conventional film, and as such, it must rely on a director's strong personality and profound preliminary preparation. It has the advantage of the immense fascination coming from contemporary events, of the truth of that which it shows. Documentary, therefore, conceived truly as spectacle, to be projected in the first-run motion picture halls, with many, many people watching it. This is the documentary."[7]

Recently I decided to rewatch a few of these old Mondo favorites, to see if they still held up or if they should simply be filed under "juvenile fascinations":

> *Mondo Cane* (Gualtiero Jacopetti, Franco Prosperi, Paolo Cavara, Italy, 1962)
>
> *Kwaheri: Vanishing Africa* (Thor Brooks, Byron Chudnow, United States, 1964)
>
> *Africa: Blood and Guts* (Gualtiero Jacopetti, Franco Prosperi, Italy, 1966)
>
> *Mondo Magic* (Alfredo and Angelo Castiglioni, Guido Guerrasio, Italy, 1975)
>
> *Of the Dead* (Jean-Pol Ferbus, Dominique Garny, Thierry Zéno, Belgium, 1979)

My evaluation was that both options apply. But I also found some fascinating aspects that in many ways amplified the age-old SSC crystallizations even more. One aspect was definitely the hysteric tone and verbose hyperbole of the narratives themselves—usually a bastardized mix between original Italian hysterics and, in attention-grabbing translation, American marketing pizzazz.

In order to perhaps write an essay about the film genre as such, I decided to transcribe the narratives from these five films through an online "artificial intelligence" (AI) transcription service. The software simply "listens" to what is being said, and then turns it into editable writing. As we all know, technology nowadays is great but very far from perfect. In fact, the transcription created a whole new narrative in which the "real" was thoroughly enhanced by the technologically perceived.

Not only was this narrative a blast to read, it also brought to mind two aspects of interpretation. The first was that, just as the original narrations definitely told "a story and a half" through formulation, exaggeration, and contrapuntal clashes with the images, so this transcription contained "random" bonuses that were close enough to be acceptable but still jolting in an uncanny way.

The second aspect of interpretation was my own connection to a literary as well as magical tradition: the cut-ups as developed and implemented by William S. Burroughs and Brion Gysin from the 1950s onward, and, slightly later, by Genesis P-Orridge and others. Using randomly chosen selections of basically any expressed source material in randomly assembled new montages created a whole new narrative (and style). These pioneers claimed that these new montages could prophetically "leak" the future and definitely reveal what was *really* being said in the source material. It was a literal (and literary) disruption creating revealing fodder for an associative imagination.

My AI-produced transcriptions of these already quite hysteric and hyperbolic cinema-not-so-vérité narratives simply reminded me so much of the early experiments by Burroughs and Gysin that I decided to edit some of the pieces together.

Working on this essay, I was also reminded to check my archive for something that I felt had relevance. When visiting the American artist Peter Beard in New York in 2005, he showed me a part of his amazing collection of Africana: a framed original letter written by British missionary and explorer David Livingstone. Some weeks later, Beard sent me a transcript of the letter (addressed to anti-slavery "activist" and fellow missionary Horace Waller). Reading through this letter, I couldn't help "hearing" it read through a voice that sounded exactly like a Mondo film narrator . . .

. . . the most startling disease I have seen among slaves is not earth and clay eating which too is a disease per se but what really seem to be broken heartedness. It does not attack those who have been slaves in their own land but those who have been free—I saw a party taken across Lualaba by a slaver and when they saw this mighty river roll between them and home they seemed to lose all heart . . . Twenty-one who were then considered "safe" were unchained and scuttled off to the mountains but eight still in the chain and in good health died in three days.[8]

Although Livingstone was certainly the real deal compared to hysteric Italian filmmakers, I can see some similarities. Livingstone wrote his letter less than one hundred years before the Mondo films were beginning to be made, but it was the dawn of a hundred years that would change Africa forever in irreparable ways. What the original explorers and colonizers exploited, the Mondo filmmakers exploited to an equal degree—or at least the bloody aftermaths of both colonization and decolonization. Thus a trail of actual imperialism donned a new filmic frock; one of media-savvy cynicism and gently mocking both genuine traditional customs and desperate attempts to shake off the yokes of yesteryear.

And what is Joseph Conrad's 1899 masterpiece, *Heart of Darkness,* if not an eloquent precursor to the narratives of these speculative displays of shock and sensation?

I steamed up a bit, then swung downstream, and two thousand eyes followed the evolutions of the splashing, thumping, fierce river-demon beating the water with its terrible tail and breathing black smoke into the air. In front of the first rank, along the river, three men, plastered with bright red earth from head to foot, strutted to and fro restlessly. When we came abreast again, they faced the river, stamped their feet, nodded their horned heads, swayed their scarlet bodies; they shook towards the fierce river-demon a bunch of black feathers, a mangy skin with a pendent tail—something that looked like a dried gourd; they shouted periodically together strings of amazing words that resembled no sounds of human language; and the deep murmurs of the crowd, interrupted suddenly, were like the responses of some satanic litany.[9]

I am not sure that these edited snippets from the Mondo films will reveal any truths or prophecies at all. They are, however, remarkable excerpts from an era that was perhaps becoming self-consciously anxious in apocalyptic apprehensions but that for commercial reasons couldn't really leave behind the perspective of ridiculing those less materialistically fortunate.

The interpretation of this, in many ways old material by a new intelligence self-admittedly "artificial," perhaps shines the light on where we stand today. Instead of relying on our own capacities of interpretation (and transcription!), we rely on technology for efficiency. When things are not perfect (are they ever?) perhaps we far too easily accept the situation? Instead of critically working with and evaluating a given material, we instead spend our time editing technologically sanctioned fragments into a basic coherence.

Please note the surprising presence of large tech names that certainly didn't exist in the films, nor in mid-1970s, period! How these seeped into the main text is mysterious, or perhaps even "occult" in the prophetic sense. Perhaps they rank on top in the reservoir of accessible interpretation possibilities? Perhaps their secrets codes and markers of ownership were somehow squeezed to the surface by too much primordial African weirdness? If so, perhaps an invisible battle between sensual sources and appropriating forces has been initiated by your own very reading of this essay? Or perhaps it's simply an SSC-induced, intellectualized declaration of love for Jacopetti, Moravia, the Castiglione brothers, and all the other cinematic sensationalists?

However, I hope the following offering gives something beyond all of the above, and then some.

It simply is what it is, or . . . whatever you make of it.

Their Cosmic Ties Come Dressed

Many times before the camera has ventured into the dark continent, but never before has its darkest secrets been revealed with such starling staggering sights. You actually see more fertility rites, rhythmic orgy of sexual frenzy culminating in a binary sacrifice of a virgin. The world's most fantastic husband, a witch doctor with 49 wives and 212 children, never before seen dance of puberty, as new bio maidens cross the threshold into womanhood, the eternal drama of jungle survival . . . Remember founder Justin Young was gone, was in the shower. My goal is to assemble means, Nikita notice your nose. She must have a fairly scary Santo Nino Kalyan Tito Tito Cynthia was via yoga marijuana, she didn't come today, may come from within us countries. Morning Good morning welcome. Young eager yo yo do not intend to use this area set of women, and women were chemo for tourists I don't recall. If you can hit the broadside of a barn you can lose that Reddit gun, so powerful it could demolish a dinosaur, get him anywhere. That shot killer is bound to knock him down . . . This one's a must for the latest most up to date brochure for a trip through the animal paradise, that inviolate sanctuary of our planet's disappearing wildlife. That sacred shrine of nature where even whispering was forbidden. Because today your trip can be a lot more jolly. You can shout scream curse and romp around to your heart's content . . . Land of great beauty, in Africa is also a land of great brutality, a continent of desperation. Here in Africa, all this beautiful and Google's uniquely, after all, this is disappearing. Here the ancient thing, and the ancient ways as well are giving way to all that is new, and modern . . . The following day after the remains are on, the following day their cosmic ties come dressed. I will cosmic tie this hand first. Meaning that nails they do, jaw, jaw they so john dangerous job shackle day sat down to town to go to town to do. Auto auto things come on down, Mama got one. The Union, your power application, Santa Ros, to go on being my mom got a nice nice title. I'm sorry, I thought a long time to go to Coachella or go to college, climate change, Toby multizone, I can only speak for myself and I do . . . They really don't, they know it's inevitable, it's gonna happen, but they're not anxious for it to happen anytime soon. Actually, what we were saying before maybe I find that rather than maybe I'm not afraid. Maybe it just shows that there are as well and me there. No matter what you say, or do, it's gonna happen anyway . . . Besides, the duty of the chronicler is not to sweeten the truth, but to report it objectively to the east of New Guinea. This is the law of the Jimbo deep in the heart of New Guinea. There is still one place on this earth where there is not much difference between the life of a child and that of a pig. Under a huge sky at the top of very high mountains that seem to lift the earth for the very source of light man lives still surrounded by darkness . . . Therefore, only their ancestors can build the planes. The spirits of the deceased cannot know the white man. Therefore all those wonderful things that the planes carry were meant for their descendants. They've left the mission. They forgot their prayers. And here they are. Waiting faithfully at the doorway to the sky . . . The American woman on the other hand, must lose weight if she wishes to be successful in love. We're in Los Angeles, one of the many big panic gyms. Famous health clinics specializing in remodeling women, come hundreds of American women, some to spend a good part of their most recent widowhood in the hope of losing the extra weight accumulated during their latest marriage. And to get back in line with the laws of gravity while waiting for the next inevitable wedding . . . In complete absence of doors or windows, flirting and sexual play is done in the open for all to see. However, the erotic games never go beyond innocent foreplay, and rarely stimulate the male to the point of erection. When a couple decides to make love, they simply take three steps into the privacy of the forest. Even in this part of the world dog is man's best friend, with the exception that here they take the friendship a bit more seriously. For example, a young Yana warmer woman doesn't think twice about breastfeeding her puppies or child, cycling at one breast and a puppy at the other nearly doubly satisfies her maternal instincts . . . Penetrating deep into the patient's flesh with their fingers. They remove incurable cysts and tumors. When the operation is over, blood is wiped off the wound with a wad of cotton and for some unexplainable reason, not a trace of the operation is visible. The patient who had been operated on without any anesthetics is simply declared healthy and politely told to leave. But is he really healthy? The British leave the garden, the government halls are opening to the black rulers for the first time, somehow giving away everything lively with race, religion, Mr. Lee, and again, here the bully Canada. Europa League leave your review and your opponent, Africa's nursemaid. But Africa grew up through fast food . . . The white woman is descended from the monkey, and her hair is a straight as a monkey. The white woman has bloody bread, and the men white back. But it's a hard lesson to learn here, the state run beauty contest . . . But when you are slowly dying, slowly progressive disease is mostly used to be is that you get weaker and weaker you know and less degrees of mobility as you go along. And this is how this is kind of hard to overcome at times I guess. But I have been getting used to it. One more time on your red bag. JOHN dive will diagnose, diagnose when we find your phone can bang bang Dong Dong Dong, dong, ba ba, ba, ba, ba, ba ba ba by one bye bye enjoy my day bye ma ma ma ma ma ma ma ma ma ma ma ma ma ma ma I rarely bring a coffee instead of cremated and it's just for me I've ever been putting the rocks as I think brain advisor waste to me the body is nothing but a vessel raised to contain your soul . . . It's just very routine to bring people back from the dead. And a person who has just been pronounced dead is very little different from from the from that same person 5, 10, or 15 seconds earlier when he was presumably still alive. To be a suspension member, you have to provide funds for your suspension . . . Must be familiar can do my God continue to bless Hello Bellona . . . Indeed know shall shall shall retire. Software Defined, what a wedding you live you will never ever megos per hour of the day. You're going to hear me say please come on home, I've got to get some lunch . . . All this is vanishing. All this which man has lived with for 1000 1000 years. The great beasts of the land, the beasts of Might and muscle to man always gave wide berth. They are disappearing, for man no longer gives them wide berth at all. Instead, he slaughters them, for the marketplaces of the world. The whole thing is a dirty business, big business, Africans staying alive by marketing the living resources of their land, new and old, and they battle and the new is slowly winning out . . . Once the male is captured, he is democratically destined to the healthy and quick amorous appetites of the community . . . They are bred, chosen, cared for, fattened, and then cooked according to ancient and complicated recipes to please a vast category of connoisseur restaurants like this one. Whether clients can choose the most appetizing puppy directly from the cage a common all over the island. In this part of the world, terriers, bloodhounds, pumps, poodles or St. Bernard pups are appreciated, but child dogs are preferred, some dogs that in other places are valued for their intelligence and loyalty . . . You can't even mouth a few words of their sweet language. They're singing Welcome, welcome, strong and manly white man. Welcome, welcome. Oh seductive and beautiful white woman. You will teach me the secret of the elegance with which you seduce your men. And I will teach you the secret of a dance with which I seduce mine . . . For a primitive African movement is akin to prayer. And as such unbinds the soul from its earthly feathers. Only slow motion does justice to the structural beauty and glamour of the nylon attic race in action. Mock battle is a joyous dress up affair among the mondai, many come to the ceremony girded with colourful ostrich feathers. Those who can afford a more solid defense come in tortoise shaped suits as male meshed with tiny pearls . . . It doesn't know that the atom is killed, the seeds of life within atomic contamination is at an even *more tragic effect on the sea turtle. When it's last sad, maternities finished. Can't find its way back to the sea. Contamination has destroyed all sense of direction. Lost. Instead of heading toward the sea, she drags herself in the sun and fatigue. . . This death house for automobiles is in the United States. California alone kills three of them every two hours. Then they are piled up here in these huge cemeteries where however, the rest will not be eternal. Compressed for reasons of space 1000s of Ford, Chevrolet, Chrysler, Oldsmobile, Cadillac, Lincoln and Buick won't need repair any longer, and yet their destiny as cars is not finished. In a short while, in fact, they will be sent to the large European automobile industries where modern mechanical genius will bring them back to life again as other cars but of a smaller size . . . They have been banished to the most inaccessible and dangerous parts of this region. Their unfortunate encounter with so called civilization has left its mark on their language, not without reason, not the word, and Yanomamo, which means white man also means cruel and treacherous . . . The reason for this phenomenon described by Freud in reference to the behavior of young girls is that the men distinguish themselves from the uninitiated by tying their penises to their bells. Obviously, even in the Amazon jungle, a child is unaware. How fortunate he is to be young, only to come of age.*

8

The Prisoner Will Set
You Free

*I will not be pushed, filed, stamped, indexed, briefed,
debriefed, or numbered! My life is my own.*

NUMBER 6 IN THE "ARRIVAL"
EPISODE OF THE TV SERIES *THE PRISONER*

The most valuable art is that which inspires a reaction and an inner process in the partaker. Art that confesses, confounds, confuses, and caresses our minds with its desire to communicate something of urgency. If it doesn't, then perhaps it's better to call it "illustration" (regardless of medium). And if it pushes too hard and *demands* that we read the enclosed manual or manifesto, then that battle is also automatically and immediately lost.

When genuinely expressed through a personal and preferably unique aesthetic grid, art has the potential to grab one and reflect something to or onto one. This takes place not in a demagogic fashion but rather with a compelling insistence that one is somewhat missing out if one doesn't look again (or listen, or whatever the form is).

Sometimes it works best in terms of communication if the message isn't too clear—meaning not primarily addressing some *mental* faculty in the partaker. The artwork needs to overwhelm, seduce, and seep into our minds and souls to fully communicate. Hence the integrated use of form, aesthetics, seduction—creating a flower-like center of attraction that will pollinate the curious and encourage new flowers in other meadows.

To make attractive sense in the present, art needs to use a form that immediately appeals, and one that has the ability to do more than just secure a second glance. The motivation to get to that point of "coalescing creativity" within the artist usually stems from reactivity—a need for catharsis, acknowledgment, resonance—success, even. The artist's compensating cogs of creativity must never be underestimated when looking at a particular work of art. Nor should we disregard the outer context of the creative mind in question. Nor should we ignore the time and space in which the art-inducing psyche exists.

Yes, these are indeed somewhat meandering generalizations to some degree but none the less accurate in or for most things I choose to look at. And it's especially true for me in the case of one of the most astounding TV series ever made, *The Prisoner*.

With its seventeen episodes originally broadcast in 1967–1968, the psychedelic spy drama *The Prisoner* managed to confuse audiences wherever it was shown. There was star recognition through its main creator and leading actor, Patrick McGoohan; an attractive big-budget surface; plenty of fanciful intrigues; some kind of narrative continuity; themes of contemporary interest; a modern aesthetic, and . . . a whole lot of mystery.

It was (and still is) a TV series like no other, and I won't hesitate to designate its actual mythic potential. It simply carries so much signal both in its narrative arc and in its details—in each episode—that it draws one in and won't let one go. It won't let one go, that is, unfortunately until the episode is over (by which time, of course, one can skip to the next episode or simply watch the recent one again).

The Prisoner is a veritable feast of swinging '60s zeitgeistishness as well as a philosophically stimulating timelessness. Its level of ambition and immediate impact not only via British TV but also American ditto (and beyond) sent active ripples throughout the culture. And as much as it in many ways—consciously or not—celebrates a very colorful intersection of time and space in Western culture, it also puts a lid on it through its massive doses of paranoia, confusion, and inherent criticism of (specifically) British society.

The Prisoner is a ball of yarn that one can never fully disentangle, a knot that cannot be untied, and a mystery that (probably) can never be solved. This of course only adds to its appeal and generates a cult following in seemingly each new generation. Why? I would argue that *The Prisoner* is a skillfully assembled gesamt artwork that is filled with mythical force and magical clues to one of the most important mysteries there is: that of individuation.

As Number 6, in the episode "A Change of Mind," said: "You still have a choice. You can still salvage your right to be individuals. Your rights to truth and free thought! Reject this false world of Number Two . . . reject it NOW!!"[1] And as the president in the episode "Fall Out" stated: "He has revolted. Resisted. Fought. Held fast. Maintained. Destroyed resistance. Overcome coercion. The right to be a person, someone or individual. We applaud his *private* war, and concede that despite materialistic efforts, he has survived *intact* and *secure!*"[2]

No wonder then that the series was screened right after the summer of love in 1967, the very apex of a new age (Aquarius? Horus?) that unleashed interest not only in LSD and other hallucinogenics, but also in individual freedom itself. Where the outer form and narrative structure constantly nod to zeitgeistish occurrences, its main hard core is not one of daring design, jolly hopes of enlightenment, and world peace. Rather it is one of a paranoia-driven fight against repressive and draconian forces. Hence it packs a different and in many ways more powerful punch than the eye-candy-infested messages of unconditional love that were also present in the culture at exactly the same time.

Where to even begin? Well, the recurring intro to the show is undoubtedly a great place. In an efficient montage or mini story we can see the actor Patrick McGoohan's character drive his Lotus sports car through London and into a garage, from which he walks through a tunnel to an office. A man at a very formal desk receives a letter of resignation from a very upset and agitated McGoohan. In an ensuing montage we see his old portrait photo being crossed over with typewritten Xs, and filed in a cabinet drawer marked Resigned.

He then heads home to pack a suitcase. However, an arcane-looking man in a black frock and top hat arrives in a hearse-like car and gasses the former employee through the keyhole of the front door. Thus begins each episode of *The Prisoner.*

It is a very intense beginning that creates both familiarity and verfremdung at the same time. In each episode, the man henceforth known as Number 6 wakes up in a weird place called the village, which seems to be a tiny fishing village with colorful, Mediterranean-looking houses, parks, and streets. No wonder he's confused.

The people he encounters are friendly and helpful but none provide any real answers as to where and who they are. His identity is now simply Number 6, and when he's taken to meet Number 2 he becomes even more confused. Because in each episode there is always a new Number 2 . . .

The clash between what seems to be a coastal, idyllic fantasy and the seemingly strategized confusion imposed by Number 2 obviously leaves Number 6 in a terrified and angry state of mind. This isn't helped by the fact that there is no way to leave the village, and every little move is heavily monitored by technology and other people.

And so it continues throughout the following sixteen episodes. There is always a new Number 2, no clarification as to who Number 1 is, an enforced, sedated, pleasant lifestyle, seemingly fully indoctrinated and content villagers, and no way to escape. There is no willingness to listen to divergent opinions (such as those of the adamantly individualistic Number 6), and there's an array of revealing incidents in each episode that enhance the brutally Kafkaesque existence we encounter.

Although the absurdities of time and space allow for plenty of humorous incidents in his meetings with oppressively jolly characters, it is Number 6's increasing frustration that is so brilliantly portrayed by McGoohan—who possibly displays the very stiffest of all British stiff upper lips.

The very brief summary above only provides the tip of the narrative iceberg. Wherever one scratches the surface, a multicolored pus of angst oozes out, and it always runs in more directions than one. The shock tactics and elegant ambiguity of both form and content distinctly echo the work of the surrealists. Is it all a joke or is it a scathing critique of petit bourgeois morals and habits? Or both? But the signal of the content goes way beyond the consciously unconscious approach of the surrealists. Here we rather dive headfirst into existentialism—and perhaps specifically the British kind so eloquently formulated by Colin Wilson in his 1956 classic, *The Outsider.*

> The Outsider's problem amounts to a way of seeing the world that can be termed "pessimistic." I have tried to argue that this pessimism is true and valid. It therefore discounts the humanistic ideals of "man rising on stepping stones of dead selves to higher things, etc.", and criticises philosophy by saying that there is no point in the philosopher's trying to get to know the world if he doesn't know himself. It says flatly that the ideal "objective philosophy" will not be constructed by mere thinkers, but by men who combine the thinker, the poet and the man of action.[3]

Despite the confusing reality of being trapped and controlled by the powers that be of the village, the frustrations of Number 6 go beyond mere passive confusion. He is also the prey of very active draconian forces that insist on knowing exactly why he has resigned (as witnessed in the opening credits). We gradually get the impression that Number 6 has been a secret agent of sorts and that he simply cannot be allowed to be set free. For Number 6, this is of course highly irritating—not primarily because he actually *has* been some form of agent and thereby could probably foresee some form of authoritarian reaction, but because the rest of the villagers live under similar conditions, and they have definitely *not* been secret agents.

Here we come to the first and most basic building block of *The Prisoner:* the secret agent. In the early 1960s Patrick McGoohan was a highly successful and highly paid British actor. Coming from a serious theater background, his good looks and very British behavior made him the first choice for the role of Ian Fleming's successful secret agent: James Bond. But as McGoohan liked neither guns nor making out with beautiful women on-screen, he left the unlit torch to Sean Connery, and instead moved on to an extremely successful TV series called . . . that's right: *Secret Agent* (aka *Danger Man*). He starred as John Drake in the show's eighty-six episodes and enjoyed all the benefits of massive stardom.

But over time, McGoohan became more and more creative himself—perhaps as a reaction to boredom or discontent. He envisioned a new series about a *former* secret agent who simply wanted to leave but apparently wasn't allowed to. As a meta-infused in-joke, the portrait crossed over with Xs in the opening sequence of *The Prisoner* is actually one of John Drake from *Secret Agent.*

McGoohan's clout and stardom made it relatively easy to find funding for the new project despite the fact that he was aiming high in production values. And in 1967, that magical year of life-enhancing and mind-expanding cultural explosions, the new series went into production.

One episode of *Secret Agent* had been shot in Portmeirion, Wales, a brainchild-village built by the eccentric Bertram Clough Williams-Ellis in the 1920s (and onward) to architecturally emulate his own beloved Mediterranean memories. McGoohan realized that this particularly über-pretty, weird, and anomalous village would be perfect for housing Number 6's nightmarish existence.

Bringing in a number of writers, actors, and directors to this already widely talked-about sequel of sorts to *Secret Agent,* McGoohan quickly made most of them disappointed. Either there was no prefabricated, overarching story, or he simply wouldn't divulge any details about it for them. A creative adventure was launched in which Portmeirion itself played an important role. Fanciful sets, colorful costumes, and the jolly behavior of the characters all contrapuntally clashed with Number 6's increasing dread—and his resistance. The entire team played along with McGoohan's visionary whims and apparently whimsical visions. Manifesting the sometimes very vague story line turned out to be not exactly problem-free, but at least it became a memorable experience. And there's no denying that *The Prisoner* turned out to be an absolute masterpiece, cemented into the bedrock of TV and movie history.

Where the story both is and is not a continuation of *Secret Agent*, for McGoohan it must have been a relief to go from the causal, habitual, and very expected, into the totally unknown. He worked with a number of well-respected writers, all of whom constructed full episodes based on opaque and seemingly absurd notions or concepts. The strange (and beautiful) thing is that it not only eventually worked out, but that it still works today.

Although at first glance the surrealisms, absurdisms, and questions are many and frequent in the viewer's mind, after a short while one gets used to it. The abnormal and unexpected become the norm in the ever-so-friendly prison in which Number 6 exists. I wonder if this isn't a result of McGoohan's apparent refusal to have everything too mapped out. His vision may have been strict, but the key people were basically allowed to create what they thought would fit. This was regardless of speculations about whether the audiences had the capacity for understanding what was actually going on or not. This devil-may-care attitude would probably not have been possible without the presence of McGoohan's star power, in addition to his vision.

Although there were fallings-out with directors, crew members, and eventually the show's main producer, McGoohan refused to budge an inch. The American backers sensed this and only allowed for a total of seventeen episodes to be made when thirteen had already been shot.

The final four episodes therefore differ slightly in tone—not least the very last one in which Number 6 is finally faced with Number 1!

I'm not going to spoil the outcome or spill any beans if you haven't yet watched *The Prisoner,* but suffice to say that the actual end created much further frustration for the series's large audiences. The switchboards of the TV networks were overheated by calls from angry and confused people. This was truly a TV series like no other!

It contains brainwashing, escape attempts, mind games, humiliations, suicides, surveillance, dream recording, schizophrenia (even in physical form given that the rulers of the village seem to be able to clone people), strategic false hopes, false friendships, organized deceit, condescending cruelty, assassination plans, sedation, sedition, seduction (attempted only, as Number 6 seems to be a true reflection of the quite Apollonian McGoohan), fights, torture, and so on. There is never a dull moment for the villagers—especially those who ask uncomfortable questions.

And should anyone try to escape or physically deviate, a large white balloon called Rover shows up and hunts the person down. What at first seems ridiculous—a big bouncy balloon actually hunting people—becomes convincingly eerie enough as we hear its sounds. Among other things the sound designer mixed in human roars, screams, breathing at different speeds, and Gregorian chants in reverse to give Rover its haunting sound. As McGoohan said, "The Rovers are the sheepdogs of the allegory. When people start to ask too many questions or assert their individuality, the Rovers act as a stifling force. If one begins to stray from the herd, the Rovers are sent out to bring them back. Again, The Prisoner is an allegory, enabling me to express this suffocating society in that way."[4]

Over the decades there have been many attempts at interpreting or clarifying what the show is really about. Although the overarching theme of individual verses stifling collective is more than crystal clear (and perhaps that should suffice?), one can of course look at the story from many different perspectives: political, philosophical, and spiritual, for example. It can also, of course, be looked at from the perspective of McGoohan's own process of liberation from *Secret Agent.*

This merging of playful form and philosophical-spiritual content was in no way unique to this TV series. The entire decade of the 1960s was one of experimentation, and externalizations of inner processes became as common as internalizations of outer expressions in a boundary-bursting, cinematic feedback loop. One could point to LSD and psychedelics, Eastern romanticism, a hangover from the ultramaterialistic 1950s, war, antiwar, cold war, and to many other things in order to at least try to explain all of this.

The open-ended format of *The Prisoner* of course lends itself very well to interpretation, and this was true of many things in these turbulent times. A playful evasion of the causal, rational structuring of the world had become a new and powerful norm in Western culture. Whether this was related specifically to people in many walks of life trying LSD, and thereby at least temporarily shifting outlooks, or to larger movements, we will never really know. Did McGoohan at some point try LSD? Or was he simply a sensitive artist who was affected by proxy by what was going on around him? No matter what, throughout his later life McGoohan was hesitant about talking too much about *any* aspects of the series. He did say this, however:

> One can attribute its long life to the allegory. Everything is not explained. It can be seen, I hope, a second or a third time, and there are new meanings. Because in an allegory you can have a new meaning, because you've had more experience in your life and can interpret things a little differently. In some ways, maybe I shouldn't be doing this? Talking to you, and to the people who are going to view it and hear it, and explain "The Prisoner." Myself, I am still getting new interpretations of it and I feel fortunate that in parts of it, I hit lucky.[5]

One important British presence in the early to mid-1960s was the author John Fowles, and perhaps especially in regard to our esteemed *Prisoner*. Fowles's first novel, *The Collector*, was published in 1963 and told the terrifying story of a man who kidnaps a girl and keeps her captive, just as he has done previously with butterflies. The book was turned into a successful film, and Fowles was lauded as a bright young literary star.

Quite surprisingly the follow-up wasn't another similar novel but a collection of philosophical essays, aphorisms, thoughts, and speculations called *The Aristos* and published in 1964. After this followed the 1965 publication of a novel Fowles had actually written prior to *The Collector.* It was entitled *The Magus* and, in 1968, was turned into a film starring Michael Caine, Candice Bergen, and Anthony Quinn.

This remarkable book tells the story of an English teacher who takes a job at a school on a Greek island, to a great extent to get away from his frustrated life. It doesn't take long before he gets entangled in the mind-altering power dynamics of a wealthy Greek man on the island. What seems at first to be a nice and cultivated environment and a charming host's eccentric whims gradually turns into manipulation, mind control and, eventually—as the boundaries are completely blurred—real disaster. The psychic abyss that opens up thanks to his host's manipulations literally drives the protagonist to the brink of insanity.

Fowles tells this fascinating story in a conventional yet experimental way. The narrative structure helps us feel the confusion experienced by the teacher as he gradually breaks down from external tampering—or is that perhaps to an equal degree internal ditto?

When looking at Fowles's initial work we can see a fairly clear blueprint for *The Prisoner,* and it would seem highly unlikely—if not absolutely improbable—that McGoohan hadn't at some point come across Fowles's "oeuvre" so far. The film version of *The Magus* conjures up many striking resemblances to *The Prisoner* but must be seen as parallel—it wasn't released until 1968. If anything, we might see a scenario in which *The Prisoner* might actually have inspired the visual aesthetics of the *Magus* film. No matter what, Fowles's book, which had the original/working title *The Godgame,* was already around and culturally present as McGoohan was percolating thoughts and ideas as John Drake in *Secret Agent.*

The book received a mixed bag of reviews, but looking at them it strikes me that they could be more or less interchangeable with reviews of *The Prisoner*. According to the *Financial Times*, *The Magus* was "A splendidly sustained piece of mystification . . . such as could otherwise only have been devised by a literary team fielding the Marquis de Sade, Arthur Edward Waite, Sir James Frazer, Gurdjieff, Madame Blavatsky, C.G. Jung, Aleister Crowley, and Franz Kafka."[6] And Bernard Bergonzi in the *New York Review of Books* said this: "I won't attempt to summarise or recapitulate the plot, since there is far too much of it: *The Magus* is like a colossal *bouillabaisse,* combining black magic, occultism, psychological brainwashing techniques, Mediterranean travelogues, forgery, flagellation, Nazi atrocities (described in loving detail), voyeurism, hypnotism, battle scenes, *fin de siècle* naughtiness, and venereal disease: There is something for everyone here."[7] He went on to say, "At the end the elaborate, glittering structure collapses into anti-climax and absurdity. What was it all for, one wonders. Unless, indeed, this very dissatisfaction is deliberate, the final product of the author's sadistic animus."[8]

Secret agents were all the rage at the time—a real zeitgeistish gestalt within the context of a very hot cold war between Western and Eastern blocs. Because of his massive success as John Drake, the role of James Bond was first offered to Patrick McGoohan. When he turned it down, in part due to his aversion to guns and, as mentioned before, making out with beautiful women on-screen, he instead recommended the Scottish milkman Sean Connery for the part. And when Connery had had enough, after the 1967 film *You Only Live Twice,* the offer returned to McGoohan, who again turned it down. This was not surprising perhaps, because this was the same exact time that he was knee-deep in making *The Prisoner,* which was everything but a conventional spy thriller.

One film that shouldn't be forgotten in our context is *The Ipcress File* (directed by Sidney Furie in 1965). It's a spy drama filled with deceit, brainwashing, and a trust-no-one scenario, all masterfully personified by the same stiff-upper-lipped Michael Caine who later starred in *The Magus*.

And let's certainly not forget Joseph Losey's pop masterpiece adaptation of the comic book adventures of Modesty Blaise from 1966, aptly called . . . *Modesty Blaise*. But where there's a sense of tongue-in-cheekishness and a sense of humor in all of these precursors— in James Bond, *Secret Agent,* in *The Ipcress File,* and certainly in *Modesty Blaise,* there is absolutely none of it in *The Prisoner* (nor in *The Magus*). Paranoia rules supreme, fueled by a sense of existential dread and futility, as the protagonists of Number 6 and Nicholas Urfe (in *The Magus*) fight not only exterior manipulation, but also their own internal dissolution. "When the individual is being attacked on all sides by the forces of anti-individuality; by the nemo; by the sense that death is absolute; by the dehumanising processes of both mass production and mass producing: the affaire represents not only an escape into the enchanted garden of the ego but also a quasi-heroic gesture of human defiance."[9]

But these outer cinematic expressions in British/Western culture only reflected larger processes in which the individual's relationship to the collective, and by extension the state, literally was all over the place. Reactions to the cold war and the problems of both French and American energies in Southeast Asia created a reactive monster of a far too uncritical acceptance of communist and socialist ideals. In 1949, China was turned into a dictatorship of the proletariat through revolution and mass murder. Only some ten years later China invaded Tibet and immediately initiated both genocide and "cultureicide." China then also tried to destabilize and overturn other countries in Asia.

The safe and secure middle-class students at European universities saw no part of the bloodshed and terror, only the vague romanticism of ideas that *still* weren't working in the Soviet republics. Although probably mostly an arrested development or teenage kind of rebellion against classic imperialist structures, there's no denying that leftist ideas got a grip on the intellectual and cultural life of Europe and beyond, for a while. The originally healthy individualistic streak of existentialism was cleverly appropriated by an unhealthy new collectivism, thus sowing immediate seeds of paranoia and surrender to "groupthink," "doublethink," and "newspeak" (to paraphrase another highly influential and paranoid pioneer of societal dynamics fiction: George Orwell).

Then of course one needs to look at the spiritual movements available specifically for the same younger generation that now opened their minds via hallucinogenics and flirted with ideas of not only peace and love, but also of any political movement that could challenge Mommy and Daddy's rigid attitudes.

As of 1947, India was no longer under British rule, and in many ways this allowed for a deeper relationship between the countries. It didn't take long before increasingly independent Western youth started seeking out yoga, meditation, and Hinduism, as well as all kinds of drugs, on what became known as "the hippie trail" (which stretched from Europe, over the Middle East, Afghanistan, India, Nepal, and all the way to Thailand).

The same was true of the exodus of Tibetans after China's invasion, with the Dalai Lama even setting up his government in exile in northern India. From there the highly influential Tibeto-Buddhist teachings spread, including the seminal text that was to become a psychedelic staple all over the world: *The Tibetan Book of the Dead*. The massive upheavals set ideas and ideals in motion, and technology and affluence made traveling easier for people from the West. As such, an active interchange was made possible in entirely new ways.

And then there was LSD. After having been used primarily by psychologists, psychiatrists, and military intelligence agencies, the word got out that Albert Hofmann's magic potion was something else—literally. Some medical doctors, who by their profession were allowed to order the substance from the Sandoz laboratories in Switzerland, became so enamoured with LSD that they consciously decided to distribute it beyond their clinical work. One such doctor was the British pediatrician John Beresford, who was in cahoots with the cultural trickster figure of British drug researcher Michael Hollingshead. From this duo,

LSD was presented to emerging protagonists like Timothy Leary (who at this time, in the early '60s, had been predominantly interested in psilocybin research at Harvard).

As LSD became not only an elitist experiment of choice but also a real mass phenomenon—and perhaps especially when its distribution got out of the hands of the professional, clinical people via renegade chemists and networks—the impact on the culture was immense. LSD changed the disciplines of music, art, literature, filmmaking, consciousness exploration, and most others that were predominantly young. This changed not only outlook but also aesthetics. And forms within those disciplines, which were appealing to the turned-on sensibilities, became predominant irrespective of whether they were old (like, for instance, art nouveau) or new (like the LSD parallel occurrence of pop art, and very soon, psychedelic art mainly stemming from the American West Coast).

Pop music became the cultural gate-crasher par excellence. Whereas the Beatles had been somewhat long-haired, cute, and charming in the early 1960s, when they were turned on to LSD and other psychedelics the ball game changed entirely. With the release of their album *Sgt. Pepper's Lonely Hearts Club Band* in May 1967, the battle had already been won: LSD was out in the open and changing millions of minds daily. This was exemplified on a literally cosmic scale when the Beatles performed their single "All You Need Is Love" on *Our World*. It was the first-ever live global television broadcast, and it used a satellite link to facilitate it. The broadcast went out to approximately 400 million people in twenty-five countries; they got to see (and hear) the band's message on June 25, 1967. The song was later included on their following album, *Magical Mystery Tour*, and in their animated feature film *Yellow Submarine*, in 1968.

Quite surprising (or not?) is that this song was also used in the very final episode of *The Prisoner*: "Fall Out" (both written and directed by McGoohan himself). The song obviously conveys a message that could be said to be pretty eternally philosophical (and vice versa). But the use of a pop song in this way simply hadn't been part of the *Prisoner* toolbox—neither as a statement nor contrapuntally. But then again, this episode was extraspecial.

Critics and interpreters have swung from looking at the finale as being completely thought through and elaborately developed, to it being a sloppy and haphazard attempt from McGoohan's side to simply kill off an unyielding beast that attracted no further financial investment. In a way, the use of the song catapulted the series into a known territory: *contemporary* British culture. We are brought back from the paranoid enchantment to a distinct time and place—in a way, we are allowed to leave the village.

McGoohan's acknowledgment of the Beatles by the inclusion of the song (and its message) also makes possible a not too far-fetched interpretation by looking at probably the most iconic record sleeve ever created, that of *Sgt. Pepper's Lonely Hearts Club Band*. In its famous montage of important people (created by Peter Blake and Jann Haworth), we can see many potential sources of inspiration for McGoohan and the other people involved in *The Prisoner*. Some notable ones are Aldous Huxley, Aleister Crowley, William S. Burroughs, Carl Jung, Sigmund Freud, Edgar Allan Poe, Terry Southern, Yogananda, George Bernard Shaw, and Lewis Carroll. They weren't necessarily unique because of their presence on the record sleeve but rather because the sleeve itself caught a slice of culture that was already very much alive and present.

Aldous Huxley's interest in mind-expansion, as well as his talent of conveying philosophical and religious ideas in popular fiction, made him a pioneering, psychedelic paragon—perhaps especially to those of a slightly more conservative bent who didn't immediately ascribe to "hippie" values or its lifestyle. Although the American band the Doors had already acknowledged his influence by their very name, Huxley's main appeal was much broader and transgenerational.

Huxley's 1932 dystopian science fiction novel, *Brave New World*, is another important blueprint for *The Prisoner*.

Suddenly, from out of the Synthetic Music Box a Voice began to speak. The Voice of Reason, the Voice of Good Feeling. The soundtrack roll was unwinding itself in Synthetic Anti-Riot Speech Number Two (Medium Strength). Straight from the depths of a non-existent heart, "My friends! My friends!" said the Voice so pathetically, with a note of such infinitely tender reproach that, behind their gas-masks, even the policemen's eyes were momentarily dimmed with tears, "what is the meaning of this? Why aren't you all being happy and good together? Happy and good," the Voice repeated. "At peace, at peace."[10]

Huxley wrote continually about his own psychedelic experiences, including in a voluminous correspondence with his British psychiatrist friend Humphry Osmond (who was the person who'd originally coined the term *psychedelic* in 1956). In a 1964 anthology of essays on LSD dedicated to the "guru extraordinaire," we find another Huxley gem that exposes the seemingly eternal dilemma between the state of awakened individual and that of the sleep-inducing culture.

Genius and angry ape, player of fantastic tricks and godlike reasoner—in all these roles individuals are the products of a language and a culture. Working on the twelve or thirteen billion neurons of a human brain, language and culture have given us law, science, ethics, philosophy; have made possible all the achievements of talent and of sanctity. They have also given us fanaticism, superstition and dogmatic bumptiousness; nationalistic idolatry and mass murder in the name of God; rabble-rousing propaganda and organized lying. And, along with the salt of the Earth, they have given us, generation after generation, countless millions of hypnotized conformists, the predestined victims of power-hungry rulers who are themselves victims of all that is most senseless and inhuman in their cultural tradition. [11]

Occultist Aleister Crowley's main philosophical dictums, "Do what thou wilt shall be the whole of the Law," and "Love is the law, love under will," were parts of an ambitious system of religious adherence and magical technologies called "Thelema" (Greek for *Will*). But the key Thelemic theme was essentially always philosophical: the inviolable freedom of the individual. In his condensed declaration of personal liberty, *Liber OZ,* Crowley even declared that "Man has the right to kill those who would thwart these rights."[12]

American author William S. Burroughs, whose experimental prose more or less chronicled his own personal shadow-world journeys through drug addiction, problematic homosexuality, and (wo)manslaughter (he had accidentally shot his wife in 1951), had one theme that was even more consistent: control. Burroughs's obsession with repression and oppression from the state (and similar power structures) trickled down into an enemy worth fighting: control itself. In many ways, the paranoid Burroughsian worldview corresponded hand in glove with that of Number 6 in the village. As such, control existed to only keep feeding more control, and any divergence or individuality becomes the proverbial nail that needs to be hammered down.

Burroughs lived in London for most of the 1960s and was a visible cultural presence there, influencing the young generation who was turning on to not only the existentialism of the beatniks but also to an enlightened yet critical approach to authority in general.

Terry Southern was another interesting contemporary of McGoohan's who also made an impact in exposing power dynamics gone wrong. Although Southern was a versatile and productive writer, it is perhaps as the screenwriter of Stanley Kubrick's 1964 hard-hitting satire *Dr. Strangelove, Or How I Learned to Stop Worrying and Love the Bomb,* that he is most well-known. Kubrick's dystopian comedy about war-hungry, top-ranking officers from different countries is a masterpiece of surreal satire that was widely written about. The trail of absolute individual freedom in opposition to the "squares" was manifested again in Southern's manuscript for Dennis Hopper's *Easy Rider* film in 1969.

There is also an interesting bagatelle anecdote that connects *The Prisoner* with Kubrick, albeit on a more symbolic level than a substantially philosophical one. The *Prisoner* team needed a night sky for one of the episodes, and basically just borrowed a very elaborate one from another film that was being shot at the same time at Shepperton Studios, Kubrick's *2001: A Space Odyssey*.

These people, plus the other ones culled from the *Sgt. Pepper* artwork, plus of course a multitude of similar free spirits, were all parts of the zeitgeist, as were the ideas and notions they propagated: from yoga and magic to psychedelics to an attitude of basic anti-authoritarianism and quasi-anarchism.

Most of these individuating processes are inner processes. One travels inside; reaches personal epiphanies; meditates; reasons; connects the glowing dots; cherishes silence; encourages forethought, thought, and afterthought; and simply resonates with oneself in a way that isn't possible when involved with the neuroses of others (whether on an individual or collective scale).

No wonder then that the loud invasion of privacy and attention, of solitude and silence, is a key instrument of this opposition to such endeavors.

In *The Prisoner* we recognize much of what is even more predominant today than in the mid-1960s: surveillance, enforced entertainment, infantilist edutainment, democracy as sacrosanct yet hollow and malleable, a monitored financial system, and so on. Even in the general greeting in the village, there are overt hints of surveillance: "(I'll) be seeing you!"

The all-present eye of control, parents, society, and surveillance was in a way (re)appropriated by the 1960s psychedelic movement's usage of the hermetically charged "eye in the triangle." This emblem had previously been used in freemasonic symbolism, not as a charge to necessarily blindly obey authority, but rather as a symbol of an all-seeing god beyond humanly defined religions.

The overall theme of *The Prisoner* seems to be not only the reactive fight of the individual against oppression, but also of continually developing the individual herself so that oppression simply cannot occur. This is the ideal outcome of individuation, whether it actually has an effect on a larger (group) scale or merely in the sovereign integrity of the individual. The very beginning of both the story and each episode indicates a *re-sign-ation*. This is not merely taking a step back from the present situation but is also an active redefinition of the *sign* and its meaning altogether by the *a-sign-ee,* not so much by an external *de-sign-er.*

In this sense, *The Prisoner* constitutes a Thelemic myth to be further analyzed and worked with, as it does a Gurdjieffean wake-up call, a McGoohanesque allegory, boarding a Wilsonian outsidership, and many other mindful matrices that can be helpful.

However, what makes the series continually intriguing and strong in its mythical force is its balance, relative reticence, and its shying away from allegiances beyond the basic and human(istic) one. It is quite enough to convey a spark, an ignition, in those who care to see—and specifically in those who have the capacity to do so. As always, John Fowles phrased it eloquently, "Freedom for me is inalienably bound up with self-knowledge. I would say the two words are almost synonymous in this context. And so it's really *that,* you know, the ability to withstand the appalling brainwashing that we all get now through the media, to think of yourself and know yourself. I must see that as a vital kind of freedom. And, honestly, it's an unhappy freedom at the moment because it doesn't exist very much."[13]

He continued . . . "To most people it is a pleasure to conform and a pleasure to belong; existentialism is conspicuously unsuited to political or social subversion, since it is incapable of organised dogmatic resistance or formulations of resistance. It is capable only of one man's resistance; one personal expression of view; such as this book."[14]

9

"Our Life Could at Least Be Doubled"

Is our existence now actually at a turning point in history? Are we living in the very eye of an apocalyptic storm (or hurricane, even); inside the very core of a critical mass?

It is tempting to believe it, if we judge by the so-called media flow—"real" and "fake" alike. Never before has there been such an avalanche of chaotic memes and schemes. However, this is mainly a technological phenomenon, not one of information proper. The messages, reactions, pros, cons, and attempts at manipulation and coercion are basically the same as they were one hundred years ago. But the digital gadgets and gizmos facilitate an unprecedented and amplified onslaught that temporarily shuts down critical thinking and instead opens up the floodgates of clashing emotions, thinly disguised as debate. It's a weight issue considerably more than a wait! issue.

These platforms of encouraged shortsightedness are of course used by all sides, and in all political arenas. Those citizens who are anchored outside this onslaught in terms of time and background have an advantage in

---

"Our Life Could at Least Be Doubled" was originally written for the German magazine *Wendepunkt,* 2017.

98

realizing that what we're experiencing is something out of the ordinary; they have experienced a time without these gadgets and platforms.

For those immersed in technology since birth or at least youth, it's considerably more problematic, because what's inside the technology is inherently regarded as true. The technology is both consciously and unconsciously part of a reality in which the truth is somehow embedded. If a critical thinking process or a historical perspective isn't integrated early on in contemporary schooling, the children will be absolutely helpless in what could definitely be seen as a negative turning point in human culture. Those with an agenda to sell are overjoyed.

But what about the other side then? Critics of technology, myself included, are usually very quick to react emotionally, too, and they often loudly remember some distant golden age in which there was surely some other kind of (criticized) technology, but not on a level this invasive.

It consists of diametrical dualism pushed to the extreme in simplified messages and a parallel, gradual dismantling of judiciary systems and general ethics. Noise drowns out the signal but instead of fixing it, everyone just raises the volume. As Machiavelli said in *The Prince:* "Thus it comes about that all armed prophets have conquered and all unarmed ones failed; for besides what has been already said, the character of peoples varies, and it is easy to persuade them of a thing, but difficult to keep them in that persuasion. And so it is necessary to order things so that when they no longer believe, they can be made to believe by force."[1]

Is contemporary reality just a Machiavellian wet dream made manifest by unenlightened cynics? Or are we witnessing, as some claim, a well-needed challenge of static political behavior, primarily contested via amazing new tech?

The answer to both questions is a resounding no! What we're witnessing is merely a "critical mass-flirting" or petting, and an "eye-of-the-storm voyeurism." None of these phenomena will change anything—unfortunately.

The extremely compensatory behavior in puerile political pendulums, technological worship, the fetishizing of space travel, the immense wealth generated by home shopping, and an uncritical approach to "artificial intelligence," for example, all leads to the very same conclusion. That is: in actual fact, nothing is really happening on the overall human level except for a massive denial of guilt. On a higher level though—the bird's-eye view—we are witnessing firsthand how the tangibility of our own wreckage is creeping closer. And creeping closer to home very quickly. That can be quite painful to realize.

The reaction to this is (as we're experiencing each day in the media flow) supremely compensatory: no really rational agendas beyond existing bureaucracies churning away on the detail level; cherishing artificial intelligence instead of our own to create an optimally dystopian scenario (don't these people read science fiction?); abandoning climate change treatises in defiance while adhering to infantile religionisms and fairy tale moralisms; longing desperately for a safe place in space (where, of course, "no one will hear you scream!"); bickering and bitching; and letting lawyers sort out the endless aftermaths.

But still I argue that this is of no real concern to human existence. Our essential needs are profoundly basic, and we are profoundly adaptable when push comes to shove. We have more than enough of everything. It is, however, of great concern to a phenomenon that has now taken over large chunks of the (mainly) Western mind frame: the human death wish. It's a thing. It's a thing in itself. The unconscious drive to destroy, kill, and most importantly, to be killed, is now so strong that it's going to be quite hard to stop it. Perhaps even impossible?

And maybe that's actually a good thing? Maybe it's a good thing that it all breaks down before all the death-wish projections through technology and weaponry destroy too much for sensitive biospheres in general and for other species? A systemic change is obviously needed, but I suspect that even such a phenomenon will be sublimated into a kind of denial of denial—not to be escapistically arrogant but rather to inspire by courage in the same arena as the death-mongers. In this, the same platforms and media are used to deny the death drive, deny the moronic media flow, deny unintelligence, deny compensatory simpletons. If enough people stick with their own individual visions, no one will have a need for an imposed, attempted collective suicide.

The intelligent people will stay safe when the unintelligent crumble in their own rubble and dirt. Then, hopefully, we can get back to being constructive and creative human beings again, smiling and minding our own little businesses. Then the children (of all ages) can finally grow up, individuate, and enjoy life in peace—and create amazing things, as real humans do.

A healthy dose of egotistical survival instinct filtered through poetry and humor could very well be the best way forward. We should allow ourselves to be guided by Salvador Dalí (quoted below, in *50 Secrets of Magic Craftsmanship*),[2] rather than by an army of unindividuated engineers and businesspeople who simply wish to die, and preferably take the rest of us with them. Let's deny them that ambivalent pleasure. Let the rest of us get on with life. Amor fati!

Proust's *Remembrance of Things Past* is not the hyper-individualistic lucubration of a blasé. It is the very healthy basis of a whole Dalinian system by virtue of which the physical span of our life could be at least doubled. For you could then tell yourself that what you are now living you could live again better, at the same time that you were living something different. I especially. Everything which I miss living at every instant, everything that I am wasting at present, all the ineffable, congealed cascades of sensation and emotion which escape me at this moment without my even being aware of it, this whole treasure of life, of time which I am losing, one day I shall find again, with a fresh wonder, in a new and real terrestrial paradise.

10
Embracing Magical Realism

What exactly is magical realism? I would argue that it's much more than a literary genre that's usually associated with Latin American authors with a slightly surrealist bent. I would argue that it's much more than a slight distortion technique in fiction in general, which has the potential to elevate the reading or viewing experience. And I would argue that two essentially complicated words don't necessarily create a less complicated construct together.

However, I would also argue that embracing magical realism as a cultural phenomenon can help us understand our own confusing reality better than clearheaded rational and intellectual analyses ever could. The reason for this is simple: magical realism is a discernible bridge between the two extreme realities that our specific culture consists of: fact and fiction, or, if we allow some logically speculative slack, truth and untruth.

We could list a large number of authors who would fulfill academically constructed criteria of being magical realists: Borges, Márquez, Murakami, Hesse, Calvino, Akutagawa, Jünger, Pirandello, for exam-

"Embracing Magical Realism" was originally presented as a lecture for the Austrian O.T.O., 2020.

ple; there are far too many to mention, really. Also, it's not as easy to define this genre as it is others because the backbone is always an actual deliberate vagueness; a transparency that isn't fully translucent in a way. Normal everyday scenes may be described, but there is always something extra: a word, sentence, or a passage that distorts, tilts, jolts, makes one question what's just happened. The experience becomes a suprareading induced by skill and intelligent eloquence, and/or thematically dazzling or weird material. It's not fantasy, satire, absurdism, surrealism; nor is it necessarily thematically magical or marvelous. The stories of the every-day often contain the most magical nuances—if expressed in an evoca-tive enough way.

Borges, as well as magical realism in general, appropriates a well-known form and gently corrupts it, which leads to dislocation. "What did I just read? A newspaper? A short story? A film treatment?" This is especially true of Borges's *A Universal History of Infamy* (con-taining stories written in the 1930s), with its gallery of weird characters presented almost matter-of-factly. If we are unsure whether these char-acters ever actually existed, perhaps it's because we would like for them to exist. This thought contains something like an expression I heard in Werner Herzog's documentary film, *Nomad: In the Footsteps of Bruce Chatwin*, about his author friend and fellow fabulist Bruce Chatwin. It was said that Chatwin told "a truth and a half."[1]

Perhaps the doubt embedded in the fantastical narrative evokes a need in us to be amazed—either in escapist counterpoint to a dreary life, or in affirmation of an imposed uncritical or even anticritical attitude. Are we really surprised at the number and force of bizarre conspiracy the-ories in the wake of the memetically induced dissolution of intelligence recently? Reveling in the false, as a mainly emotional critique of the true, which apparently has no room for their own worthlessness—or their own perceived sense of the same—is a naive yet potent use of black magic.

The passage between conscious irony and unconscious acceptance of the power of a collective leverage is a stretch in which the price is high. It represents a complete negation of individual traits in favor of a mass movement of illusory safety. The meme- and slogan-swallowing herd in the American Midwest is completely interchangeable with the proletariat of Russia that made the manifestation of the Soviet Union possible. It's also analogous to the anxious German middle class who used democracy to elect their favorite Nazi authority, who could then fill their disgruntled lives with some kind of meaning, and who collectively still worship at the scientifically justified materialist altar while always making bloody sacrifices to the totem animal of the scapegoat.

A lie that is repeated often enough will eventually be accepted as a truth. This is especially true in a culture that confuses challenging a point of view with defaming what's called a "freedom of expression." It's the same corrupt and corroded pseudo logic that confuses justice with an aggressively minute interpretation of arbitrary legal paragraphs.

The British, Catholic author G. K. Chesterton, who was so influential for Borges and many other magical realists, once wrote: "A madman is not a man who has lost his reason: he is a man who has lost everything except his reason."[2]

In actually creating fiction, there has always existed the important concept of the suspension of disbelief. When one goes to film school and learns how to make a fictional film, one doesn't want anything to make the viewer aware of the making of the film. The form has to be flawless, smooth, seductive, and make the viewer get sucked into whatever the narrative is. The language is not just the story itself but also the storytelling structure.

But in news or overt propaganda the flawed form may actually amplify the potency. A blurred phone camera clip of basically any group of people could, for instance, be used together with an emotional narrative, saying, "These people stole our jobs/raped our women/sold drugs to toddlers/whatever." In a sense, the fictional form is unsuited for the blatant propaganda of the moment but very suitable for the propaganda having to do with lifestyle and consumer choices. The immediate news form, which inherently conveys a sense of truth, is unsuited for the propaganda of lifestyle but very suitable for assaults on the senses and a shutdown of critical thinking. Then add the power of repetition that commercial advertising has refined for over a century. In this relentless onslaught even one's own frustration of having seen the same message hundreds of times is not a defense mechanism but actually rather just an amplification of the message because one vents their frustration about the brand in question to others. They then will recognize the brand on the shelves of the supermarket, on the skyline, on the TV, in the social media "feed," and eventually in the election ballots.

Mechanical repetition is a sure way of grinding down resistance in order to facilitate literally demented behavior of STOP/GO and YES/NO.

Wisdom no longer lies in the Akashic Records of Blavatsky and other tender theosophists, but in the Aphasic Records of power-hungry sophists, pure and simple. And perhaps this has been going on longer than we care or dare to believe. Hermann Hesse, yet another wonderful magical realist, wrote in his classic story *The Journey to the East:* "The whole of world history often seems to me nothing more than a picture book which portrays humanity's most powerful and senseless desire— the desire to forget."[3]

Just as poets, authors, and other artists are often intuitively inclined and thereby prescient—like eloquent fortune-tellers—their works, just like that of the fortune-tellers, can also help *set* the stages of the future by mere description. This can in equal measure lead to good things as much as bad ones, but it seems the bad ones are willing to negate or deny their fictional roots to a greater extent. No matter what, the sphere of the apparently irrational and poetic will always be filled with displays and pre-interpretations of what seem to be inevitable developments in our forgetful futures. Ernst Jünger, in his book *Der Waldgang* or *The Forest Passage,* has this to say on the subject: "Where the automatism increases to the point of approaching perfection—such as in America— the panic is even further intensified. There it finds its best feeding grounds; and it is propagated through networks that operate at the speed of light. The need to hear the news several times a day is already a sign of fear; the imagination grows and paralyses itself in a rising vortex. The myriad antennae rising above our megacities resemble hairs standing on end—they provide demonic contacts."[4]

And Hermann Hesse (in *Steppenwolf*) weighs in as well. "And in fact, if the world is right, if this music of the cafés, these mass-enjoyments and these Americanised men who are pleased with so little are right, then I am wrong, I am crazy. I am in truth the Steppenwolf that I often call myself; that beast astray who finds neither home nor joy nor nourishment in a world that is strange and incomprehensible to him."[5]

Taking this powerful position into consideration—that of being able to create the future not by the violent demagogic programming of the moment but by magical, sensible, and intelligent formulations carrying hope and creativity—the author realizes a great power. But unfortunately most authors are not consciously aware of this magical metapotential. They are as human and susceptible as everyone else—perhaps even more so because they share the artist's neurosis of needing a lot of attention and acknowledgment. Many are the poets and artists that have been swayed into the the bellies of the collectivist beasts because they enjoyed the attention they got so much. At least temporarily.

I'm not certain whether George Orwell, author of *1984* and *Animal Farm,* was a magical realist or just one of the greatest satirists ever, but he certainly had some interesting things to say:

"To suggest that a creative writer, in a time of conflict, must split his life into two compartments, may seem defeatist or frivolous: yet in practice I do not see what else he can do. To lock yourself up in the ivory tower is impossible and undesirable. To yield subjectively, not merely to a party machine, but even to a group ideology, is to destroy yourself as a writer. We feel this dilemma to be a painful one, because we see the need of engaging in politics while also seeing what a dirty, degrading business it is."[6]

Seen from this perspective, magical realism can be a more powerful weapon than combatant sloganeering—especially in dangerous times.

Two books that come to my mind as great examples of this are Jünger's *On the Marble Cliffs* and Anna Kavan's *Ice*. Both are masterpieces of uncanny criticism not against this or that tyrant but against tyranny in general. The reader fills in the irrational voids with his or her own projections, and a literary collaboration between writer and reader begins in the best possible way.

The effects of reading magical realists like, for instance, those I mentioned, bring for me—and I suspect for others, too—an elevation of the mind and a sense of awe of what's always possible literally between the lines. It's an encouragement to remain in a state of mind that encourages irrational and experimental ways of connecting the dots. We're not talking about a strict passage from point A to point B as in a straight narrative, but rather jumping barefoot in a dyslectic playground that contains all the letters and all their possible combinations. Not only can new words and sentences arise; so can new meanings, perspectives, facets of truth, and perceptions of reality.

Is it modernism, postmodernism, surrealism—or nothing, or all of it? It really shouldn't matter, and that's one important key to it. We simply enjoy the experience itself. We don't always need to know why. But . . . if we absolutely do *not* enjoy whatever it is, then we are more inclined to go analytical. And yet what the academics dissect and disseminate eventually loses its potency. The discernible smallest common denominator doesn't necessarily contain *the* truth—or any truth at all. It's only that the picture is so big we cannot see the totality of it that can properly convey the truth—if there even is such a thing as truth.

Displacement, jogging, and distortion of the expected almost paradoxically allow for a clearer image, just like the psychedelic experience of LSD comes from the brain trying to recreate order after the initial chaos brought on by the chemical agent. It makes things connect again after the chaos that challenged inertia, through a temporary increase in synaptic activity. And that not only brings eye candy and new connections, but also—potentially—deep and joyful insights about how one is to live one's life, and why. We can see then that magical realism is not merely a literary technique or tradition, it is very much an attitude to life itself. Enhance a little, and experience a lot!

The expression of inner, subjective truths is not only the territory of the poet or magical realist: it is also the territory of myth. Our most vital myths have most often *not* been transmitted via straight narratives of "he said she said," or in soberly rational records of who killed whom and then took what. They have instead been transmitted via enchanting fairy tales, fantastic stories and images that are literally—and this is important—beyond belief!

In this mythical sense it's not surprising that the magical realism of the early to mid-twentieth century experienced a renaissance during the psychedelic 1960s. Not only did Hermann Hesse sell millions more copies of his books like *Siddhartha* and *Steppenwolf*, but more highbrow authors like Borges found new audiences in the chemically enlightened generation of post-World War II. These authors could already see through the seductive language of advertising that had been perfected in the American 1950s, and that always seemed to bring with it a coup d'état somewhere on less fortunate shores and continents.

Is there an inherent mythic force or function in magical realism? I would say so, because it caters to nuances that are willing to accept accentuations that are not based in the strictly rational. There is also an important comparison we have to make here, to what I call "memetic manipulations." If we think back to the past five, six years, we have seen a lot of that—specifically in politics. Brexit was a result of it; Trump's political reign, also. The memetic manipulations also appealed to the irrational—and more specifically to the emotional and the symbolic— spheres, but these were not created to elevate but rather to debase the receiving end of the stick.

Could there be a mythic force within this memetic manipulation? Can it generate educational roots that affect the cultures of the future? I believe that its form already has (in the form of reality TV, news, and in the contemporary "documentary" style, etc.) . . . But what about the content? Isn't it just absurdist ranting? Demented slurring? Involuntary jesters hell-bent on self-destruction? Primitive diversions?

Some inebriated rabble-rouser taking selfies inside the Capitol in Washington is surely not on par with the storming of the Bastille or the residence of the tsars in St. Petersburg. The answer is, of course, "No, it isn't." But given the chance, and assistance with formulation and dissemination, the rabble-rouser could definitely become an American folk hero à la Jesse James, Billy the Kid, Bonnie and Clyde, or even Charles Manson. Let's not forget that Charles Manson is the American president in J. G. Ballard's highly prescient 1981 novel of "magical hyper-realism," *Hello America,* in which Manson is running the United States from the new political power hub of Las Vegas.

Is there a distinct relationship between magical realism and the shadow side of memetic manipulation? Both essentially state that whatever we perceive and experience isn't fully and truly true. Our perceived reality is malleable. Both set the expected narrative aside and create a new interpretation of reality—sometimes literally, as mentioned above, beyond belief. Both challenge the present hegemonic structures, albeit in different approaches: in subtlety on the one hand and blatant screaming on the other.

I would say that magical realism has an altruistic agenda of opening the mind up for the sake of its own well-being. Memetic manipulation wants to fill that same mind with an arbitrary agenda, not for the sake of that specific mind's well-being but for that of the formulator's.

Some people will analyze demographics, statistics, sociology, anthropology, and other academic constructs in order to try to understand what's already been spelled out for decades in the United States—and also beyond, of course, thanks to their grand scale media imperialism and monoculture. All scenarios, strategies, and mind frames have already been presented in the most palatable form there is: fiction, thereby programming rather than merely entertaining. Fiction rules supreme.

Fiction is not only the new fact, it is also at the core of contemporary identity formulation. We are no longer simply who we are, but mainly what we consume in terms of fiction, and also how we display that consuming process to others. We live in a culture of attributes rather than essence, and if someone offers a more pleasing or more refined attribute, to which our identity is already more or less connected, people will change along with any changes made to the attribute in question. This goes for clothes, styles, catchphrases, discourse, behavior, consumed fiction, and so on.

In this sense, it's not only a Nietzschean but also an Orwellian nightmare. What we so politely and nicely call "sharing" on social media is a complete masochistic resignation to blurring the boundaries between a private sphere and a public one, in which our data is not only "mined" like minerals but also thoroughly exploited and commodified for the benefit of the highest bidder. The memetic manipulations we have been exposed to over the past decade are a result of exactly this process, in which the language of fiction (both formal and narrative) has been used to seduce and coerce until the mass reached its critical point and the relationship roles were ultimately reversed. In this, fiction became fact, and vice versa. Lies are now the truth, and vice versa.

And all those cynical euphemisms that are so much fun and always new: the "story" we "share" and which the platform in question removes after twenty-four hours; the verbs that arise from the platforms ("I will text you, please DM me."). Or "Snap Chat" or "Tik Tok" . . . all alluding to the enforced impermanence and aggressive devaluation—worthlessness, even—of the individual human expression.

There is an indefinite number of examples of how exposure to fictional form and content paved the way for this critical mass point. Let's watch some TV: *West Wing, Boardwalk Empire,* and *Succession,* for example. All of them normalize the abnormal through the seduction of fiction—that is, from a civilized perspective. And of course, there's "reality" TV, too: *The Apprentice* and *Keeping Up with the Kardashians,* for instance. And let's not forget all the "idol" and "talent" shows in which the best possible copycats or emulators are rewarded in perfect humiliation of self-negating mimicry. It's a bizarre blur far too complex to fully comprehend or take in.

I guess we all remember Kim Kardashian in the Oval Office suggesting ideas for prison reform to the reality TV star president—something her father, Robert, had already touched upon back in the media blitz of the O. J. Simpson days, surely? And another instance, from my own experience: In an episode of *Boardwalk Empire* the colored staff of the hotels on the boardwalk in Atlantic City go on strike, picketing with their signs and demanding higher wages. Almost exactly one hundred years later in our general timeline I was in Atlantic City with my wife, and we saw an exactly similar scenario—a magical realism simulacrum!—with hotel workers picketing on that same boardwalk, in front of the casino and hotel called the Trump Taj Mahal. (This is a place that, just after this moment, went bankrupt, by the way.) Let's not even delve into the actual reality TV show *The Apprentice*...

These are all blueprints upon blueprints, which over the years have been written about, laughed at, discarded, and ridiculed. But they are blueprints nonetheless, and as such highly successful ones. Inside your own refined ivory tower of ultimate understanding, most people on the outside seem ridiculous, unintelligent, and pathetic—until... they start tearing down your tower because... someone told them to.

Most of us are familiar with the expression "Hindsight is 20/20"—meaning it's easier to see clearly when we look back at what's been. But if you take into account that most people and generations repeat the same mistakes over and over, I'm not so sure it's all correct. It seems that even perfect vision doesn't guarantee that there's an adjoining understanding of what's seen.

The relationship between clarity and *potential* understanding has been present in basically all our magical history, as well. Individuals or groups can receive or provoke epiphanies and great insights in various ways—almost as if these are inherent within us—but that doesn't mean or lead to anything if the surrounding power structures aren't willing to validate at least the brave attempts at developing these existing structures. As we all know, the agency of self-preservation within power structures is definitely as strong as that within human individuals. No one wants the boat to rock—unless there's someone in the boat who's uncomfortable or ostracized for being too odd, challenging, or creative.

There's always a rebel who gets up, rocks the boat, and builds his own vessel eventually. Or he or she simply hijacks another boat and flaunts a newly designed pirate flag to rewrite a history of utter subjectivity, not seldom with a new and improved message that will convince acolytes new and old that they need to join in.

The year 2020 was also a specific year—one permeated by a global pandemic and a general unrest because of an upheaval of the well-known and a violent takeover by a displaced shadow to deliberately force others to wallow even more in chaos. What I mean by displaced shadow is a being that is out of its own element, in the misdirected belief that it does belong there. The political and other ramifications this confusion always automatically brings are disorder and anarchy; an uprooting of building blocks and foundations such as courtesy and decency and upholding the rules of law, for example.

There are many examples of how new technological platforms have been used to analyze and sway populations for purposes of no real use to the populations, but rather only to the strategists, architects, and well-funded, well-paying, and displaced shadows themselves. Large segments of the population, mainly based in Anglo-Saxon, Christian cultures, were easily taken over by the use of very simple demagogic techniques, amplified by costrategist-owned media until chaos reigned supreme. What a year!

At best, this has been interesting to watch as an entertaining historical tidbit shining the harsh light on the actual causality of mass manipulation. But whereas we have previously associated this kind of behavior with the well-documented "dictatorship of the proletariat" in Soviet Russia or Nazi Germany, the year 2020 and the years preceding brought to our attention the fact that the most susceptible proletariat masses exist in the Anglo-Saxon cultural sphere. It will be interesting to see the effects of Brexit on England in the long run, especially after Wales and Scotland will have left the once "Great" Britain. As for the United States . . . Oh boy! As I write this, it feels like the entire world is finally exhaling after a four-year-old's four years old tantrum. Everyone is trying to figure out how this could happen here—meaning more specifically, in the United States and the United Kingdom.

And let's not forget the critical aftermath that perhaps doesn't become so critical after all, because of its packaging *inside* fictional frameworks. What exactly is that film about Brexit? *The Uncivil War*— starring Benedict Cumberbatch as the campaign director? Fiction? Fact? A critique? A double agent double entendre? Or any documentary about Brexit? Or any documentary about Julian Assange, or Edward Snowden, or Chelsea Manning? Whose whistles are actually being blown, and which tune are these whistles really playing?

Basically these are documentaries that display the so-called truth but in a form that makes them a mere tree in the forest of similar-looking documentaries about thousands of topics available on hundreds of streaming platforms for one's tens of gadgets ready to receive and display them. They are complete with the same dramatic documentary film-stock music, and endless drone shots, and emotional close-ups of teary-eyed faces asking, How could this happen here? Fiction is not only content—it is also very much a form.

By their very form and distribution, these potentially critical expressions become parts of the same stream: a malediction through "malefiction" or a "metafiction" or a "metafriction" that is quickly dissolved by zapping when there is something a bit too disturbing on the screen. In a way, the display of harsh facts in seductive forms is the screen-based equivalent of the opioid crisis of the United States. In this, a substantial and predominantly proletarian section of the population was sedated and literally made void through the dark magic of "pain relief"—a euphemism of course for profitable addiction, plain and simple.

On a more hands-on level, exchanging fact for fiction has been one instrumental key to unlocking the dictatorial door. And yes, I do refer to lies . . . But we should never forget that the door didn't open overnight. Fictional appropriation of reality, whether for fun, profit, or political strategy, is as old as mass media itself. What we have seen recently are just the inevitable results of this dissolution and confusion—the blatant upheaval of very basic concepts and contracts like truth, law, and honesty.

So, okay. . . enough of realism for a while. . . what then of the magical itself? Of what relevance is it that some cognoscenti occasionally paraphrases the writings of "chaos magic" from the 1980s in their comments on current political methods? Here chaos, memes, and sigils are celebrated as cool tools of political manipulation, readily available to the highest bidder. I have seen this happen both pro and contra memetic manipulation—as if both sides try to score bonus points by affixing themselves to a magical system that was created in order to *not* be a system at all in the first place. If there was any allegiance within the chaos magic of the Illuminates of Thanateros (IOT) at all, I would define that as ultra-individualistic. It would also contain a possible streak of paranoia in regard to draconian structures and cultures—no doubt influenced by their most well-known member, William S. Burroughs.

And in this, it's not at all unlike Thee Temple Ov Psychick Youth (TOPY), who at the same time also made great use of memetic magic in the form of networking, sampling (in music and writing, for instance), and generally antidraconian streaks—all included in a package that also contained taking on the magical heritage of Spare, Crowley, Burroughs, Gysin, and many others. Basically, the meme or sigil's function is magical and essentially apolitical in its pure form. Unless, of course, some magician or savvy technician wants to have the meme or sigil behave within some political process. That then literally creates a whole new desired scenario or narrative.

Magic as such is never an objective ideal. It's a cluster of attitudes and methods that can be used by people of differing mind frames and opinions. From this utilitarian perspective, magic is not at all unlike politics. It's a structure, method, and lifestyle that allows for manipulation of others under the banner of subjective idealisms.

Whether we write, read, or perhaps even read what we write ourselves, the elevation that magical realism brings allows for a wider and more colorful perspective. The use of memetic manipulation and other techniques of fiction for immediate causal gain should probably best be called realistic magic. It's the sphere that is rationally quantifiable rather than perceived with the senses and inner feelings. That's not evil or bad in itself; in a way, we all do it in the working of our magic for personal purposes when dealing with real life. But perhaps the dividing line is really about when you use other people—third-party individuals—as leverage for your own gain, and you do it in a scheming and cynical way. Good? Bad? I don't know, but we can see that magical realism isn't the same as realistic magic, nor is it its absolute diametrical counterpoint. They are certainly related, but one is for you and your relationship with yourself, whereas the other has to do with your relationship with others.

Realistic magic, for me, is also somehow quantifiable, visible, apparent to others. The equation or association between cause and effect certainly doesn't need to be apparent to others in order to function, but for the magician it probably should be. One could then perhaps say that magical realism is an attitude toward life, and realistic magic one particular kind of causal application of this attitude.

Louis Aragon, one of the masters of a magical realism bordering on the surreal and the fantastical, produced many great insights about these dynamics: "Reality is the apparent absence of contradiction. The marvelous is the eruption of contradiction within the real."[7] He also said, "The property of the poetic image, as opposed to the essential image, if I may rely on this mediocre epithet, is to incarnate this quality of materialization, one that exercises a tremendous power over man and is quite capable of making him believe in a logical impossibility in the name of logic. The poetic image presents itself in the form of fact, adorned with all fact's necessities. But fact resides not in the object but in the subject: fact exists only in terms of time, that is to say of language."[8] And this: "Men pass their lives in the midst of magic precipices without opening their eyes. They manipulate grim symbols innocently, their ignorant lips unwittingly mouth terrible incantations, phrases like revolvers."[9]

I think what Aragon is referring to is that essentially whatever we look at can be a means to an end. Whether it's art, technology, or politics, it's all used by people of different persuasions, and in quite similar ways. He also wrote that, "The image is the path of all knowledge."[10] Meaning, I suppose, that the smallest element that literally contains more than an intellectual understanding of words and messages can be even more powerful. Here we drift into the symbolic, and also therefore touch upon the mythic. The clearer the symbol, the stronger the power. But as with all things, the force can also backfire.

As we exhale, we can now delve forever into analyzing the data, the experiences, and the reports—whether they be firsthand, secondhand, or thirdhand—as well as smartphone video footage, and a million memes, pro as well as con, of whatever it is we're looking at . . . I certainly hope someone will delve into that and report something smart back that we don't already know. But as for intuitively grasping the bigger picture, embracing the intelligence of magical realism might be a better path than throwing oneself headfirst into the fierce combat zones of intellectual and moral rigidity. The slight distortions—and their reactions—always reveal more than loud, vulgar causality.

In a way, our current discourse is like a medieval magician screaming his spells louder and louder when no benevolent spirit initially arrives to do his bidding, to the degree that his God-fearing neighbors dial 6-6-6 to the Inquisition. Instead of changing the individual perspective, mind frame, and understanding—weaving in intuitive interpretations of a process that is never causal or simple and expressing himself in eloquent poetic form to attract and then command the spirit—this disgruntled magician simply expressed and displayed his own frustration. In so doing, he thereby played right into the scenario or narrative of the draconian powers that be. All the while the spirit looked on and hoped for better and smarter magicians to come along—regardless of which side of the "moral" fence they might stem from.

As a hopefully suitable or suitably hopeful end to this harangue of contemporary pessimism, I would like to offer a morsel of light based in and on our conclusion. It's a very short story called "A Universal Infamy of History," and it goes like this:

> After having indulged in a harangue of contemporary pessimism—
> unsure of whether anyone had listened—the author wanted to offer
> a morsel of light based in and on his conclusions. He got up from
> his desk and exited his apartment. Down on the street, on the pave-
> ment, he undressed until fully naked; then spread his wings, ruffled
> his feathers and flew up and away. From his new perspective he
> could see his entire city with all its people rushing, stressing, and
> hunting for illusions constructed exclusively by others. "Alas, there is
> no point to any of this; nor to anything, really," he sighed, and then
> flew away to the forest where he built a nest together with a bird-of-
> paradise that had eloped from the tropics. They relaxed and enjoyed
> their simple life until it ended.

11
Literchoor, Kulchur, and a Damned Fine Friendship

On the Symbiosis of Ezra Pound and James Laughlin

Looking at the relationship between Ezra Pound and his principal publisher, James Laughlin, not only gives us an interesting insight about their specific relationship, but also one about the cultural environment they were both in, and became key players in. There is something of the magical in this, both thematically and dynamically. We have a relationship that is at first imbued with the dynamic of master and apprentice, but that later changes into a more concrete working relationship and constructions of mutual creative universes and careers. The master also roams freely through religious, philosophical, mythic, and magical spheres. In so doing, he disseminates enlightening symbols or fragments through his vibrant poetic mind. He does this both in his work proper but also in correspondence with the disciple, who realizes already from the very beginning what a privileged situation he's in.

"Literchoor, Kulchur, and a Damned Fine Friendship: On the Symbiosis of Ezra Pound and James Laughlin" was originally presented as a lecture at the conference "Re-writing the Future: 100 Years of Esoteric Modernism and Psychoanalysis," in Merano, Italy, 2019.

This fundament was laid out already in 1933, when eighteen-year-old Laughlin wrote to forty-eight-year-old Pound, then situated in Rapallo, Italy. Pound welcomed students and friends to come join him in what was called the "Ezuversity"—Ezra's University. If one simply stayed around, one got to hang out with one of the world's most famous modernist poets, and one could try to integrate as much or as little learning or inspiration as one saw fit. No other curriculum necessary—or even extant.

Pound at this time gave teaching as such a lot of thought, and had plans to eventually set up an academy based on quality minds and quality source material, yet always within a nonrestrictive framework. In his text, "The Teacher's Mission," Pound stated didactically what the important things were: "All teaching of literature should be performed by the presentation and juxtaposition of specimens of writing and NOT by discussion of some other discusser's opinion *about* the general standing of a poet or author."[1]

In the same text, Pound elaborates on what seemed to be of equal importance to him at the time: teaching culture as a kind of sacred mission. "Artists are the antennae of the race. If this statement is incomprehensible and if its corollaries need any explanation, let me put it that a nation's writers are the voltometers and steam-gauges of that nation's intellectual life. They are the registering instruments, and if they falsify their reports there is no measure to the harm that they do."[2]

James Laughlin had been recommended to go see Pound by a friend and teacher at Harvard, Dudley Fitts. Laughlin was one of the hungrier students at the Ezuversity. After having arrived, he got a dose of Pound's acerbic yet probably well-meaning advice, along the lines of: "Your poetry is no good; why don't you start a publishing company instead? I'll help you find authors that matter." Had Laughlin been a pathological poet, he would of course have stormed out in anger. But he was more insightful than that and actually heeded his master's advice.

The publishing company New Directions began humbly but was supported by Laughlin's father and an aunt. Upon graduating from Harvard in 1939, Laughlin's father (a steel industrialist heir) endowed him with one hundred thousand dollars. Laughlin was smart, as he didn't invest all the money in the publishing but in his other passion: skiing. He opened a ski resort in Utah, which soon turned a profit. These profits were invested in championing modernist icons like Pound, and the result remains with us through the publishing company he founded: New Directions. It's still a heavy-duty player when it comes to fine literature and poetry. And each title still has the same line on the impressum page: "New Directions Books are published for James Laughlin." One could argue that during the first decade of their friendship, the books were to an equal degree "published for Ezra Pound."

Laughlin knew the value of the pound (pardon the pun!)—but more so in the poetic sense than the commercial one. His mind was set already from the get-go of New Directions to always keep Pound in print, as a kind of religious devotion to a poet so brilliant and important that Laughlin owed it to the world. That makes you think: What if . . . ? What if this young entrepreneur hadn't had this unconventionally devotional attitude? Where would Pound's legacy be today? In Laughlin's words: "These days ND is abubble with a frenetic roil of switched wires and tangled gargles as we struggle to get out a lot of new books. Ruin hangs like a large garbage pail over the Halloween doorway because costs are way up and sales are way down. But who knows, who ever knows, who does? Important and gratifying: keeping all the books of Pound and William Carlos Williams in print, which I could do because I inherited money. A normal commercial publisher would have had to remainder many books ND keeps in print."[3]

Pound's own publishing history up to that point had been a mixed and often paradoxical bag, which very much reflected the overall modernist environment. Radical authors and poets like Pound, Joyce, and Eliot were mostly published in small literary magazines, and quite often the authors themselves were part of the editorial boards of these and other magazines. There existed a rich cultural climate if we look at the "signal" and personal engagement. But then as now, peer-produced media didn't really have a strong and wide outreach. The esoteric dynamic of preaching to the already converted needed to be overcome. Pound was good at this, for his books had already started coming out via bigger publishing companies.

This, however, was not an easy situation for Pound and the others. They shared a sentiment that the really powerful publishers were "commercial" and hence infected somehow by a kind of base "unseriousness" and lack of comprehension of what these modernists were trying to achieve. More often than not, this can be ascribed more to narcissistic neurosis than anything else. In fact, there were many publishing companies interested in what these new pioneers were doing, but the poor sales discouraged them from carrying on at the same pace as these wild, formal experimentalists. So that mix between small literary journal freedom, and unwillingly willingly trying to secure better publishing deals, was a normal situation at this time. One could complain in vitriolic rants to fellow poets about the corruption and inefficiency of big publishing companies but at the same time gladly accept invitations from these same companies.

How perfect then for Pound that there came along a really smart and potentially wealthy young publisher—a poet at heart who would soon be washed clean of those aspirations by an elder with many ulterior motives. But Laughlin didn't mind. Not at all. He understood the dynamics right from the start. Not only would this mean an incorporation of an already existing and inspiring friendship but also access to a very strong network of the very best poets and writers of the era. Let's not forget that Pound had, by this time, for decades defined and refined both the work of others and authorships proper. Indeed, T. S. Eliot dedicated *The Waste Land* to Pound, who had edited the masterpiece into full glory. Eliot wrote "For Ezra Pound, Il miglior fabbro," which means "the better craftsman."[4] For Laughlin, hosting Pound's authorship also meant hosting Pound's mind and friends. Already in 1934, Pound put Laughlin in touch with William Carlos Williams and Louis Zukofsky, who both became solid literary workhorses in his stable. Pound also made sure Laughlin became the literary editor of Gorham Munson's "social credit" magazine *New Democracy*. The literary page was called "New Directions," which set a snowball in motion that is still rolling today.

The two were working on editions of Pound's already overwhelming oeuvre—focusing mainly on the many variants and developments of the massively ambitious and all-immersive *Cantos* project. As they did so, the correspondence soon integrated other topics dealing with the most important things in life, which are "literchoor" and "kulchur." But it became clear as time passed, and Laughlin in many ways individuated himself out of the pure acolyte stage, that he was well-aware of a situation of gratitude vis-à-vis Pound—they both were—but that Laughlin was also his own man, with his own views. As Pound's radical economic reform ideas merged with literally classical forms of anti-Semitism, Laughlin objected and said straight-out he'd publish none of that.

In a way there was a streak of a Christic archetype in Pound. His work in itself was not enough, it seems. It needed to be contextualized in perhaps unnecessarily complex ideas and marketed to the world, but with himself as a clearly visible instigator. The economic reform ideas are one such example, and one that was actually already actively taken care of by other instigators at the time. When these economic ideas were padded in anti-Semitic clothing, it's another Christic gestalt taking form—that of Golgotha, and of Pound as not only a poet-thinker but also a martyr.

After the war, Pound was back in the United States and interned at St. Elizabeths Hospital in Washington, D.C. His work on a utopian academy that would define a certain Poundean learning, and also way of learning, could be seen as an example of the same phenomenon: Pound's mind was so advanced and lofty that he probably couldn't see that these structural issues or constructions actually hampered his strictly poetic flow—not to mention his career.

In the context of his books, like *ABC of Reading* and *Guide to Kulchur,* there is a strong didactic, pedagogic streak, but even here, when the teacher disseminates his wisdoms to us, there is also lofty poetry at work and in motion, and aphorisms that still stick: "It doesn't matter which leg of your table you make first, so long as the table has four legs and will stand up solidly when you have finished it."[5] And "Literature is news that STAYS news."[6] Pound also said, "Without gods, no culture. Without gods, something is lacking. Some Stoics must have known this, and considered logic a mere shell outside the egg."[7] He said as well, "A civilized man is one who will give a serious answer to a serious question. Civilization itself is a certain sane balance of values."[8]

Basically, when Pound's ideas leave the lofty arena of poetry, developed during a lifetime of advanced learning and creative association, and drift into pseudo-political demagogia and a perhaps compensatory need for majestic structures, they lose their mythic and inspirational value. Laughlin saw this very clearly and could therefore be adamant about saying no to certain works. Laughlin saw the value and brilliance of the *Cantos*—as did many, many others early on. They appreciated that it included an entire universe, perhaps even more, of thoughts, ideas, and emotions; of past, present, and future; of experimental theory and pragmatic poetic practice. To stretch beyond the experimental perfection of Pound's poetry (and by all means, also prose) was simply not necessary, according to Laughlin.

Even if he had wanted to, Pound would have had a hard time decontextualizing his own approaches. It was simply one cluster of attitudes and ideas in which everything was connected and relevant. It seemed impossible for the maestro to untangle personal poetic perspectives from a general Nietzschean legacy that so often seeped through. In 1918 Pound stated, in a piece about Henry James: "The whole of great art is a struggle for communication. All things that oppose this are evil, whether they be silly scoffing or obstructive tariffs. And this communication is not a leveling, it is not an elimination of differences.

It is a recognition of differences, of the right of differences to exist, of interest in finding things different. Kultur is an abomination; philology is an abomination, all repressive uniforming education is an evil."[9]

Even a literary overview of an admired author apparently couldn't be spared from general demagogia! If we are kind and diplomatic today, we could call this attitude passionate. But it is also an example of Pound's recurring tendency to drift from the poetic or descriptive center to his own web of strained associations and almost justifying ideas, although, essentially, no justifications are necessary. In literary criticism this was fine, as a kind of highbrow seasoning in a heady soup that a fair chunk of Western intellectuals ate with a great appetite and also found nutritious. But when one group or culture was targeted in similarly eloquent flows that could never be read as anything *but* political, having severed all ties to any literary, poetic, or even general cultural contexts, the situation naturally became more problematic.

As Laughlin was preparing for new editions of the ever-swelling *Cantos* in 1940, he and Pound wrote back and forth about clauses in their contract that would release New Directions from any litigations stemming from anti-Semitism, or perhaps to even have an introduction in the new edition explaining and perhaps even justifying some of Pound's ideas. Laughlin: "I think that I ought to write a preface, or something, to these new CANTOS, explaining what is what: I mean, linking them up with what has gone before and giving a summary of the earlier ones. You see the attitude over here is that the CANTOS are incomprehensible."[10]

To this Pound was strongly opposed but at the same time more than willing to suggest various improvements to appease Laughlin's publishing conundrum. Thereby in some ways he admitted, if not guilt, at least awareness of the controversial sticks of dynamite they were tossing back and forth; Laughlin respectfully striving for avoidance of headaches and disaster; Pound striving for an almost gleeful pushing of the boundaries.

Pound: "I don't mind affirming in contract, so long as I am not expected to alter text. You can put it this way. The author affirms that in no passage should the text be interpreted to mean that he condemns any innocent man or woman for another's guilt, and that no degree of relationship, familial or racial shall be taken to imply such condemnation.—But no group national or ethical can expect immunity not accorded to other groups."[11]

And so it went on, back and forth, and in minute detail. In 1941, Laughlin heard of Pound's radio broadcasts from Italy.

Laughlin: "You are pretty much disliked for your orations. Your name in general might be said to aspire but not attain to the dignity of mud. I would rather fill this unfortunate interim with fairly uncontroversial things like cantyers/Cantos selection and the Cavalcanti . . ."[12]

Pound wrote back: "No use your saying I am disliked. I want to know HOW, and by whom. Details welcome. What you need is a little trip to Europe as refresher."[13]

As the United States entered into World War II in 1942, that little refresher trip literally wasn't on the map for Laughlin. The two remained in touch sporadically during the war to keep business going, but Pound's destiny now seemed as sealed as Italy's, as well as that of the axis powers in general, and this in a very Wagnerian sense. Götterdämmerung is real, so let's stoke the funeral pyre! Pound's insistence, eloquence, and stamina, and his active integration of not-so-symbolic anti-Roosevelt orations, eventually led to his arrest and to being placed at first in a cage and then later in a hospital tent in Pisa. A Jewish chaplain provided him with writing materials so he could write his classic *Pisan Cantos*. This was a strange twist of destiny for Pound, I'm sure.

Laughlin wrote to Pound in September 1945: "I'm afraid that things are going to be kind of tough for you here, but rest assured that though you have many spiteful enemies, you also have a few friends left who will do their best to help you. No one takes your side, of course, in the political sense, but many feel that the bonds of friendship and the values of literature can transcend a great deal."[14]

In many ways their correspondence both during the war and then afterward, as Pound was interned in the United States, is endearing and genuine but also in many ways "pussyfooting." There is no straight-out clarity, especially not when it came to problematic issues that could inflict damage on both men's careers. I think this stems back to the very first communications in the early 1930s, when on the surface there was mutual admiration for energy and zest but underneath the surface a mutual reckoning and evaluation going on. The poet saw a young publisher who could keep his old and new works in print and develop a career on American soil while he himself enjoyed Italy and was, at least before the war, out of reach of tangible hostilities. Laughlin saw a mentor and a source of inspiration. He also saw an open door to a pretty vast network of authors and poets whom he could exploit under the umbrella of "mutual benefits." And since the formula worked so well from basically day one, no one wanted to rock this boat.

As Pound grew increasingly infirm during the 1960s, Laughlin stepped forward and took on more of the role of literary agent. He helped set up deals of recordings, editions with other publishers, translations, and so on. Their correspondence was never really personal or emotional but rather continuous eruptions of wit and puns, of agreements and disagreements. When Pound was back in Europe and living right here where we are assembled today, this position of Laughlin's became even clearer. He was at a vital fifty in 1965 whereas Pound was at a dwindling eighty. The power dynamic had changed quite diametrically, but there was still plenty of loyalty both ways.

In a letter from May 22, 1965, Pound wrote Laughlin: "I hope you will find some way to print something that will remedy past errors. If you do that I will sign it 200 times."[15]

At this time Pound was depressed and often questioned his own value as a poet. Laughlin did his very best to inform Pound that the world looked at him differently. There was a strong upsurge of editions and translations in the final decade of Pound's life. With a few exceptions like certain people wanting to publish Pound's clearly pro-fascist radio broadcasts, he could actually enjoy his autumn years knowing Laughlin was still out there and pushing his poetic genius onward; if not to the masses then at least to new generations of intelligentsia. This was certainly, again, to both men's advantage, and with age the relationship graduated from epiphytic to actually symbiotic. There is in many ways, symbolically at least, a big difference between "living off one another" and "feeding each other."

In the times of hardship, it was Laughlin who brought forces together to make things easier for Pound. He reached out to old friends like Ernest Hemingway for money for Pound's attorneys, or to make sure he had reading and writing materials at St. Elizabeths, or any other important thing. In this, Laughlin was the great facilitator who went well beyond the expected. This also included continually feeding the American intellectual environment with plenty of Pound. This also led to many cochampions appearing, who saw beyond (or simply neglected) the politics and preferred the poetry. One of these champions was Allen Ginsberg, who in many ways became a poet laureate of sorts of the American underground, just like Pound had been in the 1910s and '20s. In a conversation in the Pound studies journal *Paideuma* in 1974, Ginsberg sums up the attitude of, I think, many younger American intellectuals at the time, many of whom were Jewish.

Pound told me that he felt that the Cantos were "stupidity and ignorance all the way through," and were a failure and a "mess," and that his "greatest stupidity was stupid suburban anti-Semitic prejudice," he thought—as of 1967, when I talked to him. So I told him I thought that since the Cantos were for the first time a single person registering over the course of a lifetime all of his major obsessions and thoughts and the entire rainbow are his images and clingings and attachments and discoveries and perceptions, that they were an accurate representation of his mind and so couldn't be thought of in terms of success or failure, but only in terms of the actuality of their representation, and that since for the first time a human being had taken the whole spiritual world of thought through fifty years and followed the thoughts out to the end—so that he built a model of his consciousness over a fifty-year time span—that they were a great human achievement.[16]

Whether Pound appreciated Ginsberg's comments I don't know. But I think it's a valid perspective. Although Pound was absolutely correct when he claimed that artists are the antennae of the race, these antennae need to stick to a mythic language—whether written, visual, musical, whatever—or else they will be painted into a corner that will be very hard to get out of. This period of history is filled with examples of genuine artists, genuine antennae, who were far too easily flattered and cajoled into being poster boys or girls for devious people and movements going on around the fairly well-insulated antennae. Pound's good fortune was his network of family and very loyal friends. It's to them we owe the gratitude for the preservation and repackaging of Pound as our modernist genius and master.

He opened the floodgates to the subconscious—his own and that of our culture—in a much more powerful way than did aesthetically accessible, psychedelic surrealists of the same era. Pound drew from the source of the classics of many regions and eras, filtered it all as a scholar, and expressed it as a truly unique artist. In this he bridged not only space and time but also his inner sanctity and the outer chaos of twentieth-century Europe. In that sense, a shamanic archetype who freely roams and shares his findings, although unsure who actually understands them. In that sense also a Don Quixotic paraphrase, in which James Laughlin played the part of Sancho Panza—ever willing to make sense of a confusing world to the pure and good-hearted romantic knight; and vice versa.

12

Spare Me a Pound

An Initial Look at the Sui Genericism of Austin and Ezra

The human need to create is essentially a central part of the cluster that is usually termed the *survival instinct*. If our beloved forefathers and foremothers hadn't been on the forefront of foresight and developed a trust in their immediate intuitions—and a forceful application of their ensuing impulses—this book that you now hold in your hands would never have existed, nor would our general culture as we know it.

We constitute the direct result of a long period of time of constant refinement of the battle against *any* kind of inertia, because we know instinctively that inertia equals death—the very antithesis of survival.

In our modern and chaotic culture, people still carry traces of this primordial creativity, but for the most part it has been relegated to "professionals"—whether that be politicians creating safe environments, the military protecting this specific habitat, or the artists who are trained at prestigious schools to be sensitive in their reflections of what's going on around us.

"Spare Me a Pound: An Initial Look at the Sui Genericism of Austin and Ezra" was originally written for the anthology *Outsider Inpatient,* Trapart Books, 2021.

This compartmentalized institutionalization of survival is neither good nor bad; neither constructive nor destructive. What has happened, though, is that the view of creativity as such has been narrowed down to a time- and space-specific activity, and *not* as a comprehensive extension of an instinct we all actually share. Needless to say, this has diluted the quality and potency of the original function of art; of making people aware of necessary survival mechanisms. Art should present and represent *potential*—the very first (and perhaps therefore the most important) game board upon which we evaluate where we should move next.

Traditionally the artist was much more powerful than he or she is today. Why? Because the artist had that power of presenting and representing potential. This position of reverence and respect has traveled onward genetically as well as culturally. It's often contained within a sociocultural complex we could describe as "individual survival by outstanding excellence." If our tribe members project respect and awe on us, our own chances of survival greatly increase. (This exclusive position could of course backfire, too, if the presentations and representations of the artist turn out to be erroneous or threatening to the well-being of the tribe itself.)

Talented and creative children should be encouraged to develop their skills and creativity. But even if that's not the case, their need to create and express doesn't go away. It just becomes stronger than any external discouragement. In some milder cases this manifests as honing a skill within the boundaries of a hobby—that is, a time- and space-relegated ventilation mechanism. In other cases, where the need for acknowledgment is stronger (usually because of active external oppression/repression), the need becomes part of a pathology in which talent and need become united, overheated, and disregarding of convention and accepted behavioral patterns.

Examples of this would be the troubled genius or the starving artist, whose forceful and sometimes (paradoxically) self-destructive drive to not only create but also to *display* the creations in question constitute a shard or a remnant of another facet of the atavistic artist archetype. It's that of a shaman who goes beyond the senses to bring back information and inspiration from other strata of consciousness—even at the risk of being ridiculed.

A discrepancy between sender and receiver, for instance, because of autistically fragranced inabilities or insensitivities within the sender, only increases the fervor or temperature in an already overheated mind. One way of dealing with this inadequate level of acknowledgment is by adding the dimensions of *contextualization* and *systemization;* that is, a metalevel augmenting the great skill one already (supposedly) has. In this way, the original art or signal is repackaged and enhanced through its own contextualized reverberation. These systems can be advanced, elaborate, and eloquent to the degree that they eventually even overshadow the original expression or talent. And thus they can become new avenues or even career opportunities in the ever-developing process of acknowledgment and survival.

Looking at two prominent twentieth-century creatives—American poet Ezra Pound (1885–1972) and British artist Austin Osman Spare (1886–1956)—we can clearly see this fascinating aspect of the development of added levels of neurosis.

Both gentlemen were prodigious, and developed not only skill and expertise but also a transcendence both in process and expression. In other words, they both engaged so fiercely in their creative process that the rational mind with its many inhibiting forces was set aside—sidetracked or short-circuited—so that irrational and subconscious signals could pass through and into the creative process. Furthermore, they were both highly ambitious and productive, yet not in striving for mainstream acceptance.

They both focused on refining their tools and languages; their approaches and symbologies. In this they acknowledged the influence of contemporary psychology and its importance. At the same time, they strove for a distanced aloofness by attaching themselves to a "classicism," or an aspect of cultural eternity only expressible in a specific art form for which they felt a strong affinity.

Pound not only wrote beautiful and mind-expanding poetry and essays. He also early on assumed the position of teacher and authority. He did this not only by displaying quantitative objective knowledge that could be imparted, but mainly through his own insight and systemization, being presented as uniquely his own. *ABC of Reading* and *Guide to Kulchur,* for instance, are two book titles prominently displaying a position not only of expertise but of prerogative.

This quasi-hubristic position both helped and hampered Pound when he was confined to St. Elizabeths mental hospital in Washington, D.C., between 1946 and 1958 (following his support for Benito Mussolini's fascist Italy during and after World War II). The defense argued insanity (basically so that Pound would escape a considerably more draconian punishment), but it was also apparent that Pound at this time exercised an authority in certain cultural spheres (literary, poetic), but that it was essentially self-sustained over a long period of time.

From teaching curious acolytes at his positively ad-libbing "Ezuversity" in rural Italy during the 1930s to writing a great number of literary reviews and essays *judging* the quality of other authors' writings and attitudes, Pound rode the high horse. It was for that reason that the avant-garde and supremely talented poet expanded his own assumption of authority as a survival mechanism.

After Pound himself had been *judged* insane, his main spokesperson and aide Julian Cornell wrote to Pound's wife, Dorothy, that she ". . . need not be alarmed about the report on your husband's mental condition . . . I feel quite sure that you will find, when you see him again, that he is his usual self, and that the mental aberrations which the doctors have found are not anything new or unusual, but are chronic and would pass entirely unnoticed by one like yourself who has lived close to him for a number of years. In fact I think it may be fairly said that any man of his genius would be regarded by a psychiatrist as abnormal."[1]

Austin Osman Spare was a highly skilled draftsman and painter who received praise for his talents early on. However, instead of pursuing a successful career of portraiture, for instance, Spare spent most of his life in financially dire straits, painting pub punters for small sums and seemingly cherishing his "splendid isolation."

Spare also wrote several books outlining his own perspectives on psychology, sexuality, and magic of the occult, supernatural kind. An example is his 1913 magnum opus *The Book of Pleasure (Self Love): The Psychology of Ecstasy*. He often connected these writings with his own artistic process. His manic creativity simply wouldn't settle for merely visual expressions, although clearly marked by his own artistic genius. There was also an apparent need to contextualize his own creativity and place it on a philosophical and magico-religious level that he and he alone could systematize and assume authority over.

Where Pound was in every way a radical classicist looking back to antiquity (both Eastern and Western) and finding solace in his own position as caretaker of a legacy, Spare looked back even further. He argued that through his construction of an "alphabet of desire," it was possible to magically reawaken atavistic layers of the human psyche. (This would be for purposes of increased self-knowledge, sexual prowess, power, and problem-solving capacities, for instance.) In this way he acknowledged that we all carry the tangible traces of evolution within us—as displayed physically in the gradual development of a human fetus.

Spare's "atavistic resurgence" could be willed, he argued, by using his "magical alphabet" and creative techniques (such as "automatic" drawing, painting, and writing), and by mentally focusing on "sigils" (ideogrammatic symbols of the desired outcome) while in ecstatic mind frames (such as the orgasm).

The potential empowerment of the individual here comes through the position of pupil; a subjugation to the theories and practices of the artistic master magician and psychologically *very* liberal systematizer-teacher. This was of course exactly the situation at Pound's classes in Italy, too.

Pound often reflected upon the very nature of teaching, and shared his thoughts in works like *ABC of Reading*: "The man who really knows can tell all that is transmissible in a very few words. The

economic problem of the teacher (of violin or of language or of any-
thing else) is how to string it out so as to be paid for more lessons."[2]
He also said, "Real education must ultimately be limited to men who
INSIST on knowing, the rest is mere sheep-herding."[3]

Even this apparently critical attitude toward conventional teaching becomes a telling decoy of sorts, making our attention move from
Pound as poet to Pound as teacher, and onward to Pound as arbiter of
teaching. This abstraction and detachment is clever and often demagogically eloquent, as could be expected from a brilliantly overheated
mind like Pound's. But at the same time the intricacy and intelligence
in many ways reveal a deep fear of being scrutinized by others.

> As the press, daily, weekly, and monthly, is utterly corrupted, either
> from economic or personal causes, it is manifestly UP TO the teach-
> ing profession to act for themselves without waiting for the journal-
> ists and magazine blokes to assist them. The mental life of a nation
> is no man's private property. The function of the teaching profession
> is to maintain the HEALTH OF THE NATIONAL MIND. As
> there are great specialists and medical discoverers, so there are "lead-
> ing writers,"' but once a discovery is made, the local practitioner is
> just as inexcusable as the discoverer himself if he fails to make use of
> the known remedies and known prophylactics.[4]

The same argument can be made for or about Spare: the detachment in his case is not only simply writing about the tools of his apparent trade in passages about "automatic" drawing and writing. It goes
even further when the magical thinking becomes systematized, and he
thereby can offer a perspective on not only changing himself but also
others. It's another level of attractive distancing; a glamor spell of sorts.
"The Ego is desire, so everything is ultimately desired and undesirable,
desire is ever a preliminary forecast of terrible dissatisfaction hidden by
its ever-present vainglory. The millennium will come and quickly go.
Men will be greater than the Gods they ever conceived—there will be

greater dissatisfaction. You are ever what you were—but you may be so in a different form!"[5]

What is the hubristic hen here, and what is the ensouled egg of excellence? I would argue that the "passion of immersion" in talents like Pound and Spare, both definitely touched by genius, can create psychic overheating in the human mind, which then needs to be justified in regard to the outside world—so as not to be discounted as belonging to someone "crazy."

Both gentlemen to a great extent discarded the outer in order to refine the inner. But as that, for distinctly neurotic reasons, apparently wasn't enough, they both added the dimension of systemization and thereby assumed a constructed authority.

Spare self-published his books and had occasional exhibitions of his art. Pound's books were published and were definitely well-respected, mainly in an environment of modernist letters. As both men had this kind of external agency, we cannot claim that their assuming of authority was *purely* compensational (as in cases in which neurotics or psychotics create manically in more or less total isolation because they have no other choice).

I would argue that it's here more a case of *sui genericism* (the amplification of one's own sense of greatness through systematized interpretation and dissemination). It is not a case of hubris pure and simple, nor of narcissism per se, nor of a fascistoid character type (à la Fromm) demanding "followers."

The extra dimension of systemization never took away from their core need: to express themselves in a unique, creative way. The systemization was rather an accumulating reinforcement via shared monologues that eventually crystallized and became real, solid legacies. Spare's books are kept in print and written about, mainly in the world of contemporary occultism, and Pound is revered as an inspiring and educating classicist mind as much as an introspective and groundbreaking poet. They may have been in a league of their own—genuine "sui generis" individuals—but their own reinforcements are equally valid keys to understanding their legacy in general, as well as inspiring springboards for new generations of acolytes.

It is interesting to note that both gentlemen were quite critical of psychology and of the gradual acceptance of this relatively new science in the mainstream culture. Spare called Freud and Jung "Fraud" and "Junk," but according to his friend, disciple, and biographer, Kenneth Grant, Spare apparently "sent a copy of *The Book of Pleasure* to Sigmund Freud who described it as one of the most significant revelations of subconscious mechanisms that had appeared in modern times."[6] If this actually happened (as yet unconfirmed!) it would surely have made Spare supremely happy in his own sui genericism. The ultimately desired is always external acknowledgment.

Pound was less ambiguous in his views of Freud, calling his teaching, "unmitigated shit . . . laid out in most elegant arabesques."[7] Pound's general hatred of psychology also got meshed with his blatant anti-Semitism: "the vienese poison . . . whole pewk of kiketry, aimed at destroying the will/introspective idiocy/non objective."[8] Whether this was a shield of defense against the potential scrutiny of *any* critical naysayers or just a poundful of elegant arabesques enforcing the position of the poet-classicist as untouchable master, the main insight remains the same: The intellectual movements of Pound's time to a very great extent embraced Freud's theories on sexuality and the unconscious, and also lauded Freud himself as a "prophet" of sorts. Although Pound was interested in many of the same zeitgeist topics, he could never deflate himself to *not* be the main casual "expounder" of wisdom in his own particularly fragmented style, and just accept someone else's formulations of the same insights—especially if those formulations were coming from a Jew!

For many creatives, the time and space to concentrate and let ideas flow unhampered is absolutely essential—in the case of neurotics and psychotics these prerequisites can even seem to be *vital*. No wonder then, that isolation was a key element for both Spare and Pound. Pound's "expatriotism" was established already in 1908, when he first moved to London. From that time on he stayed away from the United States as much as he could. This willed expatriate isolation greatly helped him immerse himself in studies and creative writing. In no way a total introspective, Pound's estrangement from American culture seems to have been one of preference and cultural inspiration rather than anything else.

Pound's stay at the mental institution St. Elizabeths Hospital between 1946 and 1958 was also an isolation, but certainly an unwanted one. Here Pound could read, write, and see friends and family members, but the stay actually brought with it exactly the mental imbalance that he was there to be "cured" of.

Spare's isolation, on the other hand, was always wholly self-imposed. He retracted to his inner spheres and brought out fantastic vistas to paint; apparently transcending time and space. Spare seems to have been needing peace and quiet. As he had already been subjected to some degree of fame early on in life, he certainly knew what he was missing. His own artistic and occult experiments simply seemed more important. I suspect that an extroversion in terms of nurturing a career would also have meant an increased sense of dreaded scrutiny and criticism. I believe Spare felt safe and optimally creative in his own self-imposed poverty. Spare's sui genericism needed to be controlled and directed by himself, and not be exposed to the potential threats of outer criticism.

There are other similarities beyond parallel existences in time, basic psychological constitutions, and using far-off, distant times as romantic escapisms. Both men integrated an ideogrammatic method for reaching communicatory clarity. Pound's interest in, and occasional obsession with, Chinese characters of writing was a part of a strong, seemingly pathological drive to join the dots in poetic expression for it to bloom into a "total" expression beyond the "normal."

The desire to break down elements, phenomena, and even the psyche into the smallest possible unit was undoubtedly a zeitgeist phenomenon. The early twentieth-century development of atomic research for purposes of energy and eventually warfare suddenly transcended history, as it grew out of Greek antiquity by association with the very word. The original Greek word *atomos* means "indivisible," signifying the smallest possible building block. The scientists of Spare and Pound's day were looking for a way of harnessing the huge amounts of energy stemming from either fission or fusion. So too did the radical poets and artists, and so were the pioneering psychologists and psychoanalysts. Breaking down something inherently meant laying it bare, and as such it could be evaluated and then reassembled in desired ways.

For Spare, the literal stripping of conventional meaning from a word by not only decimation of superfluous characters but then also by reshaping the remaining ones into an ideogram meant to be immediately forgotten, post-ecstatic experience, became a central part of his teaching and system. Weaving these new and sentient symbols into his mind via automatic images and writings became an even greater artwork in itself: a psychic gesamtkunstwerk that he was the creator of.

For Pound, the main power of language, and of poetry specifically, was the evocative potential of bringing forth images in the mind. His reverence for the Chinese characters, which have developed from pictograms to ideograms over time, became a tool in his own poetic creation—as did the entire specifically Confucian philosophy. Making no distinction between times, spaces, and cultures, Pound pragmatically brought the small evocative units into his own machinery of leverage. For instance, by "translating" and editing the beloved Shih-Ching (the classic anthology of Chinese odes defined by Confucius), Pound was basically also writing his own book.

"No one is going to be content with a transliteration of Chinese names. When not making a desperate effort at mnemonics or differentiating in vain hope of distinguishing one race from another, I mainly use the French form. Our European knowledge of China has come via Latin and French and at any rate the French novels as printed have some sort of uniform connotation."[9]

Pound's frequent integration of the actual Chinese characters throughout his masterpiece *Cantos* (along with Greek and Egyptian hieroglyphs) is not solely an attempt at being clever but also a way of creating an intellectual assault that leads to an emotional-psychic release in the immersion of the images evoked. What has made Pound one of the most respected poets of the twentieth century is exactly this audacity: taking whatever source inspires you and using an uninhibited artistic and poetic license to refine and define them.

For Pound, the admiration for—and perhaps identification with—the Chinese philosopher Confucius is essential to understanding his psychic constitution. Pound looked beyond time and space and assumed authority (again) by translating/formulating Confucius, thereby bringing someone else's thoughts and language under his own umbrella of definition. This is evident in the strictly philosophical perspective as well. Pound demagogically challenged the status quo of Western academia by placing himself in this role as interpreter. We can see a similar occurrence in Pound's critique of contemporary financial systems. His was a genuine interest in alternative currencies and financial methods (like taxation only of financial sectors but not of sectors of manufacture), but the potentially constructive demagogia was hampered (to say the least) by Pound's vocal adherence to an anti-Semitic prejudice that permeated much of his thinking.

According to Pound's son-in-law, the Italian anthropologist Boris de Rachewiltz, he was " . . . constantly at work breaking down outworn symbols into their original components, once more restoring them to some of their earlier power by making them new. This is, after all, quite an appropriate function for a poet in his role as a perpetuator of traditions temporarily lost from sight."[10]

For Spare, the development of his "alphabet of desire" had proto-creative or metacreative potential. He presented his method in *The Book of Pleasure* and other texts; outlining his core idea that it's not so much his aesthetic approach that is the key but a wholly individual *formation*. Basically, anyone could use the method, regardless of artistic skills. Writing the desire as a word or a sentence, for instance, one then strips out any repeated letters, then takes the remaining unique letters and recomposes them into a graphic glyph—*formed* out of the written desire, but no longer discernible as "rational" writing. This glyph is then, according to Spare's schematic magical view, "dropped" into the subconscious during an ecstatic mind frame, from which it blooms as a desired manifestation of events. A traditional, rational, smallest common (/communion) denominator is reshaped by will into an ideogrammatic unit to be integrated in a magical worldview—disseminated by the master magician, of course.

Reconstructing protoletters via unique expertise is an important part of the respective defense mechanisms of both men. They wanted to strip down the norm and chisel out an innermost meaning that could then be put to new poetic-magical use in their own systems. Both wanted to expound a new meaning and then spare (pardon the puns!) the mind the inert machinations of the normal/rational. And both used their creative genius as the main constructive agents or tools. The times couldn't have been more perfect for artistic experiments like this, and I believe that the zeitgeist itself was more instrumental for them both than they cared to admit.

In many ways, Spare was the quintessential surrealist in both form and content, ever experimenting with both, as well as acknowledging psychology and the subconscious as a very real and useful sphere. Pound was as affected by World War I as everyone else, and actively sought out a constructive contrarian position in modernist letters as student-teacher-editor-reviewer, and then as an ambitious poet laureate of a disgruntled post-World War I world seeking new meanings and new forms.

Through their brilliance they also helped (re)shape their times. This was more immediately true of Pound, for he actually made an impact during his own lifetime. Spare had to wait a few decades after his death in 1956 before real, outer acknowledgment took place—mainly thanks to occult-related people rather than an art world as such. Strategic mentions by key people like Kenneth Grant, Genesis P-Orridge, Jimmy

Page, the Atlantis Bookshop in London, and the publishing company Fulgur have made Spare a thoroughly revived British treasure, and one whose esteem is now also reflected in the art market's increasing prices of his work.

There is another very interesting trait that unites these two men and their quite unique psychic composites, and we could literally call it a seminal one. Spare's active use of the vacuity or psychic void at the moment of orgasm (or other ecstatic experiences) was a central part of the ritual aspects of his teachings. Being an avid masturbator helped his creativity reach new heights, he claimed, and he also used local women and prostitutes of the poorer areas of London where he lived. To Spare, it didn't matter if these women were beautiful or traditionally arousing. For him, these sexual partners were merely vehicles and vessels for him to charge his magical sigils during orgasms, and to induce post-orgasmic trances during which he saw subconscious vistas and landscapes that he then recreated in stunningly eerie and beautiful images. "The conception is the absence of its indisputable reality or reality within! When the conception is memorial to forgetfulness—it may be the chance of its reality for you? When the prayer—(you are always praying) has transmitted to its blasphemy—you are attractive enough to be heard—your desire is gratified! What a somersault of humility!"[11]

He also said, "Ideas of Self in conflict cannot be slain, by resistance they are a reality—no Death or cunning has overcome them but is their reinforcement of energy. The dead are born again and again lie in the womb of conscience. By allowing maturity is to predicate decay—when by non-resistance is retrogression to early simplicity and the passage to the original and unity without the idea. From that idea is the formula of non-resistance germinating. 'Does not matter—please yourself.'"[12]

Pound's perspective was equally out of the ordinary. Highly inspired by the French author Remy de Gourmont (1858–1915, whose writings Pound also translated—probably more correctly than those of Confucius), Pound claimed that the orgasm, and the semen specifically, sets free aspects of genius that otherwise remain passive. " . . . it is more than likely that the brain itself is, in origin and development, only a sort of great clot of genital fluid held in suspense or reserve . . . "[13] He added, "The spermatozoid is, I take it, regarded as a sort of quintessence, or at least 'in rapport with' all parts of the body; the single spermatozoid demands simply that the ovule shall construct a human being, the suspended spermatozoid (if my wild shot rings the target bell) is ready to dispense with, in the literal sense, incarnation, en-fleshment. Shall we postulate the mass of spermatozoids, first accumulated in suspense, then specialized?"[14]

In our view of these gentlemen as supremely creative but also overheated, leading to the necessary defense mechanism of sui genericism, this ultimate, creative perspective fits as well. Taking on the role of someone who is not only a master of their overall individual creative aspects—their "tools of the trade"—but also the role of the divulger of mysteries pertaining to one of the most absolute and attractive core essences of human preoccupation (and life)—sex!—they write and paint themselves into a desired position of mastery. And they succeeded, albeit to varying degrees.

In the contemporary art world, Spare is lauded as an underestimated British genius and, as mentioned earlier, the prices of drawings and paintings are constantly increasing. His occultism is well respected and never overtly criticized or questioned. New studies, biographies, and occasional exhibitions feed an increased interest in this quirky character who obviously had something going for him.

As we've mentioned, Pound was confined to a mental hospital for twelve years, which understandably broke down his general sense of joie de vivre, and yet he retained his ideas, positions, and his creativity upon returning to his beloved Italy, albeit in a more fragmented output.

To say that these specific creatives were outsider artists is not correct. Both of them exist in the real, acknowledged world of their respective expressions, and they certainly do so by their own design and agency. Thus if any outsiderisms are to be taken into account, they exist by willed positioning rather than, as is more traditionally accepted when we consider the term, as an attempt of making virtues out of necessities. Many outsider artists lack the agency to be on the inside, and therefore take pride in their position rather than try to overcome it.

There are many art historians and theoreticians who argue that the so-called outsider art is a more genuine form of art, given that it is more clearly related to the origins of art and its functions thanks to the pure pathology of the artist. If so, we could consider Spare and Pound as existing in a grey area in-between "outsiders" and "insiders." Fervently seeking acknowledgment for their brilliance by developing sui genericism, they never compromised their essential sense of integrity nor the quality of their output. But at the same time they did undeniably invite extra praise via complex structures of supra-agency.

Perhaps we could even conclude by stating that their respective magic actually seems to have worked very well indeed?

13
Some Thoughts on a Recent Paradigm Shift

The first premise of magico-anthropology is that "magic is." Whatever magic is according to a seemingly indefinite multitude of definitions, it always simply *is*. Wherever we look in and into time and space, there is that one fundamental phenomenon that seems more ingrained and integrated in the human psyche than anything else. Soundly embedded inside the survival instinct, the human being's relationship to magic has never really disappeared. It has, however, externally developed into different subforms like religion, philosophy, psychology, and the "natural" sciences, to name just a few disciplines. These various manifestations and developments are results of the increasing complexity of human structures in which we could schematically say that the more we increase the distance from a literally natural habitat, the more our magic will drift from its natural source.

What is this source? It is the link between the human mind and all other sentience(s). Meaning: the roots of magic are embedded in the individual's connection to a holistic, intuitive, instinctual understanding of itself. When a human society deteriorates, this connection will seek new forms in order to survive. It is in many ways an inner

"Some Thoughts on a Recent Paradigm Shift" was originally written for *The Fenris Wolf 10,* Trapart Books, 2020.

reflection of the outer circumstances that continually dictate challenges for the human individuals and tribes alike.

As we know, most of these human "superstructures" are ephemeral and wholly interchangeable. All empires collapse; all political systems crumble; all religions eventually find themselves too far from the source and then give in to reactive chaos that will end up becoming their own nemesis. Underneath the surface of human chaos lies the ever-pulsating life force itself: the will to live (biology), the will to structure life (science), and the will to enhance that life (culture).

Regardless of whether magic is thematically present in some or all of the disciplines mentioned above, its fundaments are always present, more so in constructive phases than in destructive ones. But then again, all of the motions and movements are mere counterpoints and reflections of each other. We simply cannot escape that all movements tell the same story, albeit in different chapters.

Creativity, communication, cooperation, collaboration, community, conspiration (meaning literally breathing together), and *careful contemplation* are merely words beginning with C, here mainly chosen as an amplification of the essence of its sound: "see." But they are also distinct phenomena and absolute building blocks of human life. When one (or more) is lacking, there will be disorder and imbalance.

How should one cope with this imbalance? Using traditionally "magical" skills such as trust in inner abilities and visions, foresight, sympathetic logic, intuition in itself, and also trusting the wisdom and insight that stems from a genuine communication (*genuine* here signifying "stripped of ulterior motives"). Following this, one should make manifestations of these wisdoms and insights external and accessible through art and technology. And finally by structuring and passing on positive and negative deductions and conclusions for coming generations through language and further, transtemporal art . . . These are just some examples of the basic view and approaches of fundamental magico-anthropology. In each detour or deterioration there will be many possibilities to research and evaluate instigations and results. This is the bedrock of each new balancing act.

Magico-anthropology states that the basis of human behavior stems from shamanism. It's inherent in the advanced human mind to constantly pose self-reflective questions. It is only natural that these then spill over and take on proxy forms (the tribal shaman, priest, magician, healer, et al.). But the need to ask existential questions is a unique trait of all human individuals, and this is very much the key to the constant development of human intelligence.

As the simple techniques and wisdom of globally present shamanism have been pushed to the side in favor of organized religions and psychologies, the trust in proxies rather than in one's own conclusions has greatly increased. But this does not in any way decimate or diminish the original human needs. On the contrary: in our chaotic cultures and times of (self) denial and mindless destruction of our own habitat, it is not surprising to see a necessary return to the roots. No matter how grasping and seemingly desperate the "occult" and "new age" communities are, they do seem to have a joint key message: to change the perspective, to transform the oppression of too much destructive dogma into a liberating reconnection to something that is perhaps often naively described yet genuinely felt on intuitive levels.

If shamanism is the root of all human culture, then magic can be seen or described as a term for all the derivatives—as all the branches of the tree of human life. A schematic model could look like the image on page 147.

I have chosen an atomic model to represent this. It resembles a flower in some way, and that is deliberate on my part. Whether the movements of the individual phenomena leave aesthetic traces in the shapes of petals or leaves, or whether they are like planets revolving around a sun, they all signify a relationship that seems eternal: whatever humans develop in terms of abstractions and systems, it is always connected to the "magnetic" pull of the source.

Is deterioration then simply a matter of distance from the source, whether temporal or spatial? No. Deterioration in human culture

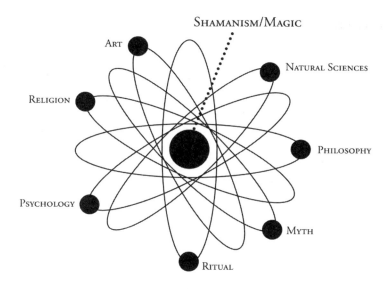

Atomic depiction of magico-anthropology; related, yet discrete realms of ideas orbit their central source, shamanism.

comes when there is *a consciously strategized negation of the heritage; of the very roots.* Time may pass, but the fundamental questions remain and always need to be answered. When a proxy structure becomes too enamored of itself and the power it wields, its capacity to genuinely help humans understand themselves automatically decreases rapidly, both in the small individual and in the big communal picture. The proxies will then also actively discourage any individual quest or adventure to find out more.

In a similar way, space may pass by/in the human perspective. Human migration throughout history has led to many syncretistic mergers, and quite often healthily so. As the source is never static (just look at the vibrant sun as a metaphor of a central core that vitalizes an entire dynamic habitat), neither should the derivatives be. Movement is crucial, but that is usually a matter of constructive shape-shifting, and not necessarily one of movement "away" from the source. In order to survive, cultures have to adapt to both external and internal developments. If they stray too far from the magical interpretation of life, these cultures will die, or desperately take on new and more hopeful shapes.

All sciences, philosophies, and systems that help interpret, categorize, and develop human life are subordinated to the central phenomenon of magico-anthropology. It is not possible to fully understand *any* human endeavor or phenomenon without first filtering this understanding through magico-anthropology.

How human beings relate to magic (again, "magic" being the central and direct derivative of a shamanic understanding, in both theory and practice) is indicative of both individual and overall human health, and possibly even of global health. Each individual human being inherently and instinctively understands this as a child, interpreting signals through an enchanted or ensouled filter. As this filter is usually (and unfortunately) ground down and removed/discouraged because of arbitrary cultural preferences, the child learns that the sense of wonder that he/she could notice when looking at the big picture with an open and uninhibited mind is, according to the peers, simply untrue. This of course creates an unhealthy imprint in the child to not trust him/herself (nor the big picture) but instead rely on culturally imposed proxy interpretations.

It is interesting to see how the power of myth transcends even these imposed boundaries. Parents happily tell the same fairy tales to their children that were once part of the cluster that they themselves had to abandon as they grew up. If myths aren't necessary to our survival, they simply wouldn't exist, let alone feel so resoundingly relevant. Anything of mythic value is directly connected to the shamanic source, and hence to our survival.

Magico-anthropology isn't necessarily the study of magic itself. That could today be regarded as belonging to the study of religions, as there are many similarities. Much of the organization of magic in history (in groups, orders, societies, fraternities, etc.) runs more or less parallel to the formation of new religions, for instance. There is also very often a similar corruption in magical communities that eerily mimics that in religious ditto. It is the same phenomenon over and over again: when there is an individual dissociation from the source and its fundamental expression in shamanism, the looming structure or system will all too gladly usurp and integrate this individual in its far too often self-serving and draconian schemes.

Magico-anthropology focuses on the very link itself. Not merely on the corruption of it, of course, but also the study of pristine and healthy connections and expressions (such as in art or myth that is conscious of, and encouraging, a "re-docking" in individual lives). Although the study of corruption (deliberate or merely unconscious) is fascinating and quite often literally beyond belief, I believe that the study of positive, beneficial manifestations of the attraction to the source as a survival strategy on both individual and communal levels is more important in this current phase of human existence.

I understand that there may be scientists and other academics who have no desire to be subordinated to the authority of magico-anthropology. Be that as it may, their position and attitude is neither here nor there. Why? Because the link to all intimate relationships between their specific fields of study and magic can be so easily explained. My schematic atomic model is the first altruistic attempt to make these people and potential critics see. Just like planets revolve around their own axes, and as they do around the central sun, so are the specific fields of study (of religions, psychology, physics, mathematics, etc.) simultaneously their own entities as well as parts of the universe of magic.

To be specific: the magical phenomenon itself is concretely rooted in the human mind. The study and classification of the same phenomenon is a degree of abstraction. Regardless of whether they are concrete or abstract, all research systems are geared toward reaching the same moment. This moment embodies the ecstatic truth of revelation, preferably embedded in further revelatory contemplation/meditation. Transgression of the rational mind is the single most important key to this ecstatic truth.

Cultural differences may apply, but the dynamic is always the same. As Goethe said, "In the sciences it is very worthwhile to seek out and then develop a partial truth already possessed by the ancients."[1]

concrete	abstract
alchemy	chemistry
spellwork	poetry/music/literature
healing	medicine
barter/morality	profit/amorality
unity with the source	religion
contemplation	philosophy
predictives	statistics
myth	entertainment

Et cetera . . .

Each piece of learning we can utilize today, together, stems from a single human mind working in magical ways and then sharing the results with a community. Whether it's faith in the sun, in ancestors, or in statistics (as in empiricism), the process is exactly the same. There is speculation, desire, ritual, invocation, evocation, epiphany, declaration of intent, irrational states of mind provoked by the rational ditto, and then an ensuing methodology geared to validating the desired results.

We are no longer living in times when magico-anthropology was regarded either as aggressively anathema or as a kooky pastime for privileged, private scholars. Today magico-anthropology has taken center stage because of a cruel necessity that calls for an increased awareness about avenues of human survival. The specialized fields of study can all contribute parts to the totality of a solution (or several). But it is only by reappraising and reappreciating magic as the core activity/mind frame of human existence that we can fully change things in a more life-affirming and life-enhancing way. We all know it's there, and we all know instinctively the creative power it wields. If humans won't wield that magical power to repair damage to their habitat, then the habitat will simply wield the same power to remove us. In the great scheme of things, however, this is not necessarily so terrifying. Any magician or shaman worth their salt knows that although the human shapes might disappear, the overall life force and sentience won't. It's just constantly evolving.

One great definition of intelligence is the ability to evolve, to adapt to changes in life. If you're too inert you'll be left behind. But if you see not only the dangers but also the possibilities, and realize that you need to change in order to survive, a creativity within you—one that is decidedly magical (literally phenomenal)—will be released.

One main problem we face today is the overall lack of individuation in monotheistic cultures. For some reason they refuse to be part of nature and to listen to its greater authority. Individuation and initiation should preferably take place inside nature—not on top of it. Magic philosophy from many different cultures and ages basically tells us this same story: we are not isolated units, but rather parts of one big organism. Many people reverently practice this wisdom via magic. Whether just in approaches and attitudes (like magical thinking) or in practice through distinct "programmatic" rituals alone or together with others, the presence of a holistic approach in which one may affect change to the whole (as much as vice versa, simply because one is an active and integrated part of this same whole) is truly indicative of cultural health.

The phenomenon of magic being demonized or ostracized as merely an isolated curiosity is indicative of cultural malaise and disease.

By childishly clinging to materialism and rabid monotheism, the most ardent critics of the holistic approach display a death drive similar to that of historical figures like Nero and Hitler. The destruction of their emotionally compensative visions leads to a desire to destroy the entire world. Instead of realigning themselves and rejoining the life-affirming core, they decide to fully separate and counterstrike against the very core itself—always with tragic results for themselves and many fellow human beings.

The following is a pertinent quote from Carlos Castaneda in *The*

Power of Silence. "Don Juan has asserted that our great collective flaw is that we live our lives completely disregarding that connection. The busyness of our lives, our relentless interests, concerns, hopes, frustrations, and fears take precedence, and on a day-to-day basis we are unaware of being linked to everything else. Don Juan had stated his belief that the Christian idea of being cast out from the Garden of Eden sounded to him like an allegory for losing our silent knowledge, our knowledge of *intent.* Sorcery, then, was a going back to the beginning, a return to paradise."[2]

I strongly suggest and recommend that all students, teachers, scientists, researchers, and others of this ilk within the academic worlds of the natural sciences as well as of the humanities immediately adjust their work so that the quintessential question is contextualized in their own field: Magic is, but how is it related to what I'm studying?

The relationship between magic, magical philosophy, magical approaches, and the human being's attempts to survive is as fixed/solid as anything has ever been, and ever will be.

The humanities have tried to express phenomena along the way, as the natural sciences have tried to classify them. All fields have their own unique languages and methods. But even here, within the area of strict methodology, we see magical approaches in the driver's seat. Given that the most ardent rationalists can usually be found in fields using the method of "empiricism," it's important to allow them to understand that one needs to *always* continue to the roots. The origins of any empirical process/evaluation is the root called "speculation." How many ideas that at first seemed kooky, crazy, heretical, and "hocus-pocus" eventually turned out to be solidly established and statistically reinforced? Quite a few. But although there are surely a lot of speculations that never make it to the "lab" to be tried out, we have to stick with the reverse perspective to fully explain this. All empirical successes are founded in irrational speculations; in inexplicable ideas or concepts that simply obsess the conceptualist(s). Then they are given increasing credence as they are gradually validated by open-mindedness and an overall attitude of creativity. Each idea has its origins.

It is only when empiricism becomes a rigid belief system ("faith in statistics") that science becomes inert and destructive—and that's usually when these constructs team up with financial systems and structures that are not altruistic in any way at all. When this happens, the original creative vision becomes a kind of diametrical demon. Meaning, the original purpose becomes corrupted in a topsy-turvy way. An example of this could be that a scientist makes a breakthrough in medicine, but the full potential of its healing process is shoved to the side in favor of a maximum profitability for the corporation that has acquired the patent from or funded the project for the scientist in question.

The scientist should ask him/herself what the magic of the breakthrough could bring to people in different cultures. The corporation should simply be the distributional matrix for an improvement of something that is not only life-affirming but also potentially life-enhancing, in the sense that good health allows for an even more present creativity—and hence more magic.

There is an inherent danger in the phase when the individual loses his/her direct communication with the source. When tribes grow too big, the need for proxies takes hold, and these are so easily corruptible. The individual humans—even the decision-makers in systems of corruption—will always maintain their magical thinking and approaches. However, some will go against their own protomorals because they have been coerced or somehow threatened by others who, in a similar way, have transgressed against *their* own protomorals.

These statements in no way suggest that there is an inherent political or financial system that is more or less magical. Politics is just—or should be—a way of structuring a society. The main thing is whether it, as a society/community, encourages individual contact with the source. If it does, it will be a healthy society; if it doesn't, inertia and collapse are waiting just around the corner.

It's not so much a revolution that's needed (actually, the less dramatic reactivity there is, the better) but rather an increase in human individual awareness of how simple these relationships actually are. They are easier to grasp than people care to even assume. This is, no doubt, a reaction to the possible change in lifestyle that's required to implement the findings of the awareness.

An increase in human individual awareness will lead to an increase in human collective awareness, and that will lead to communal leverage in the process of changing the big picture and its many problematic issues.

So how do we change these perspectives as they pertain to individual awareness? An exposure to nature itself is key, if even on the most miniature level. Indulge in nature, its beauty and its philosophy. And realize that this moment is crucial and magical in the most primordial sense as you look at something that has always been there, and that will always remain.

The more of a hardline rationalist you are, the more you will need to short-circuit your simplified wires. A dramatic infusion of the opposite always brings generative creativity. The same is true of the reverse perspective. If you are basically comfortable in irrationality, mistaking that for magic or creativity, you probably need to dive deep into a fierce rationality and order.

One key to natural awareness of this most magical kind is to allow yourself to see all the facets and perspectives at the same time. What you are regarding as something external is in fact something equally internal, at exactly the same time. And because there is no "real" separation (in the sense of being tangible, measurable, quantifiable, etc.), you realize that the responsibility for *everything, all the time,* is principally yours. But the realization is not so daunting as it may sound to a logical, rational intellect. It is merely a peek into the endless possibilities and choices that have been there in each human destiny all along, from the past (so-called), and now into the future (so-called).

The discipline of magico-anthropology is important not as a singular field of study, like some exotic morsel in the history of ideas or the history of religions. It is rather the all-encompassing umbrella for all sciences, as it asks the fundamental question, based on the fundamental protoscientific premise: If magic *is,* then *what* is it?

The subordination of other sciences is not based on value or hierarchy. It is merely a way of explaining that the awareness of yourself, and your own honesty to yourself, and your own place in the bigger picture, is at least as important as what you will produce within structures that for the most part so far have proven to be nothing more than self-serving and profit-driven businesses.

If you're a scientist, the truth is what should guide your work. Before that, if you are a fully sentient human being, magic is what should guide your life. Getting back to the source is what truly propels us all forward. The source does what magic is as much as the source is what magic does.

"Have you ever been experienced?"

14
The Magic of Individuation

I didn't initially know whether I was going to call this essay "The Individuation of Magic" or "The Magic of Individuation" or "The Individuation of the Magic of Individuation," or "The Magic of the Individuation of Magic," or . . .

They are two words and concepts charged with many meanings—actually more like surfaces of personal reflection rather than straight signals or signifiers. Maybe words or concepts like this are supposed to be hard to pin down—vague in a way—simply because they carry such a lot of cultural and mythological weight. It seems that to be efficient, they must have some "interpretative slack" onto which people can project their own perspectives, and themselves. Let's begin by trying to narrow this down slightly, to get a better overview.

What I mean by individuation is a process that most of us are familiar with from the Jungian school of psychology. Individuation is a refinement process in which we try to integrate all aspects of ourselves, and interpret them, so that we can eventually find real meaning in our lives, and be as "whole" or fulfilled as we potentially can.

What I mean by magic is mainly the intuitive interpretation of both sensory and extrasensory information in a personal empowerment process. This can be helped by indulging in keys or symbols

"The Magic of Individuation" was originally presented as a lecture for the Thoth-Hermes Academy, Austria, 2020.

from history's many schools of wisdom—esoteric or otherwise—or from one's own experiments. It's generally tied in with a holistic outlook, and can be more or less imbued with signals from a specific tradition or religion.

Magic is also something that through both introspection and action often overwhelmingly reveals the malleability, connections, and creativity of the human mind in relation to the larger cosmos—and vice versa.

Magic and individuation are both processes rather than finite, causal movements. Both processes are in constant flux, and it is up to the individual to understand this and move along with them, rather than watch them move away from the comfort zone one is presently situated in.

They both deal with, and have their roots in, deep-laying psychic spheres, like the "unconscious" or the "subconscious," which often contain unwelcome or painful truths about oneself.

Although I wouldn't equate them, they seem to be connected in many ways. That is, I wouldn't say that magic *is* individuation or individuation is magic, but rather that individuation is magic-al (stressing the adjective). By this I mean that it strongly empowers the whole individual to explore more and new areas in new ways, which in turn will reveal even more. And I would rather say that magic can certainly help in the individuation process because it already works with the intuitive tools that are needed for a fuller understanding of life.

On this note, it is also interesting to see that cultures that aggressively oppose one (magic or individuation), will more than likely also aggressively oppose the other.

So an equation, no, but a mutual suggested need or link for greater efficiency, yes.

Magic is a hard nut to crack, but it is significant and nutritious enough for us to realize that no other phenomenon has permeated human culture to the same degree. Whether we are hot-headed religious zealots or coldhearted empiricists, we are all steeped in speculative, wishful thinking, weird rituals, and intuitive approaches. The louder someone claims the opposite, the more we know they're lying. If we have the intelligence to simply acknowledge magic as the most important quintessential "cross-disciplinary" human capacity there is, we can then begin to crack that nut.

There are two basic ways or approaches to how to relate; let's call them passive and active. The passive one indicates an acceptance that life simply happens, and that we can learn about magic by watching, or just living. A positive aspect of this could be detachment, the wu wei attitude of Daoism, and the philosophical concept of *désinvolture*—a learning by nonlearning, in a way. A negative aspect of this could be angst-ridden consumerism and escapism.

The active approach contains more options in its attitude of, I make life happen, and I want to learn! The initiative brings incentive, energy, desire, curiosity. We seek initiation into the mysteries and embrace the path of the hero's quest—whatever this may mean.

The active magician can work alone or together with others, and will often seek out teachers or situations to help out with guidance and empowerment. This has both advantages and disadvantages. My experience is that it's hard to fully learn on your own, because you are at least as likely to deceive yourself as you are others, if not more.

Whereas individuation can be regarded as an initiation into a higher self, beyond the inflictions and reactions of the ego, an active immersion on a path of study and gradual revelation, quite often within an esoteric "structure," can become initiation in and into magic.

In both processes it's important to be self-critical as well as critical. How else can we progress? If a ritual or a system doesn't bring real, tangible insights about oneself, then they are merely pleasant psychodrama, at most.

Eventually, it's as important to acquire one's own tools and language in magic as it is in the individuation process. One is who one is, and that's who one should be—once one has found that out. And one's magic is exactly what one makes of it—once one has found *that* out.

An example: After many decades of working in the trenches of various magical groups and orders, I have now set up my own multidimensional experiment. This group is called the Society of Sentience and is at this point very much a platform of and for experimental individuation for those involved—and thereby for itself, too.

I had to really ask myself, Why? before I proceeded, because it would definitely be possible to work magically on my own, or together with a few trusted partners. But I realized that being involved in a structure is something I really enjoy; it's a substantial part of my life. But the difference now is that I've constructed this myself—my self— on my own terms. I would define this construction as one in which my magical work and outlook have fully merged with a conscious appreciation of the very process of individuation. They are all, in a way, one and the same.

We talked about the higher self in regard to individuation, as a totality in which all levels of one's psyche have merged. In a Western magical tradition this would correspond to the holy guardian angel or HGA, which in a similar way contains one's unique ideal. Once reached and merged with, it will guide one—but no longer as a separate entity. The psychopomp has been brought up from the depths of one's soul, and when one looks at it, one only sees oneself. Regardless of which path one is on, it should lead to this same union.

I usually call the two basic attitudes to magic:

1. Gnostic-shamanic = an epistemological pipeline, direct knowledge
2. Proxy-symbolic = HGA: a method, a system, a structure along the routes of information

Both of these variants require integration of not only oneself but of one's self. The best way to integrate that is to literally express oneself: to communicate, to share, to verbalize, to create an image or a new symbol. This is equally valid for individuation. It's not really an option, either: one *should* express oneself. Because if you don't, others will do it for you. Each personal expression is a transcendent moment that will teach one something new about oneself. All the infinite wonders of life become manifest in these movements of transcendence—no matter how large or small.

Transformation implies or perhaps even requires this kind of transcendence. Each transformation is an overcoming of the present, preferably a willed one.

Even magic as a technique, or a set of techniques, that one has become comfortable with has to be transcended in order to become a proper tool of individuation. By this I mean in the sense that petty desires need to be overcome so that the process always provides more than mere causal results. If the magical "willing" is anchored in a solid subject or identity, it is never wrong to use this kind of "lesser" magic for causal results. But the focus is often much better spent or invested on developing actual identity and a higher self.

If one does that, it is my experience that whatever one is after on causal, material levels has a tendency to appear and tag along as pleasant "casual causals." But the opposite is not always true: asking for or "willing" a new sexual partner or a job promotion isn't necessarily individuating.

We cannot really will things in our magical processes if we don't know what we truly want. And I'm not talking about fickle desires or immediate needs of acknowledgment—I'm talking about real magical desires based on existential directions we feel are unavoidable.

To be substantial magicians we also need to know not only who we are right now (to the greatest extent possible) but also who we want to become (also to the greatest extent possible). Remember that both processes are exactly that: processes—never static; always flowing.

Only when we intuit the answer to the question, Who am I? can any really constructive movement begin. That movement will take you "there," regardless of where your ultimate destination is. There are many different cultural or ethnic expressions of this very same wisdom: it's the path that matters, not the goal. Even our entire life span could be seen—symbolically or actually depending on what you believe—as one single step on a greater path in and of eternity.

What constitutes an individual? Well, it depends on who you ask, doesn't it? I would define myself as X, where others would, for various reasons of their own, define me as Y. A third party might experience me as XY, or even a Z (as in *snoozzzze*). We can never escape this social dynamic of projection, in which emotions, hopes, and possible admirations ping-pong until the cows come home and the tweet about it is trending.

Add the word *self* before any chosen great word, and these will become little clues:

> self-worth
> self-awareness
> self-image
> self-confidence

When these are discussed in culture and media, they're usually associated with a "lack," as in the individual needing more of whatever it is—and of course there will be someone there to tell it to them and sell it to them. But they are all satellites around individuation—not the other way around. Focus on the main thing, and the rest will follow—or become completely redundant. The more one defines oneself under the umbrella of honesty, the more agency one's individuality will assume.

Individuation is definitely also an important weapon of self-defense; even on a magical level. Because if you don't know and define yourself on your own terms, then others will gladly define that for you. And what they project onto you may stick, to an extent that others will prefer to see that, rather than what you yourself actually have to show.

Speaking of which, a "selfie" is very rarely a Self-ie. Usually it's formally dictated by a shallow form of vanity that most often hides substance instead of revealing it. The immediate need for acknowledgment is problematic in the larger individuation process, too, because we are very prone to adapt to what others like in us.

The myth of Narcissus is relevant here. Enamored of his own reflection on the surface of the water, Narcissus becomes both passive and pacified. There is no new revelation or insight—he only sees his image on the surface. Through this, we only get the narcotic effect of anesthesia, sedation, and addiction—never a mind-expanding revelation of substantial self-knowledge.

My standpoint is this: we, as human individuals, are not tabula rasa. We don't arrive as a clean slate, or as an empty canvas. On the contrary, we arrive with a whole lot of baggage, and it's our duty to work with what we already have and improve it. That is what constitutes long-term individuation, and that, to me, is the very meaning of individual human life itself.

There are a lot of unwise people who dismiss old esoteric teachings for either being too highbrow, obfuscated, and complex, or for having been made too lowbrow, watered down, and mainstream. But it's only really you who can truly evaluate if a poem by Rumi from the thirteenth century inexplicably fills you with inspiration and meaning, isn't it? Or perhaps it's a *Book of Mr. Natural* comic by Robert Crumb from 1968, or a dark grimoire from some medieval weirdo, or an astrological analysis that one feels is so one hundred percent "spot on" but that one feels one has to contain in secret because people would feel that one is a demonic dilettante if one acknowledged it. One is attracted to all these things for a reason. It's not necessarily because of a lack or a flaw in oneself but because there is something there that speaks to one's psyche via the beautiful language of symbolic resonance.

What is astrology if not already a blueprint for one's higher self? I'm not talking about random platitudes or "cosmicisms" in ladies' magazines, but of psychologically accurate chart analysis. If the moon can affect ebb and flow on our planet, and even affect women's menstruation, why wouldn't all of the planets in our solar system have even more powerful effects on our lives—even on the individual levels?

The manifestation of a new human individual; the magical moment of undocking from the mothership; the very first breath as the first brave attempt at individuation . . . It is a unique moment in time and space. How could anyone really argue that this moment would be unaffected by forces much greater than their own quantitative data and their own petty intolerance?

My take on why entire cultures actively repress this kind of tool and knowledge is that they simply don't like to be individually reminded of what a detrimental lie they're living—and thereby, to add insult to injury, they're selling to others. It's a confrontation with the dishonesty and thereby immorality of the unindividuated human being.

Carl Jung brought forth the holistic idea that we need to integrate all aspects of ourselves in order to fully bloom. This was in conflict with the Christian morality clusters that have been present in the Western world for almost two thousand years. One main concept was that our consciousness shouldn't merely identify with the "normal" self (what we usually call the ego) but should strive for a union with a "higher" self—an ideal that is not arbitrarily constructed but that in most people is as yet simply unencountered. Sticking with the self leads to inflation, pomposity, narcissism, unnatural dualism, and many other things. We need to unite with the ideal (both the female and the male ideal) that's already inside us by thinking, feeling, intuiting, and perceiving—basically, to individuate, and to do it in the here and now. In this, we would be wise to heed the following words of Jung on this.

It is a general truth that the earth is the depreciated and misunderstood part, and so the unconscious regularly puts great emphasis on the chthonic fact. Nietzsche has expressed that very beautifully: "Ihr sollt wieder Freunde von den nächsten Dingen werden." (You shall become friends of the immediate things.) And the immediate things are this earth, this life. For quite long enough our ancestors, and we ourselves, have been taught that this life is not the real thing, that it is provisional, and that we only live for Heaven. Our morality is based upon the negation of the flesh, and so our unconscious often tries to convince us of the importance of living here and now. In the course of the centuries man has repeatedly experienced the fact that the life that is not lived here, or the life lived provisionally, is utterly unsatisfactory. It leads into neurosis.[1]

Looking in the mirror, you might ask, Who am I?

A healthy answer from the reflection would be, Who's asking?

Jung argued that our "shadow"—the integration of evil or unwanted aspects—is absolutely necessary in the individuation process. A denial of this leads to unhealthy outlooks, as can be viewed in the extreme dualistic simplifications of the monotheistic religions, for instance.

The Jungian concept of the shadow has since become part of the general zeitgeist. An early example of this was the serialized American radio show *The Shadow* in the 1930s, which featured one of the first ultimate secret "superhero" detectives. The episodes always began with the same dramatic and haunting intro: "Who knows what evil lurks in the hearts of men? . . . The shadow knows!"

It was a cultural reflection that immediately became mythic and spawned a whole army of caped crusaders and masked heroes, all fighting for the balance of their particular, larger organism. Why? Because there was a mythic need for it in a culture that was rapidly losing its view of itself as one organism. The blatant, causal, and visible forces of justice seemed unable to cope with the wheels of destiny and its malefactors; a dark-side force of justice was needed for the "greater good."

If we apply this to ourselves instead, we encounter a quality that's absolutely quintessential in both processes: honesty. If we aren't brutally honest in our explorations and the definitions of our results, how can we expect anything to end well?

If we aren't willing to integrate memories, experiences, qualities, traits, and opinions that we *know* are genuinely ours but that the outside world would disapprove of, how can we expect to fully bloom? The psychic cluster of the shadow reminds us that we are much more than a pretty picture, quite often painted by others, and quite often in the far too broad strokes of convenience.

I'm not suggesting one must always flaunt everything in one's shadow baggage. That's not really healthy, either. The honesty referred to is mainly something that should address itself from oneself and to oneself.

Without honesty, there can be no real progress. This is very, very true for both of these processes.

A sound magical process doesn't empower solely on the causal plane but also on those of self-knowledge and honesty. Vice versa, a sound individuation process doesn't empower solely on the planes of self-knowledge and honesty but also on that of the causal.

What is the evidence of these statements, should such be needed? What exactly makes me claim that?

That would be my own experience. And it says: the single mission of the past is to come back and bite us in the butt. History is a blueprint. "His story." "Her story." "Our stories." Our future will singularly be made up of memories in those who are even further along than we are.

In this context, I claim that the human being has three different kinds of memory, and they all play an essential part of our individuation process:

First: cerebral; defined as a part of the brain; "this is where our memories reside." Sensual, causal imprints and chaotic filtering and interpretations, both in waking and sleeping states.

Second: genetic/DNA; the internal blueprint, "this is what has come down to me, this is my biological program."

Third: the "soul"; conglomerated or "gelled" imprints that are pieces of sentience that can develop during a human lifetime (and have developed for many). Here there are many culturally anchored theories about what is what; like the one about reincarnation, for instance, which implies that the soul simply takes on a new body and just carries on its work.

If both magic and individuation require honesty, as I have suggested, I would say that they to an equal degree also require knowledge of where the ideal, individuated self comes from. We are not simply moving forward. We also come from somewhere. If we know that, a lot has been won early on in the process. It becomes an enticing and stimulating mix—in the best of circumstances—in which all three kinds of memories interact to help the individual forward.

We cannot escape our DNA, but we can add to the story in beneficial ways—such as a successful individuation process in life, which is automatically embedded in a new conception of life, or "merger" with another's DNA.

We cannot escape our soul, but we can add to its development in a similar way as with DNA, by integrating the experience of active refinement within our current, given life span or structure.

We cannot escape our cerebral memories—not even in cases of extreme dementia—but yes, we can definitely add to a greater bigger picture by learning (i.e., interpreting memories) to, for instance, not repeat harmful behavior.

A good cerebral memory then, is an invaluable tool in both magic and individuation. On the most basic level it would consist of thoughts like this: *Yes, I remember liking that.* Or, *No, I remember not liking that.*

A genealogical overview is a great help in terms of the DNA, especially if we know what our known ancestors did (more than merely exist). The more we know of our history, the better equipped we are to face both the present and the future.

And if we accept the presence of a soul that is distinctly ours, we should waste no time in trying to acquaint ourselves with it—quite literally a magical process! If the soul accumulates memories that help define itself/oneself, then surely whatever is in there since "time immemorial" is also exactly who we are this very day?

Goethe poetically described human happiness in this temporal sense: "The happiest man is one who can link the end of his life with its beginning."[2]

I would like to add . . . "And beyond!"

Osiris, one of our great mythic figures, is killed and cut up by his brother—thereby his genetic mirror—called Set, and the parts are dispersed. He is literally "divided." When Isis, Osiris's wife and also sister—thereby also his genetic mirror—finds all the parts and puts him back together, he is made in-divisible, in-dividable—and hence an individuated character. This is accentuated further by the fact that in most variants of the myth, there is focus on Osiris's penis—in some it's there, in others it's still missing. But no matter what, Isis magically resurrects both Osiris and his mysterious penis and then has sex with him. This leads to the birth of Horus, who sets out to avenge his father's killer.

The story moves onward. The symbolic crown of the individual, in this particular mystery, is first of all to be whole and functional, and then to be empowered to move the story onward by transcending and merging together with another individual in order to create a new individual "host."

Another interesting and revealing twist of our language in this case is that, in the myth, Osiris is "dismembered" by Set. In effect, when he's put back together again, he is "re-membered." In effect, then, he has become something remembered, that is, a "memory"—which has the potential to move on in time and space via the combined effect of the three memory types or categories I've suggested.

That this process works, we know, as we're talking about him right here and now.

In order to merge with someone else, we have to transcend or transgress our individual state. Then we can be fully remembered, but that of course also requires someone in the future actually remembering us. This is possible by one or several individual memory types acting as a memetic agent. We can worship our actual ancestors because we're connected by DNA; we can feel connected to someone's soul by the proxy of an historical artwork; and we can hopefully remember ourselves what someone said about someone else living in the past.

Jung had strong feelings about the invaluable essences of myth, and how we need them to understand ourselves.

Man has always lived with a myth, and we think we are able to be born today and live in no myth, without history. That is a disease. That is absolutely abnormal, because man is not born every day. He is born once in a specific historical setting, with specific historical qualities, and therefore he is only complete when he has a relation to these things. It is just as if you were born without eyes and ears when you are growing up with no connection with the past. From the standpoint of natural science, you need no connection with the past; you can wipe it out, and that is a mutilation of the human being.[3]

The dichotomy between myth-magic-intuition and rational empiricism is problematic and potentially counterproductive, and Jung knew it. Science and myth need to be merged, just as we need to merge all aspects of ourselves. I would suggest this should occur *not* by demythologizing myth and turning it into quantifiable fiction or analytic sociology, but on the contrary, by *mythologizing* science.

Example: Science fiction as a literary genre has already created more science than, for instance, statistic evaluation of data has created timeless stories taken to heart by several generations and brought onward in symbolic form. Transcendence or transgression bring new revelations. A union is always the healthiest outcome, and our way there now is to individuate the rational mind. One way of doing this is to be generous and inclusive in the mythic dissemination. How could one understand someone or something "higher" except by interpreting their or its own experience? Very few things within human contexts inherently *need* to be obfuscated or esoteric. Clarity and eloquence, as well as a will to communicate, should be the foundations of any soul-searching process—whether individual or communal. It's not only about the story one tells but also *how* one tells it, and to whom. A union in myth can essentially only really be achieved if there's consensual, mutual attention and respect.

Only cultures steeped or cloaked in soulful images and discernible, mythic symbols will remain. This kind of art lasts and is a powerful transcendental memetic agent that contains not only information but also value and emotion. Hence it is "individuated" art that inspires and encourages people to work with themselves.

In essence and in theory it's quite simple: if one develops into a strong and clear individual, one will become a signpost or beacon. People will react binarily in a faster way to such a person. Those who say no will disappear more quickly, which will save one some headaches. Those who say yes will want to help you and be in your presence, which could bring many beneficial results. So there is inherently something magical about the individuated person. There is a discarding of the ambiguous that facilitates substantial developments in contacts with others. Because no matter how individuated we may be, we are still social human animals who need to interact with each other, allowing ourselves some occasional "interpretative slack." That in itself is the ultimate creative sphere that we should refine over and over again as magicians and individuated humans.

But . . . let us never, ever forget . . . "Who knows what evil lurks in the hearts of men? . . . The shadow knows!"

15

Lux Per Nox

The Fenris Wolf as Libidinal Liberator

Vavtrudner said: / The Wolf will devour / Allfather, / but him will Vidar / venge; / cold jaws / he will split / in the moment / of battle.

SÅNGEN OM VAVTRUDNER

(THE SONG OF VAVTRUDNER)

The Fenris Wolf, the journal in which this essay originally appeared, is not only that journal's title, it's also the name of a mythical creature/force in the Scandinavian *Asatro* (a belief in the Asa gods) pantheon, and one that deserves careful study as possibly the most important agent of that entire pantheon. He is usually associated with the end of the world/existing order—"Ragnarok"—and therefore usually carries the heavy baggage of negative projections. But what does *the end of the world* really mean?

The Scandinavian myths are developments of basic Indo-European myths and religious stories. These usually deal with a ritualized, "religionized" repetition of the original cosmic Creation, amplifying how important it has been/is for the human being to know (or at least

---

"Lux Per Nox: The Fenris Wolf as Libidinal Liberator" was originally written for *The Fenris Wolf 10,* Trapart Books, 2020.

mythologize) one's own roots as far back as one possibly can. Conscious continuity is a quintessentially important part of human identity. When the myths and gods are allowed to act out eternal dilemmas and mysteries, it's easier to structure human culture and life in an emotionally healthy and life-affirming way.

The myths themselves usually tell us of a cyclic structure: there are eras, periods, and times in which movements of nature and destiny occur, disappear, and reoccur. Undoubtedly this is a remnant of assessment and insight deep inside the human psyche (and very likely even relegated to DNA), after having carefully watched how nature works. The greater the trauma of the unexpected or anomalous, the greater the mythic impact. So when things have turned really sour, and when there are still people around to tell that specific story, it will be an important piece of the story line; more so than tales about when everything was perfect, peachy, and harmonious—if that has ever happened!

Natural disasters, wars, conflicts, upheavals, pandemics, and other agents of enforced change throughout the millennia have all been integrated in therapeutically valid stories that have then grown to become myths—if relevant enough.

Today *the end of the world* means something quite different from what it did to people five thousand years ago, and ten thousand years ago, and so on. Even a hundred years ago. But as that horrific moment is usually intimately tied in with a very central cathartic message—the promise of a new order and new life—it's usually in these actually catastrophic tales that we can evaluate the health of the society in question. Because regardless if the end comes through an inexplicable natural disaster or through very distinct human warfare, human beings could (can) only cope with the trauma of the lost paradise by repeatedly telling the story of hope in an abstracted, mythologized fashion. If the myths are actively integrated in the culture, then the tribe, group, society, or community will be more harmonious than if there is some kind of negation or repression of these traumatic histories.

In this sense, the myths that deal with regeneration and cyclic passages of destiny are of great value because they usually connect more to the actual trauma than to its possible aftermath. The disaster in itself is always more revealing than any post facto constructions. The main question is, What are the reasons for the end?

Ragnarok is a phenomenon or matrix that could be applied to any psychological or historical process, but for the sake of Fenris himself, let's stick to the classic story here.

At the end of the world, trickster god Loke's three children do what they have to do. Hel opens up her sphere and lets out hordes of dead people (not the heroic kind that went to Oden's Valhalla, but just normal folks). The world-encircling Midgård snake, who usually keeps the world in order by biting its own tail underneath the surface of the oceans, provokes thunder god Tor to the ultimate fight (in which they both die). Fenris breaks free of the Asa gods' fetters, kills main god Oden, and devours the sun. As the old structure is slain there is mayhem, chaos, violence, bloodshed, terror, and despair.

But the old poems and sagas don't stop there, at the supposed end. Although Fenris kills Oden, Vidar (Oden's son) then kills Fenris, and there are also other Asa kids who are ready to take over. So basically, the story—although essentially catastrophic—brings not only a new beginning but also a distinct mythic attachment to the continual rebirth of order and harmony. It's a basic and violent story, in many ways reflecting the culture at the time. Yet it also contains hope, eloquently expressed in literary wealth and beauty.

To fully understand the Fenris Wolf as a mythic creature, we have to look at the ancestry or heritage. Fenris is the son of Loke, the Scandinavian trickster god, who was painted in quite Satanic colors by the main post-heathen storyteller: the Icelandic Christian historian Snorre Sturlason. Loke is a highly integrated instigator of intrigue, conflict, and provocative behavior. There are many key myths/stories in which Loke is central not only to the story as such but also to its inherent morals. In this sense—of Loke as an ambiguous *agent provocateur* in the world of the gods—we see genuine satanic semblance and function. Loke is essentially the force that provokes situations so that the main issues can be resolved. There is always ambivalence and ambiguity in regard to Loke as a necessary trickster, and there are many stories that leave the reader with a sense of comic relief and respect for him, rather than, as for the Christian formulators, as an inherently evil figure creating chaos.

The necessity of appropriating an integrated trickster has never been lost on the Christians though. As Anton LaVey, founder of the Church of Satan (1966) so aptly wrote in his 1969 book *The Satanic Bible:* "Satan has been the best friend the church has ever had, as he has kept it in business all these years!"[1] Without the "negative" example, the "positive" order cannot be upheld for long. Essentially, scapegoating is as inherently human as the capacity for suicide. The more strictly dualistic the portrayal of the trickster is, the poorer the religious culture.

In Asatro then, it seems that Loke is an irritating but still necessary element in the overall health of the culture. There is ample evidence (or if not "evidence," then at least highly illuminating pointers) that Loke was a central force in upholding rituals and communal balance through his own unique spirit of transgression.

One of the most entertaining parts in the Edda anthology is "Lokaträtan" (the Loke Arguments), in which Loke spews forth his vitriolic accusations against the gods. No one is spared, not even Oden himself. Oden and Loke accuse each other of unmanliness, and the main accusation against Loke is that he carried and gave birth to a child while in the shape of a mare. This, however, was part of a solution that benefitted all of Asgård.

To protect Asgård from attacks, mainly from giants, the gods make a deal with a giant master builder who says he can build a strong wall around Asgård. If he can do that within a limited and short time, the gods promise that he will be amply rewarded. But as they notice that the giant is about to actually succeed—thanks to a magical stallion that can keep on working even though the giant himself is asleep—the gods fear that they will actually have to pay up. Loke then transforms himself into a beautiful mare that lures the builder's horse away. The builder fails to finish in time, and the gods rejoice at both their new wall and that they won't have to pay the cost. As the result of this scheme and tryst, Loke gives birth to Sleipner, the eight-legged horse that Oden takes as his own, which allows him to swiftly and protoshamanically travel in between various spheres and states of mind.

Loke often becomes a victim of his own intrigues, as if he has a pathological need to be in trouble; to shake things up. But he also assumes, post facto, the responsibility of cleaning up the mess, alone or together with the particular Asa god concerned.

It is not only through sly cunning that Loke wriggles out of trouble. It is also by using transgressive magics that were not usually used by the Asa gods. Although basically all of the gods have shape-shifting abilities (some use this potential more than others), Loke takes the magic one step further by also shifting gender and/or sexual perspective and position.

Loke's (likely) unconscious provocations lead to a distinctly Promethean punishment: enchainment in a cave, complete with dripping snake venom as torture. The violent reactions from the captured Loke lead to earthquakes—a premonition of Ragnarok. The drops from the snake are collected by Loke's wife, Sigyn, inside the cave. Instead of integrating his painful revelations and wisdoms, the Asa gods choose to repress them.

Trickster gods/forces are present in many cultures. Two that are similar to Loke are Islam's "green man" figure of Khadir or Khezr, and the Yoruban Eshu (aka Legba in other West African spheres). "The upside-down qualities of Khezr's way reminds us of those clown societies among the American Indians whose humor consists of doing the opposite to everything normal, wearing shoes on their head, talking backwards, outraging moral conventions and authority. This clowning hides a deep wisdom in ridicule and whimsy, and such societies operate under the sign of the Trickster, using laughter to storm the gates of heaven—or to slip through like a thief."[2]

Loke as a devil or a demon? I think not. These much wider attributions were simply demagogic ones from Christian proselytizers like Snorre—but a highly valuable trickster figure and force, for sure. This then is Fenris's father: an integrated force of transgression—one needed for overall and eventual health and balance. What about Fenris's mother? Angerboda is the giantess who gives birth to the feared trio of ferocious forces. As Loke is also a giant (although a skilled and shape-shifting one), these kids should technically be solid giants, too, but none of them are.

The meaning of Angerboda's name has been a matter of debate. The predominant perspective is simply etymological, claiming that *Anger* is the present Swedish *ånger* (regret) and *boda* refers to the Swedish *båda* (in a sense, to provoke or conjure: *att uppbåda*). I would like to suggest an explanation that I think has more relevance for the big picture here: *Anger* is actually related more to the Swedish word for *meadow* (äng). The colloquial word for *vagina* in Swedish is *fitta* (cunt), and the original meaning of that word is a meadow, moist from either rain or dew. The word *od* is also highly relevant here. Not only is it the root of the name Oden, but also of the "concept." *Od* means "ecstatic rage" in old Swedish.[3]

Freja, the goddess of sex and sensuality (among other things), once had a husband or lover named Od. When he left to go roaming, she cried "red tears of gold" (undoubtedly a menstrual metaphor). The fallen heroes of the battlefield are divided between Oden and Freja. She was the one who taught Oden the dark, magical wisdom and methodology of the Sejd system. Considering the many similarities and interactions between Freja and Oden proper, it is more than likely that Od is in fact Oden. Seen in this light, I would argue that Angerboda is the vagina or womb Oden uses for the specific magical working of Ragnarok.

Given that Oden once mixed his blood with the very unlikely contender Loke (and thereby confused all of Asgård), the seemingly blurred identities now in many ways become quite clear. Loke often travels with Oden, and they experience all kinds of mischievous shenanigans together, many of which the other gods cannot or will not understand at all. The mixing of Oden's blood with his was the only reason that Loke was welcome in Asgård. The Fenris Wolf was therefore actually raised in

Asgård, but when he became too unruly and ferocious (puberty!), he had to be fettered.

The Angerboda progeny are all essential for the Ragnarok process, and although Oden will be devoured by Fenris, he is certainly no stranger to "sacrificing himself to himself"—given that he received the knowledge and wisdom of the runes by self-asphyxiation, hanging from the world tree Yggdrasil. Oden may be masculinely adorned with a phallic spear and two controllable male wolves (Gere and Freke), but in the shape of Loke he can not only dress and act as a female, but actually have ritual sex, receive semen, and give birth to magical creatures (like his own horse Sleipner). Loke is in many ways Oden's anima and/or shadow; the very aspect that allows for the transgressive magic that Freja taught him to manifest, and thereby to change the course of destiny. Taking into account that Oden's main epithet is Allfather, it is not surprising that even the end is conceived, conjured, and controlled by him.

In the Swedish language, the word *wolf* can be translated into either *ulv* or *varg*. Ulv is an older description of what we call "Canis Lupus," and it's also how kids have usually been presented with the concept in school: *Fenrisulven,* the Fenris Wolf. The other word, *varg,* is considerably more common today than ulv (which is mostly present in the masculine name of Ulf), but traditionally this was not associated with Canis Lupus per se, but with an outsider-ship that required draconian or punitive measures. To be "varg" was to be ostracized. For instance, a murderer would in old Swedish be a *mordvarg,* and an arsonist a *brännvarg.*

Seen from this perspective, Fenris is both ulv and varg. Scandinavian farmers were undoubtedly respectful of the ferocious Canis Lupus in their vicinity, and the deeper aspect (of fear rather than respect) surely created this mythic gestalt imprint of a somehow constantly threatening wolf or wolf pack that could certainly endanger an entire microcosm of a homestead or small farm.

Continuing on this ancestral or familial trail, let's also look at

Fenris's two siblings by Angerboda. They are the Midgård snake and the "goddess" Hel, who rules over the queendom of the same name.

Hel is fully integrated in a sphere that is feared yet inevitable and irreversible. No one escapes Hel, except for the warriors who have valiantly died in battle (half of whom go to Oden's Valhalla, and half to Freja). Hel is simply an accepted and necessary sphere/state.

Although visions and cultural concepts changed over time to actively include resting places such as the burial mound itself or even designated mountains of death, Hel as a mythic afterlife sphere was the predominant one. And that surely keeps Fenris's sister continually busy, up until Ragnarok proper when she opens the gates and lets the dead roam free.

Midgård is the name of the human sphere in the Scandinavian mythology/cosmogony, just like Asgård is that of the Asa gods. The Midgård snake relates specifically to the sphere of the humans, and was originally cast out by Oden to encircle that sphere, and thereby to keep it tight and safe (Midgård is an Ouroboros, biting its own tail).

As for the Midgård snake and the Fenris Wolf himself, mention in the Edda poems (and prose renditions) and other stories is mainly focused on that very final battle between cosmos and chaos. The end of the world, Ragnarok (aka the Wagnerian/Nietzschean "twilight of the gods"), pushes them both forward to fulfill their destinies: to help end the current cosmos, unleash chaos, but thereby aide a noncorrupt cosmos in being born from the debris and ashes.

If all central myths are generative or regenerative, the Scandinavian ones should not constitute any exceptions to that rule. If we stick with the ever-so-relevant magico-anthropological concept of *sympathesis,* we see that there is always more that unites than sets apart. Each specific culture evokes its own myths (or flavors of older ones) that are designed to allow for the original fodder to transcend itself. An individual self-transcendence and/or a cultural ditto is therefore the key to understanding any magico-anthropological motivations or perspectives.

Examples of this would be the rigid hierarchical structuring of religion in Judaism, and its release and transcendence in the ultra-intellectual, mental system of Kabbalah. Another would be moments of insight and possible epiphany in complex intellectual systems like the Western Ceremonial Magical Tradition (as exemplified by the Golden Dawn, etc.). The individual mind is not able to set itself genuinely free before it succumbs to and penetrates the predominant structure/system itself—whichever it may be. The inherent magic of the human mind constructs a culture that constructs a magic that will eventually allow for a transcendence of itself.

If we return to the Asa sphere and its inevitable Ragnarok, we can easily see that the issue is not merely causally "(re)generative" (as in larger mysteries of natural fertility), but rather more specifically sexual. Transcendence comes when addressing the moral problems of any more or less homogenous culture (like the Scandinavian). In this arena we have the symbolic gods as proxies for all the basic human dilemmas in times of extreme hardship, a brutal climate, and a reliance on strong bonds, allegiances, and kinships. Transcendence here makes itself manifest in a quasi-humorous acceptance of very basic desires and foibles. But when push comes to shove, one has to protect one's own sphere—with any amount of violence if need be. The structuring of violent retribution through complex aspects of Lex Talionis was another form of important transcendence in which the Scandinavian mind frame and societies developed from an emotionally reactive anarchy to a more or less orderly adherence to rules, bureaucracy, and processes of law.

Why are the Ragnarokian mysteries essentially of a sexual nature? It's because ancient cultures existed in a continual learning process in which the inner angst of death mixed with an external view of, or insight into, the regularity of nature—and of generative processes. Seeing fertility as the only weapon against a hostile chaos, it's not surprising that the myths were steeped in an acting-out of exactly these issues.

A cosmos (of any size) will always be transformed into a chaos—it's an inevitable process. As is the opposite: the new chaos will bring forth a new cosmic order. Ragnarok is not the end then. The progeny of the

Asa gods survive the antics; they are ejaculated into a new potential cosmos emanating from the dark void of Ginnungagap.

The Midgård snake is an all-encompassing phallic force, keeping the entire world together by uniting with its own tail. The actual name Midgård for this snake or dragon is only used in Snorre's *Edda*. In other sources, he is referred to as "Jörmungand" (a great staff or wand).

Hel is the dark mother of gestation and the underworld. This is not the romanticized sphere of the idealized Asa gods. This is a chthonic, earthen, soilish, regenerative sphere of heavy transformation. Fenris represents the very will to live by wreaking ferocious havoc and clearing the path. The kinship with the Greek half-god Pan (Roman version: Faun) is obvious. Whatever Pan threatens or enforces in terms of ecstatic rage/lust will benefit fertility as such, as well as the culture of fertility.

When this libidinal force is unleashed, it has the power to destroy the existing cosmos/order on many levels. Fenris is the feral principle/ferocity that lies hidden in the repressed people; the libido that cannot be held back for long. When this is unleashed in/on collective levels, it always brings a violent end to the present reign.

This seemingly chaotic trio constitutes a veritable passage for a kundalini blast that moves from the chthonic sphere via the snake, straight up to the sky. The yogic reference to the eternal fire of enlightened insight is here represented by the fire giant Surt, who at Ragnarok scorches the existing Earth in volcanic eruptions.

Is there violent sacrifice? Indeed. An entire world or era is sacrificed in this burst. Only one sperm merges with the cosmic egg—the rest are shot out into the nonfertile void. Rejuvenation always comes at a high price.

As mentioned, the Midgård snake is an Ouroboros. Oden casts it out, and it encircles the earth/world, thereby creating restraint. Oden casts out Hel to Nifelheim, which is also a walled-in space, thereby creating restraint. It's all about confining/encircling/restricting forces—both ways. These two forces of "order and death" represent outer restraint.

On the other hand, Asgård is—to gods and humans alike—an inner restraint, and that's why the deceptive walling-in for protection won't work. Tricking the giant builder is the actual seed of the moral decay that brings forth Ragnarok.

When the gods feel a need to domesticize or at least control Fenris by throwing the fettering net over him, it's psychologically justifiable (but foolish): they choose to cover up and suppress the very same force that once brought forth their own Asgård paradise, thereby suppressing the kundalini of inevitable change.

Both Midgård and Fenris are excommunicated when they grow too big and unruly. Midgård is thrown into the ocean, sinking into the depths. Fenris is restrained by a magical net or chain in the form of a very special thread. Although soft as silk, this thread, Gleipner, is constructed out of the roaring of cats, hairs of women's beards, the roots of the mountains, the sinews of bears, the breath of fish, and the spit of birds (this koan-like composite is surely worthy of further magico-anthropological research!).

Of course there are retributions: the symbol of power and valor in the form of the god Tyr loses his/its right hand when dealing with the only temporarily chained beast. Is it a mere coincidence that the hand of apparent masturbation is involuntarily sacrificed here? No matter what, it's a traumatic loss to the entire community. This is because it makes clear that we can never escape the power of our instincts, as frequently expressed by Loke—the shamanic diplomat moving between the orderly Asgård and the considerably more chthonic spheres.

In Tyr we find an interesting expression of amor fati—it is simply his destiny to lose his hand. Whereas Oden's focus lies on magical self-sacrifice, that of Tyr is causally duty bound. His valor is actually not connected to willpower, but rather to a subservience to the expected that is part of the overall systemic error that causes the eventual downfall of Asgård. It is neither Fenris, the Midgård snake, nor Hel that cause the end. Rather it is the corruption among the gods themselves. "Garm barks terribly / in front of Gnipahålan; / the fetters will break, /

the wolf is free. / I know of much wisdom, / much further I see / about the great victory gods' / final destinies."[4]

There are many speculative theories about who exactly Garm is in this drama. Garm is a canine (he barks) and could therefore be a canine entity on his own, or a poetic symbol for Fenris. The fetters break and the wolf is free, and that is, as we know, intimately connected to the ultimate timeline of Ragnarok.

Gnipahålan is a cave-like sphere—an entrance to Hel—and it has also been stated that Garm is actually Hel's own dog. In this fascinating dance of Loke's spawn, I would argue that Garm is the domesticated dog/instinct that in Fenris/Pan will break free of the restrictions of sexual moralities. We should here remember that Hel is the resting place for common people, and Garm barks by the opening of the dark goddess's cave. Garm represents the origin of the vast majority of sperm that are shot out into the void of death rather than divine (re)birth. But this barking awakens and brings forth the deeper and stronger libido, which eventually cannot be restrained. Hel may be barren, but Fenris certainly is not.

Why this is of interest here is that, depending on which source for the Voluspa poem we use, this very paragraph is repeated between three and five times, thereby making it, by the mere repetition, either a fairly redundant accentuation, or, as I would argue, an actual spell intended to facilitate the expressed outcome. This is a mythic certainty that is culturally encouraged rather than anxiously forgotten or repressed.

This is not as paradoxical as it may seem. Although it was formulated in a culture that was based on very strict kinships, loyalties, and bloodlines, people of course knew that libido is the most powerful force, whether expressed in Eros specifically or not. The Scandinavian myths and stories about gods who are often barely more than human generate a more colorful bouquet of coping skills than any monotheistic whitewashing ever could.

Sigmund Freud's schematic view of the psyche can be very useful when looking at this particular mythological structure—especially as it leads to a psychological-emotional disaster and even to the death of the "patient." Jotunheim, the sphere of the primordial giants, represents the unconscious (Freud's *Das Es*). This is not exactly identical to the instincts, but certainly strongly related. Midgård, the sphere of the humans, represents what Freud called *Das Ich* (confusingly translated as the ego). Asgård, the sphere of the idealized gods, represents what Freud called *Das Über-Ich* (confusingly translated as the super ego). When the Über-Ich protects the Ich from the underlying threats of the unconscious by allowing it to deceive itself and transgress, this can set in motion a chain reaction that will eventually lead to a psychic collapse.

The breach of the oath with the giant who builds the protective walls around Asgård is what instigates Ragnarok later. It's a corruption that opens up for even more (self) deceit. Loke helps trick the giant builder by becoming a mare and sidetracking the giant's needed stallion, and then giving birth to Sleipner—the chief superego's ability to travel/survey all the other spheres. It becomes a moral/moralistic reaction, which in turn will provoke Loke even further as the "community" of Asgård apparently will allow any amoral and corrupting trickery for the sake of its own protection. A dangerous double standard takes hold. As Mircea Eliade put it, "The construction of cosmic time through repetition of the cosmogony is still more clearly brought out by the symbolism of Brahmanic sacrifice. Each Brahmanic sacrifice marks a new Creation of the world. Indeed, the creation of the sacrificial altar is conceived as a 'Creation of the world.' The water with which the clay is mixed is the primordial water; the clays that form the base of the altar is the earth; the side walls represent the atmosphere."[5]

In many ways, it's a crude simplification to say that Fenris "allows for a rebirth" by instigating the end of the world. Although the outcome is very much accurate, the complexity of the overall mythic dynamic deserves further attention. If we assume, in some kind of Jungian sense, that all cultures share basic myths (or mythic structures)—whether by a collective unconscious or simply by mythic migration (or both)—then the Scandinavian cluster has survived its migration very well.

Taking into account that one of the main formulating historians,

Snorre Sturlason, was a Christian, his demagogic attempts are actually not that hard to wash off. Loke was not turned into a too-simplified Satan, but just enough to relay a new faith to very tough and decidedly very heathen peoples. It is the blessing and the curse of the monotheistic appropriation. If the new system is moved in too quickly and forcefully it will experience a backlash. If too slowly, the message will be lost in far too many pampering adjustments.

The strength of these myths, regardless of which cultural clothing they're in, lies in their phenomenal psychological insight. We can read any pan- or polytheistic myths and stories from basically any time, and still recognize ourselves as well as basically any contemporary dynamic. This is not so in the case of the monotheistic myths, which are consciously designed moral tales to be simply integrated in subservient obedience but not necessarily understood.

16
The Imaginary Is a Real Thing

The history of psychoactive substances and occult practice is fascinating, to say the least. Although one can probably never find an absolute equation or relationship between the two, their tandem history of "altered states" gives enough evidence of kinship. As with all things that touch or stem from the "inner reaches of outer space" (to paraphrase Joseph Campbell), both the use of psychoactive agents and irrational, ritual behavior originate in shamanism, as does the larger human construct of "religion."

All things "inner," "magical," "spiritual," and so on and so forth, can be traced back to the integration in the human mind of an intuitive, "natural" (i.e., *not* intellectually constructed by a human mind via language), pantheistic appreciation that everyone and everything is connected and ensouled, and that there is a lot more to learn from than what meets the eye (or any of the other senses). Shamanism is the very bedrock of human knowledge in general, and of inner knowledge in particular. As all later inner practices then stem from shamanism, it is this foundational phenomenon we must lean on when looking at any kind of "spiritual" or "magical" phenomenon—such as, for instance, medieval witchcraft.

Witchcraft is a cluster term for a multitude of practices, many of which are still performed/upheld/developed—in some traditions *possibly* with "unbroken lines" of teaching. In many ways witchcraft could be seen as the currently most formalized keeper of a shamanic tradition in the European sphere. Many other cultures (specifically indigenous ones) still have active shamanic legacies, but not so in the homogenized Christian cultures. The usual main shamanic foci (healing, helping, acquiring knowledge and wisdom) and techniques (inner traveling, communicating with nontangible entities and intelligences, nature worship, integrating pantheism, etc.) all stem from inner practice in its purest form (i.e., in direct individual experience, or in small esoteric groups).

The integration of psychoactive components in shamanic practice, as well as in witchcraft, facilitates the necessary "flight" into other, inner realms. There are other and perhaps more central techniques (for instance drumming and/or using other rhythms of different frequencies, as well as induced physical exhaustion), but the history of human spirituality and protoreligion has indeed been one steeped in intoxication. When shamans go to different spheres to find their answers, it's a rationally irrational and active use of the human imagination integrated in a supportive cultural context. Integrating elements in and from nature—from macrocosmic speculations to microcosmic experimentation ("protomedicine")—witchcraft has been an active keeper of human and shamanic wisdom (as well as of a rich psycho-pharmacopoeia) since linear time was invented.

Medieval witchcraft is a strange research subject because so much of the documentation stems from antagonistic or decidedly malevolent sources. The witch craze contained deeply and morbidly absurd instructional tomes for amateur inquisitors and public officials alike, unfortunately resulting in very tangible torture and genocide. Occult practices and the use of psychedelics have of course never been condoned in Christian tyranny, but I suspect the medieval witches were victims of unfortunate general circumstance rather than of specific esoteric and psychoactive practice.

There are similarities throughout the many centuries of persecution, as well as in different regions. Many of the so-called trials were at civil courts, and accusations popped up from ordinary people more than from centralized clerical quarters. Witches were scapegoats picked out for their outsider status and for keeping (and fanning) a flame that wasn't condoned by accepted norms and behaviors. When people needed a love potion, a sexual partner, a child, an abortion, or some kind of secret counselling everything was fine and dandy, but when famines, plagues, and infant deaths so common to the era hit the poor population all over Europe, witches became very convenient targets for compensatory accusations. This served the church very well, as the witches were obviously dealing in some kind of original natural wisdom that had been appropriated and sanitized by their own, earlier church "fathers." No competition allowed.

As the judges in question were officially negative to anything or anyone opposed to the prejudiced doctrines of the Christian Church, we have to assume that the diametrical opposite of whatever these judges claimed actually constitutes the truth. As mentioned elsewhere, between the years 1400 and 1750 approximately one hundred thousand human beings (mostly women) were prosecuted for witchcraft in Europe and America.[1]

The accusations often had very little to do with concrete crimes (as in there being perpetrators and victims) but were mainly projected fantasies from disgruntled neighbors and perverted minds in anxious power structures that simply disliked independent women as much as they did liberating inner/shamanic experiences. The combination of the two, then, became a license not only to kill but also to happily torture innocents, while making enforced statements new truths for posterity. Some of these actually still linger on *ad verbatim* in the most retrograde monotheistic communities. This certainly explains why certain societies (as in groups, orders, or communities) have chosen to be secretive and immersed in complex esoteric symbolism.

The medieval witch craze has, unfortunately, only been one of many occurrences of this kind of draconian behavior in monotheism. It is, however, one of the most interesting occurrences to look at when we want to learn more about the dynamics of draconian transference.

Witchcraft and/or the magical uses of psychedelics weren't set back by the mock trials and dire sentences as much as the normal historian/ interpreter would believe, but rather the contrary. The romanticized or even fetishized trauma of the genocidal atrocities and all the fanciful accusations in account as well as iconography actually helped create the very worst nightmare the Christian Church* could ever envision. That their own cluster of lies would much later become an actual truth that would revisit them to bite their own behinds.

What I mean by this is that the formulation of alleged horrendous behaviors, demons, devils, and various monsters via Christian minds and mouths, and in printed "witch hammers" ablaze with "demonological" illustrations and detailed descriptions of a multitude of perverted behavior, actually did become parts of a romanticized witchcraft. This integrated a historic knowledge (of herbs, plants, and spirits alike, as well as of customs and rituals) many hundreds of years later. Today, the once so monstrous emblems of fear are integrated as semihumorous status symbols in neopagan groups flaunting expensive reissued editions of medieval grimoires. Experimental ritual behavior in these groups stems not necessarily from evanescent fantasies of some innocent antiquity via "inspired" minds like Margaret Murray, Gerald Gardner, and Alex Sanders, but from the dark sadomasochistic dungeons underneath pious Christian monasteries. In many ways the aggressively repressed Christians didn't manage to suppress anything at all but on the contrary helped unleash exactly the monsters they were so afraid of.

The witch craze of the medieval centuries brought to light not only man's inhumanity to (wo)man but also some evidence of a chemognostic relationship to folk-magical practice (very much a legacy of shamanism). Given that there was no written communication on the "folk level" during this period, intellectual concepts journeyed in other forms: myths, stories, and songs, for instance.

---

*In singular henceforth unless otherwise noted, as both the Catholic and Protestant cults were active parts of this monumental psychosis.

As these migrated and were transmitted transregionally and transgenerationally, more and more of a local, cultural flavor was added. Over the centuries, classic Eleusinian death and rebirth myths morphed into local stories, integrating local languages, symbols, divinities, and plants. The key to the mysteries lay in nature herself, for nature offered ways and techniques of letting the human being see herself in a new light. This was also a more or less wholly gnostic concept—one where the numinous touched and taught the individual directly, without any need of human structures or proxies.

What kind of knowledge has been passed on throughout the millennia? There's the protoshamanic "traveling" technique of course but also information on supplemental psychoactive ingredients like plants, mushrooms, and herbs. This entailed journeying in the inner to a netherworld, an upperworld, and other variants in-between; being guided by power animals, spirits, plants, and other nontangible sentiences; and acquiring knowledge for all possible kinds of uses.

The underlying idea is holistic and conveys that (A) it's easy to be/get "there" and (B) it's as real as anything else you perceive with your senses. Traditionally the journeys have been aided by plants and other organic agents from nature, most often within a structure of drumming/rhythmic pulses. Scientific analysis has helped us isolate these key agents within the agents, so to speak, and basically none of these have *recently* been discovered by humans. Knowledge of psychotropic herbs, mushrooms, and plants has been with us for a long, long time. It is a knowledge as distinctly human as the use of fire and the use of language. Using these activating agents in shamanic contexts has the power to set one free—to allow one to leave rational mind traps, the sensory hegemony, inherited morals, and basic concepts like time and space. The experience can be pleasurable (or not) and will leave one with truly additional information about oneself and the world one inhabits.

This pantheistic approach, in which everything and everyone is ensouled and connected, is the foundation for what later on became religion. The more the human being hubristically distanced herself from nature as such, the less she appreciated or encouraged pantheism in favor of simpler concepts like dogmatic monotheism.

The established perspective witnin academia in regard to the history of esoteric drug use has been one of resignation, all too easily forgetting that myths and the imaginary usually tell us a lot more than analyses of pipes, bowls, broomsticks, and other possible utensils. Brian Inglis, the open-minded Irish writer and TV personality, summed up the dilemma like this in the 1970s: "We will probably never know for certain what the constituents were of Homer's nepenthe; or what drug was used in the shamanist Eleusinian cult in ancient Greece, in which the initiate was given a potion designed to induce delectable visions, after which he could never be the same again. In general, the information about drugs and their social effects in classical times, and in the Middle Ages, is too scanty and unreliable to serve as the basis for anything more than enjoyable speculation."[2]

However, the very same author couldn't help but in the same text provide a petty proviso, thus indulging in "enjoyable speculation" himself.[3]

Drugs crop up chiefly in connection with witchcraft. Professor Michael Harner has recently argued that they were of central importance to witchcraft in Europe, but that this has been obscured by the fact that so much of the source material, most of it in Latin, has never been studied by anybody with an interest in this aspect of the subject. From the later evidence of witchcraft trials, it is clear that witches employed such plants as henbane and deadly nightshade— sometimes making them into unguents, and smearing them on parts of their bodies—as a way of liberating themselves, to undertake their Sabbat rides. It is also clear that, like shamans, they believed that while they were under the influence of these drugs they really could fly through the air.

It should probably be mentioned here that shamanism scholar Michael Harner's perspective was that medieval witchcraft was a "debased form of shamanism, which the hostility of the Church had prevented from coming out into the open."[4]

Recently things have changed, not only in the presentation of material previously only available in rare manuscript form and containing drug references (for instance: *Touch Me Not: A Most Rare Compendium of the Whole Magical Art*),[5] but also in the (re)formation of a consciously expressed contemporary witchcraft aware of possible mythic interpretations of legacies and lines but at the same time definitely reconstructing as much as creating anew. The strong interest in theurgical-magical systems stemming from antiquity and classical grimoires signals a desire to (re)connect with the mythic and make it both tangible reality and useful technology in contemporary and causally chaotic times.

Scarlet Imprint founder Peter Grey, a distinct advocate of working with old materials in our present time, writes in his *Apocalyptic Witchcraft* on the subject of unbroken traditions.[6]

> However you wish to cut it, this is not the case in the West. There is no evidence for the survival of a complex system, we are the inheritors of splintered bones, toppled crosses, and violated grave mounds. Our task is only beginning, though it would be more lucrative and reassuring to claim otherwise. Scraps of folklore need to be underpinned by a complete set of bones or they are simply rags blowing in the wind. Yet perhaps the Sabbath itself is the key to re-establishing our cults. We must be honest about this, and acknowledge the debt we owe to the living traditions that are helping us reanimate our own.

That Grey's own generation has integrated psychedelics in these "traditional reformations" is well-known and could be the subject of a wholly separate study (or many).

"The Empire has several other witch hunts which run concurrently. First is the War against Drugs. As witches, our use of entheogens, plant medicine and even organic and home-grown food places us on that watch list."[7]

Eminent psychedelics researcher and scholar Patrick Lundborg touches upon possible agents in European witchcraft in his great book *Psychedelia: An Ancient Culture, A Modern Way of Life.* Whereas psilocybin mushrooms were quite likely ingredients in European witchcraft, as was ergot on different corns in southern/central Europe, the most likely ones are actually from a different family, and a less pleasant one. This is the *Solanacean* (potato) family, including *Atropa belladonna* (deadly nightshade, belladonna), *Hyoscyamus* (henbane, stinking nightshade), *Mandragora* (mandrake, alraune), and *Datura stramonium* (thorn apple, angel's trumpet, Jimsonweed). These are all absorbed in the blood flow via the skin, and are most efficiently absorbed in ointment form via mucus membranes. If we speculatively enter the territories of vaginal and anal membranes, and take into account insertions of phallic items like witches' brooms smeared with ointment, it is then not far-fetched to state that the psychedelic or "deliriant" agents have been literally intimately connected also with sexual experiences—masturbatory or together with others in a possible group.

The psilocybin and lysergic histories should not be underestimated. Psychedelic mushrooms have been central to human culture and inner work for millennia. The ingestion of ergot on rye and other corns was used by midwives to induce abortions and also, in milder doses, to stop bleeding and ease birth pains. (This was the original incentive for Dr. Albert Hofmann to study this particular agent, which, as we know, led to the synthesis of LSD-25 and its massive cultural influence.) Midwifery has traditionally been associated with wise women and witches, and it should be safe to say the opposite is also true: European witches were associated with life-and-death mysteries in general folklore, which provided them not only with beneficial respect but also with detrimental prejudice and accusations of trafficking with forces larger than human life.

The *Solanacea* family is usually called "deliriant" rather than "psychedelic" because of its violent and uncontrollable nature. Ergot on various corns can easily be overdosed, too, inducing the phenomenon of St. Anthony's Fire (essentially food poisoning, often leading to death), as well as more convulsive spasms, often with ensuing psychedelic states. Perhaps we can assume—given that we have no evidence about these ancient witches' knowledge of dosing to achieve "controllable" trips—that the wild ride of the witches (broom-induced or not) was in great part due to uncontrollable physical fits parallel to out-of-body (= flight) psychedelic experiences? This sounds pretty protoshamanic in my ears. What or who these brave women found during their wild flights very likely had to do with securing concrete answers to current questions. They seem, on the whole, to not have been joyrides at all. Perhaps any sexual/pleasurable elements in the initial ingestion stages of the trips were actually deemed necessary to embark in the first place?

In various forms, the basic agrarian myths have lived on all over Europe, often with only minimal variations. The mysteries of farming were integrated in a general pan/polytheistic, pagan mind frame, and no Christian attempts could ever eradicate this—well, not before industrialization and urbanization, anyway (not a specifically Christian phenomena). The Greek drama starring agriculture goddess Demeter, her daughter Persephone, and Pluto, god of the dead, has been one of the most important myths of the Western cultural sphere. To make a massive myth a short story: Persephone is kidnapped by Pluto and taken to the netherworld. Demeter is heartbroken and furious and curses plants and crops in rage.

The gods react to this, as humans without crops simply can't offer these to the gods in sacrifice. A deal is struck. Pluto gets Persephone for a third of the year, while her mother gets her for the rest of the time (so that they can bless the Earth and grow things again, together). While Demeter was in grief, she was taken in by the royal family of Eleusis and, not being allowed alcohol while grieving, she was presented with something else . . . This was symbolically (or not) retained in the later Eleusinian mysteries and plays, which presented each candidate with this very same something else. This then led to a death and rebirth ritual in enactment and in the inner spheres of the celebrant. If Demeter's main trip (pardon the pun) were corn mysteries, what in this drama could have triggered the feeling of being reborn and also getting a younger version of oneself back from the reign of death—to facilitate new natural progress?

Gordon Wasson, the mycologist so seminal to the psychedelic movement of the mid- to late twentieth century, asked his friend Albert Hofmann (the "creator" of LSD) whether the Eleusinian rites could have had something to do with ergot, the parasite affecting different forms of corn and some forms of grass. Hofmann, being the world's foremost expert on the subject, answered yes: "Early Man in ancient Greece could have arrived at an hallucinogen from ergot growing on wheat or barley. An easier way would have been to use the ergot growing on the common wild grass Paspalum. This is based on the assumption that the herbalists of ancient Greece were as intelligent and resourceful as the herbalists of pre-Conquest Mexico."[8]

The connection between psychedelic initiation, associated inner work, and revelations in a rural framework of learning about the seasons and farming thus established, we can look at corn farming folklore basically anywhere in Europe. It basically tells the same story over and over again. Where the original mysteries allowed the natural context (farming) to become the symbol of an individual journey and development, in many regions it was also acted out communally in times of sowing and harvesting. The last sheaf of the harvest, usually called the "corn mother," has traditionally been saved until the next sowing season and even dressed up as a woman and danced with.

Corn mother in German is *kornmutter*, and a slight twist gives *mutterkorn*, which has been a common name for corn affected by ergot, and one of the first things Hofmann studied. "In German folklore there was a belief that, when the corn waved in the wind, the corn mother (a demon) was passing through the field; her children were the rye wolves (ergot). In our context we observe that of these names, two, *seigle ivre* ("drunken rye") and *Tollkorn* ("mad grain"), point to a knowledge of the psychotropic effects of ergot. This folk awareness of the mind-changing effects of ergot shows an intimate knowledge of its properties, at least among herbalists, deeply rooted in European tradition."[9]

And who essentially were the herbalists in rural, medieval European cultures? That's right: the witches. As these wise women knew how to handle herbs, plants, and mushrooms, perhaps it's obvious that they were also blamed when things stemming from nature and the very same agents took on dangerous forms? There were, for instance, several occurrences of mass afflictions of St. Anthony's Fire during the medieval centuries because people had eaten bread contaminated by ergot. This wasn't *empirically* established until the seventeenth century, hence a more intuitive blame game against the witches seems likely earlier on than this.

Already in 1582, a physician in Frankfurt by the name of Adam Lonitzer wrote that ergot had been used by midwives for centuries, mainly to precipitate childbirth (as we have mentioned earlier). By that time the problems with correct dosage, both in terms of uterine spasms and postpartum hemorrhage, were well-known.[10] This knowledge of controlling the uterine queendom must surely have been of interest to the Christian Church—specifically if the wise women could and would abort unwanted fetuses in other women in the early stages of pregnancy.

The human need to share extraordinary experiences is sometimes a dangerous one. If someone, whether woman or man, returns from a psychedelic and revelatory inner journey and relays what they've experienced to someone not initiated, the consequences could be (and in this case probably were) disastrous. Where no psychological or otherwise abstracted explanation models existed, malevolent minds that heard or overheard stories of strange inner journeys during which amazing creatures and intelligences communicated with the traveler, could so easily retell these stories in an accusatory way to people in power who could provide favors or status enhancers for them.

Thus an avalanche of persecutions and psychosis ensued, in which psychonauts and tradition-bearers became victims of simpletons and anxious monotheists joined together. As mentioned earlier, between the years 1400 and 1750 approximately one hundred thousand humans (again, mostly women) were prosecuted for witchcraft in Europe and America.[11] It remains one of the most bestial and shameful cultural genocides in human history. And it's very likely that this often happened and spiraled because of mere hearsay and ill will.

The anti-witchcraft sentiments of medieval times were not necessarily a patriarchal given/standard at all but to a great degree constituted a specific misogynistic variant of monastic homosexuality, and were instigated by common folk. What were the obvious threats to this power structure? The individual, the freethinker, the heretic, the dissident, Woman, female sexuality, nonprocreative sexuality outside of the walls of the monastery, invisible transcendence, unfettered emotional spheres, proximity to and active contact with nature, keeping secrets, knowledge of life and death (as in midwifery, healing, medicinal wisdom, magic, etc.) without supernatural, monotheistic explanations or theories. What to do about anyone or anything that contained even an inkling of these essentially quite general human qualities? Draconian counterforce, of course! Torture, enforced and constructed confessions, imaginary beings and conspiracies, the Sabbath's *osculum infame* (kiss of shame) as a projection of male homosexual desire, with the devil as a Big Top that needed to be serviced in order to facilitate for the humble ass-kisser's self-eradication through penetration, which then brings shame and self-flagellation/torture.

Christ on the cross and St. Sebastian, among others, are icons in this environment/culture because of the vivid description of the sexually repressed male. The strong male body is violently affixed to erect wood, rendered impotent but compensationally susceptible to penetration (by nails, bolts, spearheads, arrows). Please note that in the Christian mythos this is not a rape scenario but a voluntary submission to a brute, overpowering phallic force. Please also take into

196 The Imaginary Is a Real Thing

consideration another important aspect of this strange myth: a child conceived by a mother not penetrated and impregnated by the father/a human male but by a supernatural force. The primal function of the human father figure is removed and the mother is sanctified by supernatural proxy powers. Projecting this perverted construct onto a male baby will surely create interesting fantasies in the child and young adult, who will certainly be integrating compensational elements of what later became known as "the Christ complex."

A violently repressed sexuality fueled by the above story as its central myth provoked "religious" hallucinations both in monasteries and convents. This psychosis spread and was encouraged by outer worldly power structures, too (perhaps to keep the disgruntled proletariat happy with a new and more absurdist kind of Circus Maximus). Aldous Huxley's classic novel *The Devils of Loudun* (and Ken Russell's wonderful film adaptation, *The Devils*) shows the frenzy with which this was acted out in a convent, where communal sexual repression resulted in complete dissociation and hallucinatory states of mind in a form of religiously sanctioned, institutionalized insanity. Unfortunately it also had the result that many innocent women (and men, too, for that matter) were brutally murdered.

The roots of the medieval "witch craze" thus lie only in part in the ostracizing of women outside of homogenous cultures per se (because of poverty, weirdness, nonadaption, knowledge of magic, unwillingness to provide sexual favors and the like as has been suggested by many "anti-patriarchal" interpretation models). And only in part can we blame the actual occultism and drug use, as these aspects were, preferably hidden—until they were drawn out by force and justifying coercion.

The overall roots of this tragedy can be found in the power of the Christian Church (mainly the Catholic cult) to affect mundane and political affairs. When and where the Christian cult thrived, business, tolerance, progress, and culture usually did not. The Italian city-states during the Renaissance are usually thought to be a high-tide marker in the creation of Western civilization. These were places and eras where art, philosophy, esotericism, magic, and science were allowed a considerably longer leash than usual and considerably more so if one was well educated and male rather than a poor rural woman of course, but still . . . The stifling intolerance of Christianity was less present.

The problems essentially began when the monastic culture integrated learning that fell outside the purview of strictly religious learnings. The big European monasteries became libraries and intellectual centers as well as archives of many dissident teachings. Monks became students, not only of God's will, but also of human history and learning in general. This also included medicinal and healing knowledge, as well as farming ditto. As these intellectually vital environments degenerated into power-broking centers under the intolerant thumb of the Vatican, any outsiders who possessed a similar or even original kind of knowledge—whether shamanic witch or natural experimentalist—were simply deemed heretical.

Although grandiose political opponents and the odd, brilliant protoscientist were most often male and easy targets because of easily provoked male oppositional pride, the women were of a different nature—literally. This made them even more threatening to a homogenous male power structure that regarded women in general as nothing more than Christian baby ovens. What horrible things were going on in secret? What were these women up to? Of course there were pagan traces in rural Europe, through which women (and men) worked with nature in shamanic practices. But the central issue wasn't so much these actualities as the monastic fantasies that fed the power. If the supposedly crazy women didn't confess to any wrongdoing, all one had to do was torture them until they did. Fiction became fact as wise women were tortured to death.

In essence what we're seeing when looking at the relationship between medieval witchcraft and psychedelics is a scenario where actual facts are mixed with actual fiction. Ample documentation from what would appear to be the victors paints a picture of their own insanity more than that of any witches, organized or not. In the aftermath we see enthusiastic neopagans on the one hand, willing to create something new out of a mythic witchcraft, including psychedelics, whether based on actual lineages or not. On the other hand, we see more or less impotent academics regurgitating the same footnotes and troubled relationship to Margaret Murray over and over again.

These crazy medieval centuries tell a fascinating story about when and how a life-affirming, pantheistic, shamanic fertility cult was attacked by a brutal monotheistic death cult. That the former has used psychoactive agents in its important work, both in normal day-to-day situations and under cultic, ritual umbrellas is beyond any doubt. That the latter have aggressively denied themselves and their followers these same agents is also beyond any doubt.

On this (end) note, I find it an interesting insight that the same family of plants can contain such different forms and attitudes yet carry such perfect symbolic weight in this context. The Solanacean plants used by witches on their wild, ecstatic, and revelatory individual journeys to the Sabbath are related to the potato that was fermented in the strong alcoholic liquids used to enslave and numb/dumb down the populace.

17
Memento Mori Forever

About a year before my best friend died in 2014, he gave me a silver necklace pendant displaying an old woodcut image of a skeleton leaning over a table, one hand casually resting on an hourglass. Integrated in the image are also the words *Memento Mori*—Latin for "Remember that you will die." It is truly a wonderful pendant, which is further adorned on the backside with my initials, a star, and an inlaid black diamond.

My friend liked to design jewelry, no doubt an extension of his interest in numismatist collecting of coins and similar things of crafted value. At the time I didn't give this much thought. I gratefully hung the pendant around my neck, and there it still resides—some eight years later.

When my friend died, the pendant took on a weird new meaning. Why had this image and the pendant popped up at this particular moment in time? Was my friend increasingly aware of his own demise somehow? Or was it a mere coincidence—if there even is such a thing?

No matter what, a remarkable piece of jewelry was transformed from something beautiful and distant to something meaningful and close as it was touched by the experience of death itself. Speculation is certainly the prerogative of the living, but all speculation aside, this twist of fate really opened my eyes to the phenomenon of mortality

"Memento Mori Forever" was originally presented as a lecture for the "Psychoanalysis, Art and the Occult" series c/o Morbid Anatomy, 2021.

itself. The message relayed became an actual, substantial, and penetrating wisdom in a way that no other philosophy had been able to in my own life.

It's easy to intellectually grasp the concept of mortality, finality, inevitability. But it's a whole different story when it's lined with the emotional aspects of genuine loss. Everyone who's experienced the death of a loved one knows this, and for most the shock leads to a neat compartmentalization rather than a head-on collision with one's own comfort zone. One pushes the confrontation and the emotional impact aside through rituals and culturally sanctioned behaviors—like funerary rites and permission to cry loudly at home or at a funeral but not really uncontrollably at a restaurant or in other public settings, as that's slightly too disturbing. Within limits, the experience of death is easy to share, and that is probably very necessary in order to maintain a balanced mental health. But the confrontation with the inevitable is often very hard to bear—especially if it brings undesired negative implications for oneself.

This cluster of anxiety about something at the same time ridiculously simple and endlessly complex can be fetishized into negative behaviors, such as restraint of life-enhancing behavior and related feelings. This is a dominant feature of the monotheistic religions that not only promise something "better" after death but also require obedience and various forms of taxation in order to ensure the individual's continual relief from angst. Instead of celebrating life as a stretch of possibilities, joys, sensual pleasures, learning experiences, and so on, the focus lies on moving away from personal meditations on death itself and instead moving into superstitious denials in thought and action.

But of course the cluster can also be fetishized into something positive, such as an acknowledgment and celebration of life-enhancing behaviors and related feelings. It seems the best way to do this is not only by taking part in communal activities that promote life-enhancement, but also to use art as a personal reflection surface for further insights and revelations—a talismanic appreciation in the here and now of a majestic flow of ancestors as well as future forces.

With this in mind, I have often returned to the necklace for comfort and meditation. I have come to no other conclusion than that on some level, my friend's demise was expected—at least unconsciously. Sure, he created other items of jewelry not so focused on death itself, but this one so perfectly sums up where he was at the time. It's an aesthetically pleasing piece that carries a life-affirming message. It was then further made decidedly talismanic by the addition of the personal. In my case, this included my initials, a pentagram, and the black diamond. It seems my friend knew what he was up to.

I'm not entirely sure where this specific image comes from. But the main idea or image—that of a pondering skeleton—was a staple in medieval iconography. When Vesalius published his anatomical, medical masterpiece *On the Fabric of the Human Body* in 1543, it became a classic not only in the medical sciences, but also in artistic ones. Its many illustrations, created by Titian's workshop, literally opened up the human body for lay people to see. And they often put the corpses and skeletons in poses that were animated in a way, as if they were still alive. But even before this Vesalian impact, this general image or gestalt of death as an active and mischievous agent had been around for a long time, at least since the thirteenth century.

Another major book at about the same time as Vesalius, Hartmann Schedel's *Book of Chronicles,* published in 1493, tried to encompass a lot of different information. Schedel's friends and allies in the learned city of Nürnberg created a masterpiece of a book, one that has been revered for centuries and has survived thanks to its staggeringly impressive form and content. Except for maps and similar visual overviews, the history writing was basically biblical, dividing known history into sequences and tales of key persons that people were familiar with from church indoctrination. However, and this is important, Schedel was thereby smart and avoided a collision with the totalitarian Catholic Church, as he was sneaking in pieces of learning and wisdom from other cultures, too, mainly Greek. This was a real Renaissance step forward in freeing the human mind from biblical bondage (and a little bit sneaky, in the best possible way).

Hartmann Schedel wasn't by any means the sole author of the opus, though. He culled, quoted, copied, and intersected the pieces with descriptions of his own, thereby acting as editor of the most useful bits and pieces from both sanctioned and otherwise available sources. That in itself was a tremendous task, given the scope and ambition of this project. Yet his name isn't even clearly stated in the book. There wasn't even a proper title page in the original edition (this was common at the time). The *Book of Chronicles* should speak for itself, simple as that. The age of the author/editor-ego hadn't begun quite yet.

Also, one very probable reason for Schedel's not taking the entire credit for the book was that bookmaking was definitely more of a communal labor than it is now. At the facilities of the book's printer, Anton Koberger, there was room for eighteen printing presses. More than a hundred typesetters, printers, and assistants worked there, not forgetting the artists who provided sketches or drawings for the woodcutters. For this particular project the most well-known woodcutter today was the least well-known back then: Albrecht Dürer, who was an illustrator's apprentice in the book's production.

Included in this vastly encompassing volume is a beautiful image of a so-called "Dance of Death," or a "Danse Macabre." These were common as frescoes in churches and monasteries, displaying one or several skeletons grabbing or interacting with humans in different social positions, from infant to elderly, from peasant to pope. These integrated the "Memento Mori" message and often included the actual words.

It has been suggested, by historian Barbara Tuchman for instance, that the word *macabre* derives from the Maccabees, the group (and lineage) of Jewish warriors who created their own kingdom in Judea just before the Christian era began. Jews worked as gravediggers in France during the pestilent medieval periods, so they were probably very busy, and very visible. According to Tuchman, the expression was first used in the 1376 poem by Jean Le Fèvre, "I Do the Danse Macabre," but she claims it had been used earlier as "Danse Machabreus."[1]

So all through the fifteenth century the concept as such was increasingly present—initially as a reminder from the church to get in line because "we all die," but increasingly as a social comment in an overarching movement that eventually led to the reformation and the establishment of Protestantism. The Catholic Church, with its epiphytic interactions with society's leaders and the wealthy, was gradually looked upon as a blindly power-hungry structure that kept its sheep in dark ignorance for maximum crowd control and pecuniary profit.

The presence of popes, bishops, and similar corrupt potentati in the dances of death in the German sphere increased, and this was something remarkable. Something that had originally been sanctioned by the church as visual tales of moralism had in a sense been appropriated into tools of social commentary, inspired by humanistic efforts and thoughts of equality. Similar ideas had been present and integrated in art since the late thirteenth century, specifically in tales like *The Three Dead and the Three Living*. In this moral story, three noblemen meet death in the shape of three quite alive skeletons.

Hans Holbein the Younger's masterpiece series of woodcuts called *Pictures of Death* or, more colloquially, *The Dance of Death*, was completed in 1525. That he had been exposed to similar dances and Memento Moris is more than likely, as his own city of Basel even housed a sixty-meter-long painting version at a Dominican convent. This painting dated back all the way to the 1440s.

It also seems very likely that Vesalius and his team of artists had seen Holbein's published *Dance of Death*. The stand-up animated skeleton interacting with humans had definitely been part of the zeitgeist for a long time, but it seems that the mid-sixteenth century was an unusually generative era. Not only were there spots of plague and other diseases around that still terrified the European cities, but the refined printing techniques and the craftsmanship adapted to this new technology made for a blooming of artistic creation and business-minded dissemination. And the humanistic approach of the Protestants allowed for more social criticism and new ideas, more or less hidden in artistic expressions. The rattling of the iconic skeletal bones was definitely part of this. And it should be contrasted with earlier or even parallel Christian—that is, Catholic—art that masterfully displayed horrendous visions of hell or biblical scenes, but never allowed for the common man to be anything but an obedient victim of the powers that be.

To me at least, it is as if this magical skeleton figure very subtly was the agent of change in the big medieval picture, too. What once had been a reminder to obey gradually morphed into a reminder to *not* obey. What once had been an icon of seemingly inescapable life-denial gradually morphed into an icon of realization and, as a result, life-affirmation and life-enhancement. That said, one could argue that we always get what we project on the concept as such; that the best basic building blocks are always ambiguous. But that's also when they become most powerful, which contradicts the mechanics of advertising, for instance.

Repeating mindless simplicity can certainly affect behavior in certain directions on a causal level, but it will never change the person at heart, at the core. This requires a personal reflection, a meditation, a triggering stemming from something so uniquely personal that the language spoken can never be misinterpreted. And if we strip things down to a literally skeletal level, what better slogan than the one that powerfully admonishes "do or die": "Memento Mori." Remember that you will die. Everything beyond this is essentially just superstructure invested with egotistic compensations and projections in order to hide behind others. In a way, it is as if these words secretly contain a paradoxical deduction in which the true meaning is no longer "Memento Mori" at all but rather "Memento Vivere": "Remember to Live!"

The Catholic Church responded by becoming even more macabre, if that's even possible. As a reaction to the philosophical tendencies and the very tangible threat of Protestantism, Rome surrected and resurrected ossuaries and relic worship to create phantasmagorical and alluring visual spells for the impoverished populace. Human corpses were dried, pickled in vinegar, and exposed to the sun, not necessarily to salute them or try to philosophically or medically understand the mystery of death, but rather to express Jesuit and other sadomasochistic perversions. In a culture that was visually starved, the Catholic saturation of morbidity obviously held sway over the serfs, much like television and the Internet do today. With colorful and even bejewelled corpses of bishops and other higher-ups, from skeletons in ossuaries to tombs filled with mummies, and the anxious clinging to arbitrary relics, the panic was very much out in the open. A dark, blood-drenched magical thinking in cahoots with a desperate need for crowd control turned the serene Memento Mori philosophy into a medieval Las Vegas spectacle, filled with escapist bling.

And that primitive Catholic superstition seems to still exist. When recently visiting the beautiful medieval town of Visby on the island Gotland off the Swedish Baltic coast, I could read in a guide to the town about the Catholic church there, built in 1982: "The chancel contains both holy relics of Saint Perpetua who was martyred in 203 CE, and a stone from the house in Ephesos (in present-day Turkey), where Jesus' mother Mary is thought to have lived. The latest acquisition, installed in August 2019, is a sample of the blood of Pope John Paul II, sanctified in 2014."[2]

Vesalius's skeleton ponders the destiny of the skull on his table. Although powerful, in many ways it could perhaps be seen as too much of a "double whammy"? A skeleton meditating on a skeleton? Was it even then perhaps too humorous? The hourglass, on the other hand, seemed to be a perfect symbol for temporality and, in extension, mortality. As a time-measuring object or tool it had existed in Babylonia and Egypt some fifteen hundred years before the birth of Christ. But it wasn't until the early Middle Ages that it seeped into European use and iconography.

In Dürer's classic etching *The Knight, Death, and the Devil* of 1513, Death holds up an hourglass to the arrogant-looking knight, while Death's own horse looks down and points to a skull on the ground. The devil figure here seems to assume the function of comic relief in what is, overall, a very grim image. The devil is more of a Boschian cartoon demon than someone instilling existential fear—at least for us today, anyway—whereas Death looks like a bearded skull, or even something ape-like. Perhaps a pre-Darwinian wink to our simian origins? This bearded and hourglass-wielding Dürer Death has since become the icon or symbol of "Father Time." It's certainly less horrifying nowadays, but no less wise and awesome.

As mentioned, Dürer had worked as an apprentice on the relatively jolly *Book of Chronicles* with its protodance of Death, but he seems to have become more preoccupied with time itself rather than literal death as he matured as an artist. The Latin saying *Mors certa, hora incerta* (Death is certain, time is uncertain) seems to have constituted a creative challenge for Dürer. His weirdly powerful "Melancholia" images, with their integration of Saturn as the slow and powerful force of inevitable time, greatly enriched the symbolic palette of medieval art. It integrated alchemical and magical symbolism, too, and cemented the Saturnian sickle not merely as a symbol but as a tangible tool for the proverbial grim reaper.

The grand guru of this time was Heinrich Cornelius Agrippa, who ambitiously formulated cosmic, esoteric thoughts in the same kind of spirit as Hartmann Schedel in his slightly more accessible *Chronicles*. Dürer was interested in Agrippa's writings, not least in his Saturnian focus and its relation to the state of melancholia, and *its* relation to gnostic insights regarding death itself. The melancholic meditation was perhaps a refined development of the by now almost cartoonish dances of death. In Agrippa's words below, he bestows magical abilities upon, or effects of, the Saturnian meditation, which can never really be anything else but the problem of temporality and finality.

> Therefore, we understand a melancholy humor here, to be a natural and white choler. For this, when it is stirred up, burns, and stirs up a madness conducing to knowledge and divination, especially if it be helped by any celestial influx, especially of Saturn, who (seeing he is cold and dry, as is a melancholy humor, hath his influence upon it)

increaseth and preserveth it. Besides, seeing he is the author of secret contemplation, and estranged from all public affairs, and the highest of all the planets, he doth, as he withcalls his mind from outward business, so also make it ascend higher, and bestows upon men the knowledge and presages of future things.[3]

As a coincidence, or auspicious Saturnian synchronicity, when working on this text I found an LP at a flea market with a 1960s recording of Mussorgsky's "Pictures at an Exhibition" (orchestrated by Ravel). I have always greatly enjoyed this dark and dramatic musical masterpiece, and reading the liner notes definitely brought an extra dimension. The exhibition in question consisted of paintings by Mussorgsky's dead friend, the artist Victor Hartmann (yes, another Hartmann!). Each exhibited painting led to a piece of music in celebration of their friendship. Two pieces are of extra interest here: "Catacombae. Sepulchrum Romanum" (meaning Catacombs. Roman Tomb) and the related "Con Mortuis in Lingua Morta" (which, if I'm not entirely mistaken, means With the Dead in the Language of the Dead). For these particular compositions, Mussorgsky made footnotes that read, "The creative spirit of the dead . . . Hartmann leads me to the skulls, and the skulls begin to glow from within."

In the succession of musical pieces, this leads on to "The Hut on Fowl's Legs," based on an image of a Baba Yaga or Witch's Clock, and on to an architectural sketch called "The Great Gate of Kiev" (made for an architectural competition, but the actual construction of the gate never happened). It is in many ways as if a magically aware Mussorgsky brings the sketch to life in his music, thereby honoring the desires of his deceased friend. And the Catacomb paintings were perhaps a moment in their history that bonded them together, to the extent that they both had to express it creatively, albeit in different media.

This in turn led to memories in me, which are similar and actually were triggered by the actual Memento Mori pendant as a talisman of sorts. After my friend had died I quite naturally looked at the necklace, touched it, and thought about its mystery, in combination with photographs and other mementos—as one does when one is grieving. As he and I had been working together on the documentary film series *An Art Apart,* I decided that each film that I made from then on would be made in honor of his memory. This I publicly swore to keep up at his funeral in Copenhagen in August of 2014, and I've honored that vow in each film I've made since then.

It seems to me as if the actual talisman triggered a whole series of cathartic and healing processes in which simply mourning and then moving on just wasn't enough. The powerful image itself, and the fact that he'd had these pieces made for a few select friends, with personalized gems and their initials together, constitutes a deliberate act—a ritual. Its purpose? No doubt to remind us all to appreciate life while it lasts, but also, very delicately humanely, to remind us to not forget about *his* existence and *his* life. What a successful ritual that was and has been all along!

Regardless if he acted on a hunch or on actual knowledge, or if he simply liked the image and wanted to share it in tangible form, the process of relaying a message in symbolic form through art is essentially what constitutes a fully developed human being. On a rudimentary level, most of what we do, animals do much better. But are they sentient in the sense that they are aware of mortality and can convey that awareness to their kin in encouragement of life itself? No. That is a specifically human trait in which our temporarily deflated hubris can actually deal with the paradoxical relationship between our creative, almost divine, ingenious greatness on one hand and our scavenging brutality and cynical shortsightedness on the other.

I have been interested in these philosophical questions since I was a teenager and have swum across many dismally deep oceans of systems, beliefs, and esoteric structures. But this pendant (and its message) has a higher radiance and power (if you will) than *any* philosophy or theory I've come across. It transcends mere intellectual curiosity and understanding, and instead becomes direct knowledge and direct wisdom—that is, something inherently gnostic. The message—*any* message—needs a conduit that touches or moves one to become fully effective. And the best conduit there is, is art.

And here we come to an insight, and an ensuing critique against the life-denying religions: by either militantly denying visual interpretation and anthropomorphizing of the Divine at all, or by focusing on gruesome details and macabre representations for cheap shock value, the potentially practical, altruistic, and inspiring use of Memento Mori-ism is relegated to a sphere of denial and crowd control.

But it also seems that when a phenomenon or just some strong imagery turns mythic, it becomes crystalized in transgenerational minds as a necessary kind of counterforce, lingers on, and reappears over and over again. For example, I mentioned Mussorgsky, but let's not forget Rachmaninov's exquisite music in "Isle of the Dead" nor Saint-Saëns's delightful "Danse Macabre," in which he originally orchestrated a xylophone to illustrate the rattling of skeleton bones come alive. Saint-Saëns's piece was based on a poem by Henri Cazalis.[4] Part of it reads:

> *Tap, tap, tap, what a saraband!*
> *Circles of corpses all holding hands!*
> *Tap, tap, tap, in the throng you can see*
> *King and peasant dancing together!*
> *But shh! Suddenly the dance is ended,*
> *They jostle and take flight—the cock has crowed . . .*
> *Ah! Nocturnal beauty shines on the poor!*
> *And long live death and equality!*

In the nineteenth century there were still allusions and references to the medieval Dances. In our library, we have a wonderful volume called *The English Dance of Death,* originally from 1815, with lovely illustrations by Thomas Rowlandson.[5] Here we are free of the Catholic weight, and instead are exposed to an almost Swiftean mirth in the captions:

Nature and Truth are not at strife:
Death draws his pictures after Life.

On that illumin'd roll of Fame,
Death waits to write your Lordship's name.

The Doctor's sickening toil to close
"Recipe Coffin," is the Dose.

Behold the signal of Old Time:
That bids you close your Pantomime.

And let's not forget the French nineteenth-century dioramas and images containing "diableries": vistas and scenes with the devil humorously interacting with humans, and often flanked by many a skeleton. Let's also not forget the imagery of Mexican death lore and its reigning queen, Santa Muerte, nor Asian tantric meditations in graveyards, nor various ancestor worshippers from different parts of the world paying homage and reverence to their own dead. And while we're at it, let's also recall Ray Harryhausen's sword fighting skeletons in *Jason and the Argonauts* from 1963, and let's absolutely not forget Tim Burton's *Corpse Bride* from 2005, and so on and so forth.

The iconography of any culture is indicative of that culture's overall health. And the basic situation, question, or dilemma integrated in this iconography seems to be a very simple one: do we enhance life in joy, or wallow through sadness and mechanical obedience? Also, how do we look at death itself? Is it integrated as wisdom or relegated to the profitable palaces of denial?

Our contemporary times are permeated by forensic pornography in streamlined screen fiction; an existential dissection in Ultra HD. Today we seemingly have no Vesalius working his poetically medical magic in the service of science and humanity. Our tableaux consist of cold metal slabs illuminated by color-corrected muted greys, with cynic pathologists and forensic technicians in cahoots with nihilistic detectives, cutting up bloated corpses in borderline necrophiliac close-ups. All are victims of heinous crimes, of course. It's no longer a moralistic and quite humorous dance of death but rather a dismal and digital danse macabre for a culture that equates relaxation with literally "checking out" with some new and crispy "pathology-porn."

Our originally woodcut image, on the other hand, is so brilliant in its simplicity, and as a counterpoint to the cynicism of the current Occidental Götterdämmerung. Despite its age, the message couldn't really be any clearer: "Enjoy it while you can, folks. Live it up, love it up, and do it now. Because . . . Eventually, you too will die!"

18

The Quantum Quilt of Inspiration

An Interview with Carl Abrahamsson

By Iris and Matthew Samways
April 2021

What do you think the role of artists is today and how do you relate to this in your own creative pursuits?

The role of artists today is pretty much the same as it always has been and will be: to express themselves in a personal cathartic process, but one that usually also requires acknowledgment from the outside. It's an interesting and culturally necessary process/segment because it not only allows certain creatives to deal with their own neuroses, but also benefits the overarching culture as such with reflective surfaces or facets stemming from emotional, irrational spheres. These are needed for the overall health of the culture. So I would say the artist's role is twofold: one deals with personal issues and balance, and one with a larger perspective. Personally, I might be too aware of these processes

This interview with Carl Abrahamsson was originally published on the website for the Canadian record label Flesh Prison, 2021.

to be able to call myself an artist. Other people do, though, and I'm fine with that. I am quite selfish in the sense that I care more about the benefits I reap myself from these endeavors and pursuits. Whether what I do has any meaning in a bigger picture, I don't know. Time will tell, I guess.

You have met and been around many culturally notable figures. How have they influenced you? Are there specific moments/meetings that have changed your perspective in a substantial way?

Absolutely. Some people I have actively sought out, and some have come via more chance-like elements, or by association, like links in the chain of life. This has been true for artists and magicians alike. In some cases they have even been one and the same. I think they have mainly influenced me by proxy and inspiration (a very important word/phenomenon for me). I have not wanted to emulate but rather be amazed at what's possible to achieve; whether that is a mind frame, a kind of work, a technique, a language, a network, or what have you. In a way, they have basically all contributed to what I call my "quantum quilt"—a personal mosaic of impressions that leads on to hopefully equally inspiring expressions. But that's also valid for people one meets in general. The important people are not always celebrities or artists—they can equally well come from the sphere of family and friends.

In the making of your solo album Reseduction, *what was the creation process like compared to your usual collaborative releases? Did you find it more introspective by default?*

The creative process is basically the same as in a collaborative work. When collaborating, it's been a long time since I actually sat down in the same physical space with someone and worked together in the traditional meaning of the word. So basically, I do my thing—whether it's writing/reading or making the music (or both)—pretty much in creative seclusion and then I just offer it to the outside. In terms of introspection, I would say the same amount is more or less always present.

On the album it sounds like you are using recorded loops of your voice but there are also other sources of noise that make up the background (although at times the sounds do enter the foreground or blur the lines). How did you decide which sounds to pair in each track?

Very spontaneously. In each moment, there are choices to make and usually a selection of possible avenues. I just go for what sounds good. The meaning—if there is such a thing—is always in the words themselves. Perhaps whatever is mixed in (if we're talking about sounds from "reality") has an additional or amplifying potential, but the creative moment as such plays a larger part.

In some of your tracks, notably the title track "Reseduction" as well as "Do Easy Does It," you seem to make use of the cut-up technique developed by Brion Gysin and William S. Burroughs. Do you see the influence of this method in this project or do you find that other methods influence you more heavily?

The cut-up method is there at times, especially in assemblage; in the decisions about how to put things together. In terms of specific cultural background when it comes to my creativity—both in terms of words and music—of course that sphere has been hugely inspiring. But when it comes to this kind of writing that I use for the musical pieces nowadays, I guess it's more a question of stream of consciousness. I just flow and see where the pen takes me. I very rarely use the cut-up method anymore in actual writing. Instead, I use a strongly related kind of mind frame that allows for an unrestrained association process I not only favor but also advocate.

There seems to be a cultural stagnation because of the COVID-19 pandemic. What do you feel about the state of culture now? How would you compare it to your younger years when Industrial Music was emerging, Psychic TV began, and TOPY began—including the TOPYSCAN Access Point site you started. Where do you think we will go from here?

This is a big question! Public and social interactions have certainly been affected and in many ways isolated, so perhaps that could be seen as a stagnation in terms of a way of interacting, compared to what we have previously been used to. But in terms of creative processes, I actually can't see that changing too much. Certainly not in my own case—both my wife and I have been more creative than ever during this first year of pandemic isolation—and I think it's true for many other people, too. Creatives will always find a platform or an avenue to share what they've created: that's part of their psychological makeup. As for old versus new, there's always a risk of becoming too nostalgic and claiming that it was better in the old days. But I don't think so. It's just different now. A different time, with different givens. The creative urge remains intact.

As someone who has worked in the role of interviewer, listener, and recorder in the mediums of video, photography, and writing, by default you have played a role in preserving the past. What are your thoughts on the insubstantiality of the past in terms of preservation, and what do you think is the best way to share the more nuanced parts of life with future generations?

The best way is definitely through art—whatever or whichever this art may be. Seen from a short-term perspective, culture is a vibrant mosaic, and it's a very dynamic and malleable organism. It's from this pool that short-term history is written or recorded: it's a war of volume and nepotisms! In a really long-term perspective, it's more strictly only art that remains. Theories and traditions may come and go, as will trends within the writing of history itself. But those firsthand sources are always more revealing than any later interpretations of them. You could argue that Pompeii is one of the largest works of art we have when it comes to interpreting and understanding Western roots. Architecture that remains, sculptures, cave paintings, fragments of books, magical or even domestic tools and utensils—these are the real building blocks not only of the past but also of the future. Digital culture as such will be completely gone in the future. Museums and libraries will have to be protected—they have potential. As for my own part, books are without a doubt the most important thing; tangible books, stored in libraries in different places. I love to actively preserve the past, concretely through, for instance, interview work, but also in interpreting older history. Connecting the dots! I think it will be hard for future generations to understand that there actually were intelligent people around in the early twenty-first century. In a way, I see that as part of my job: to preserve those people and those minds, as well as their artworks.

What do you hope listeners will experience listening to Reseduction? *Are you perhaps looking to invite questions about disintegration/repetition, or do you have other intentions?*

I have no intentions whatsoever on that level. I just love making these weird pieces of sounds and words. One by one they create a mass that we're used to calling an "album." People will listen to that mass and be affected by it in different ways. It's a fascinating process. Of course, I hope that they will have a positive and inspiring experience, but if that happens it is more like a bonus for me, after I'm pleased with the work myself.

Notes

FOREWORD

1. Breyer P-Orridge, *Thee Grey Book*. As republished in Breyer P-Orridge et al., *Thee Psychick Bible*, 37.

2. WE'RE ON THE ROAD TO SOMEWHERE

1. Goodrich-Clarke, ed., *Paracelsus*, 144.
2. Montaigne, *Complete Works*, 451.
3. Humboldt, "Steppes and Deserts," 427.
4. Humboldt, "Steppes and Deserts," 645.
5. Jünger, *Details of Time*, 98.

3. PANIC PILGRIMAGE

1. Bowles, letter to Peggy Glanville-Hicks in Miller, ed., *In Touch*, 268–269.
2. Bowles, *Music of Morocco*, 49.
3. Breyer P-Orridge, et al., *Brion Gysin*, 377.
4. Breyer P-Orridge, et al., *Brion Gysin*, 72–73.
5. Originally released in 1986 on the album *William S. Burroughs: Break Through in Grey Room*, issued by Sub Rosa Records.
6. Burroughs, "Face to Face," 94.

4. INTO A TIME AND SPACE OF WORDSHIP

1. Breyer P-Orridge, *Sacred Intent*, 303.
2. Breyer P-Orridge, *Sacred Intent*, 293.
3. *Change Itself*, directed by Carl Abrahamsson.

4. Breyer P-Orridge, *Sacred Intent,* 20.

5. Breyer P-Orridge, *Sacred Intent,* 28.

5. TEMPORARILY ETERNAL

1. Goldsmith, ed., *I'll Be Your Mirror.*

2. Breyer P-Orridge, "Thee Mourning Nudes" in Abrahamsson, ed., *Here To Go 2014,* 69.

3. Breyer P-Orridge, "Virtual Mirrors," 271.

4. *Change Itself,* directed by Carl Abrahamsson.

5. Breyer P-Orridge, "Dark Room of Desire" in Abrahamsson, ed., *Fenris Wolf 5,* 106.

6. Bender and Taylor, eds., *Uniforms, Organization and History.*

7. Breyer P-Orridge, *S/He Is (Still) Her/e,* 274.

8. Breyer P-Orridge, "Thee Mourning Nudes" in Abrahamsson, ed., *Here To Go 2014,* 74.

6. TRIPPING THE DARK LIGHT FANTASTIC

1. O'Pray, "Derek Jarman's Cinema" in *Afterimage* (no. 12), 9.

2. O'Pray, "Derek Jarman's Cinema" in *Afterimage* (no. 12), 12.

3. Jarman, *Dancing Ledge,* 129.

4. Fowler, "Many Faces" in *Jarman: Volume One, 1972–1986,* 6.

5. Christopherson, "The Angelic Conversation: On the Music" in *Jarman: Volume One, 1972–1986,* 41.

6. Jarman quoted in Fowler, "Many Faces," 5.

7. O'Pray and Field, "Imaging October," 49.

8. O'Pray and Field, "Imaging October," 50.

7. MONDO TRANSCRIPTO!

1. Alberto Moravia, narration-text for the film *Mondo Magic.*

2. Ballard, *Atrocity Exhibition,* 70.

3. Ballard in Goodall, *Sweet and Savage,* 7.

4. Ballard in Goodall, *Sweet and Savage,* 7.

5. Goodall, *Sweet and Savage,* 11.

6. Landis and Clifford, *Sleazoid Express,* 160.

7. Jacopetti in Goodall, *Sweet and Savage,* 228.

8. Livingstone, letter to Horace Waller.

9. Conrad, "Heart of Darkness" in *Portable Conrad,* 587.

8. THE PRISONER WILL
SET YOU FREE

1. "Change of Mind," *The Prisoner.*

2. "Fall Out," *The Prisoner.*

3. Wilson, *Outsider,* 290.

4. McGoohan in White and Ali, eds., *Official Prisoner Companion,* 178.

5. McGoohan in *Six Into One,* directed by Laurens Postma.

6. *Magus,* Wikipedia.

7. Bergonzi, "Bouillabaisse."

8. Bergonzi, "Bouillabaisse."

9. Fowles, *Aristos,* 170.

10. Huxley, *Brave New World,* 214.

11. Huxley, "Culture and the Individual" in Solomon, ed., *LSD,* 38.

12. Crowley, in Beta, ed., *Equinox 3 issue 10,* 144.

13. Fowles in Vipond, ed., *Conversations,* 161.

14. Fowles, *Aristos,* 124.

9. "OUR LIFE COULD
AT LEAST BE DOUBLED"

1. Machiavelli, *The Prince,* 50.

2. Dalí, *50 Secrets of Magic Craftsmanship,* 95.

10. EMBRACING MAGICAL REALISM

1. *Nomad,* directed by Werner Herzog.

2. Chesterton in Aragon, *Paris Peasant,* 202.

3. Hesse, *Journey,* 8.

4. Jünger, *Forest Passage,* 29.

5. Hesse in *Steppenwolf,* 39.

6. Orwell, "Writers and Leviathan," 344.

7. Aragon, *Paris Peasant,* 204.

8. Aragon, *Paris Peasant,* 201.

9. Aragon, *Paris Peasant,* 177.

10. Aragon, *Paris Peasant,* 202.

11. LITERCHOOR, KULCHUR, AND
A DAMNED FINE FRIENDSHIP

1. Pound, *Literary Essays*, 60.

2. Pound, *Literary Essays*, 58.

3. Laughlin, *The Way It Wasn't*, 219.

4. Eliot, *Waste Land*, 45.

5. Pound, *ABC of Reading*, 62.

6. Pound, *ABC of Reading*, 29.

7. Pound, *Guide to Kulchur*, 126.

8. Pound, *Guide to Kulchur*, 137.

9. Pound, *Literary Essays*, 298.

10. Gordon, ed., *Pound and Laughlin: Selected Letters*, 113.

11. Gordon, ed., *Pound and Laughlin: Selected Letters*, 114.

12. Gordon, ed., *Pound and Laughlin: Selected Letters*, 134.

13. Gordon, ed., *Pound and Laughlin: Selected Letters*, 135.

14. Barnhisel and Laughlin, *New Directions*, 15.

15. Gordon, ed., *Pound and Laughlin: Selected Letters*, 283.

16. Ginsberg, "Allen Verbatim" in *Paideuma*, 268.

12. SPARE ME A POUND

1. Cornell in Carpenter, *Serious Character*, 723.

2. Pound, *ABC of Reading*, 83.

3. Pound, *ABC of Reading*, 84.

4. Pound, "Teacher's Mission" in *Literary Essays of Ezra Pound*, 59.

5. Spare, *Book of Pleasure (Self-Love)*, 26.

6. Grant, introduction in Spare, *Book of Pleasure (Self-Love)*, viii.

7. Carpenter, *Serious Character*, 395.

8. Carpenter, *Serious Character*, 395.

9. Pound, *Cantos*, 254.

10. Rachewiltz, "Pagan and Magic Elements" in Hesse, ed., *New Approaches*, 195.

11. Spare, *Book of Pleasure (Self-Love)*, 13.

12. Spare, *Book of Pleasure (Self-Love)*, 17.

13. Pound, "Translator's Postscript" in Gourmont, *Natural Philosophy of Love*, 169.

14. Pound, "Translator's Postscript" in Gourmont, *Natural Philosophy of Love*, 178.

13. SOME THOUGHTS ON
A RECENT PARADIGM SHIFT

1. Goethe, "Art and Antiquity" in *Maxims and Reflections*, 17.
2. Castaneda, *Power of Silence*, 103.

14. THE MAGIC OF INDIVIDUATION

1. Jung, *Earth Has a Soul*, 86.
2. Goethe, "Art and Antiquity" in *Maxims and Reflections*, 16.
3. Jung, *Earth Has a Soul*, 98.

15. LUX PER NOX

1. LaVey, *Satanic Bible*, 25.
2. Wilson, "Green Man," 26.
3. Ström, *Nordisk Hedendom*, 182.
4. Voluspa / "Valans Spådom," 12.
5. Eliade, *Eternal Return*, 78.

16. THE IMAGINARY IS
A REAL THING

1. Levack, ed., *Witchcraft Sourcebook*, i.
2. Inglis, *Forbidden Game*, 23.
3. Inglis, *Forbidden Game*, 23.
4. Inglis, *Forbidden Game*, 168.
5. Tilton, ed., *Touch Me Not*.
6. Grey, *Apocalyptic Witchcraft*, 102–103.
7. Grey, *Apocalyptic Witchcraft*, 80.
8. Hofmann, "Challenging Question" in Wasson, et al., *Road to Eleusis*, 44.
9. Hofmann, "Challenging Question" in Wasson, et al., *Road to Eleusis*, 36.
10. Hofmann, *LSD*, 6.
11. Levack, ed., *Witchcraft Sourcebook*, i.

17. MEMENTO MORI FOREVER

1. Tuchman, *Distant Mirror,* 505.

2. Gotlands Museum, *Explore Visby.*

3. Agrippa, *Occult Philosophy,* 186–7.

4. Henri Cazalis, "Danse Macabre," Oxfordlieder (website).

5. Rowlandson, et al., *English Dance of Death,* 112, 118, 161, 207.

Bibliography

Abrahamsson, Carl, director. *Change Itself—An Art Apart: Genesis Breyer P-Orridge. Trapart Films, Sweden.* 2016. 58 mins.

———. *The Fenris Wolf 5.* Stockholm: Trapart Books, 2020.

———. ed. *Here to Go 2014.* Stockholm: Edda Publishing, 2012.

Agrippa, Heinrich Cornelius. *Three Books of Occult Philosophy or Magic.* New York: Samuel Weiser, Inc., 1973.

Aragon, Louis. *Paris Peasant.* Boston: Exact Change, 1994.

Ballard, J. G. *The Atrocity Exhibition.* San Francisco: RE/Search Publications, 1990.

Barnhisel, Gregory, and James Laughlin. *New Directions and the Remaking of Ezra Pound.* Amherst, Mass.: University of Massachusetts Press, 2005.

Bender, Roger James, and Hugh Page Taylor, eds. *Uniforms, Organization and History of the Waffen* SS. 5 vols. San José, Calif.: James Bender Publishing, 1969.

Bergonzi, Bernard. "Bouillabaisse." Review of *The Magus,* by John Fowles. *The New York Review of Books* (website), March 17, 1966.

Beta, Hymenaeus, ed. *Liber OZ.* In *The Equinox* 3, issue 10. New York: 93 Publishing, 1990.

Bowles, Paul. Liner notes to *Music of Morocco* from the Library of Congress. Recorded by Paul Bowles. Atlanta, Ga.: Dust to Digital, 2016.

Breyer P-Orridge, Genesis, et al. *Brion Gysin: His Name Was Master.* Stockholm: Trapart Books, 2018.

———. *Genesis Breyer P-Orridge: Sacred Intent—Conversations with Carl Abrahamsson 1986–2019.* Stockholm: Trapart Books, 2020.

———. *Thee Grey Book.* As republished in Genesis Breyer P-Orridge et al., *Thee Psychick Bible,* Port Townsend, Wash.: Feral House, 2009.

———. *S/He Is (Still) Her/e.* London: First Third Books, 2013.

———. "Virtual Mirrors in Solid Time." In *Thee Psychick Bible: Thee Apocryphal Scriptures Ov Genesis Breyer P-Orridge and Thee Third Mind Ov Thee Temple Ov Psychick Youth.* Port Townsend, Wash.: Feral House, 2006.

Burroughs, William S. "Face to Face with the Goat God." *OUI,* August 1973.

Burroughs, William S. *Break Through in Grey Room.* Sub Rosa, 1986. LP.

Carpenter, Humphrey. *A Serious Character: The Life of Ezra Pound.* London: Faber and Faber, 1988.

Castenada, Carlos. *The Power of Silence: Further Lessons of Don Juan,* New York: Washington Square Press, 1987.

Cazalis, Henri. "Danse Macabre." Oxford Lieder website, Songs.

Chesterton, G. K. In Louis Aragon, *Paris Peasant.* Boston: Exact Change, 1994.

Christopherson, Peter. "The World Ended a Long Time Ago." In *Glitterbox: Derek Jarman X 4.* (DVD box booklet). Zeitgeist Video, 2008.

Conrad, Joseph. "Heart of Darkness." In *The Portable Conrad.* New York: The Viking Press, 1947.

Dalí, Salvador. *50 Secrets of Magic Craftsmanship.* New York: Dover Publications, 1992.

Eliade, Mircea. *The Myth of the Eternal Return: Cosmos and History.* Princeton, N.J.: Bollingen Series, Princeton University Press, 1954.

Eliot, T. S., *The Waste Land,* Ann Arbor, Mich.: Borders Classics, 2007.

Fowler, William. "The Many Faces of Derek Jarman." In the booklet *Jarman: Volume One, 1972–1986* that accompanies the five-disc BluRay box set. London: BFI Studio, 2017.

Fowles, John. *The Aristos.* London: Pan Books, 1978.

Ginsberg, Allen. "Allen Verbatim." In *Paideuma: Modern and Contemporary Poetry and Poetics* 3, no. 2 (1974): 268.

Goethe, Johann Wolfgang von. *Maxims and Reflections.* London: Penguin Books, 1998.

Goldsmith, Kenneth, ed. *I'll Be Your Mirror: The Selected Andy Warhol Interviews.* New York: Carroll and Graf, 2004.

Goodall, Mark. *Sweet and Savage: The World Through the Mondo Film Lens.* London: Headpress, 2018.

Goodrich-Clarke, Nicholas, ed. *Paracelsus: Essential Readings*. Wellingborough, England: Crucible, 1990.

Gordon, David, ed. *Ezra Pound and James Laughlin: Selected Letters*. New York: Norton, 1994.

Gotlands Museum. *Explore Visby*. Visby, Sweden. 2020.

Gourmont, Remy. *The Natural Philosophy of Love*. New York: Rarity Press, 1931.

Grant, Kenneth. "Introduction." In Austin Osman Spare, *The Book of Pleasure (Self-Love): The Psychology of Ecstasy*. Quebec City, Canada: 93 Publishing, 1975.

Grey, Peter. *Apocalyptic Witchcraft*. London: Scarlet Imprint, 2013.

Herzog, Werner, director. *Nomad: In the Footsteps of Bruce Chatwin*. BBC, UK, 2019. 85 mins.

Hesse, Eva, ed., *New Approaches to Ezra Pound*. Berkeley: University of California Press, 1969.

Hesse, Hermann. Author's note in *Steppenwolf*. Harmondsworth, England: Penguin Books, 1965.

———. *The Journey to the East*. Eastford, Conn.: Martino Fine Books, 2011.

Hofmann, Albert. *LSD: My Problem Child*. New York: McGraw-Hill, 1980.

Humboldt, Alexander von. "Concerning the Steppes and Deserts." In *Selected Writings of Alexander von Humboldt*. Andrea Wulf, ed. New York: Everyman's Library/Knopf, 2018.

Huxley, Aldous. *Brave New World*. Hamburg: Albatross Verlag, 1933.

Inglis, Brian. *The Forbidden Game: A Social History of Drugs*. New York: Scribner, 1975.

Jacopetti, Gualtiero. In Mark Goodall, *Sweet and Savage: The World Through the Mondo Film Lens*. London: Headpress, London, 2018.

Jarman, Derek. *Dancing Ledge*. Minneapolis, Minnesota: University of Minnesota Press, 2010.

Jung, Carl. *The Earth Has a Soul: C. G. Jung on Nature, Technology and Modern Life*. Berkeley: North Atlantic Books, 2002.

———. "Projection and Imagination in Alchemy." In ed. Nathan Schwartz-Salant, *Jung on Alchemy*. Princeton, N.J.: Princeton University Press, 1995.

Jünger, Ernst. *The Details of Time: Conversations with Ernst Jünger*. New York: Marsilio Publishers, 1995.

————. *The Forest Passage.* Candor, N.Y.: Telos Press, 2013.

Landis, Bill, and Michelle Clifford. *Sleazoid Express: A Mind-Twisting Tour Through the Grindhouse Cinema of Times Square.* New York: Fireside Books, 2002.

Laughlin, James. *The Way It Wasn't: From the Files of James Laughlin.* New York: New Directions, 2006.

LaVey, Anton. *The Satanic Bible.* New York: Avon Books, 1969.

Levack, Brian P., ed. *The Witchcraft Sourcebook.* New York: Routledge, 2004.

Livingstone, David. Letter to Horace Waller. February 5, 1871. Private collection.

Machiavelli, Niccolo. *The Prince.* New York: The New American Library, 1952.

Miller, Jeffrey, ed. *In Touch: The Letters of Paul Bowles.* New York: Noonday, 1994.

Montaigne, Michel. *The Complete Works.* New York: Everyman's Library/ Knopf, 2003.

O'Pray, Michael, ed. "Derek Jarman's Cinema: Eros and Thanatos." In (No. 12) — *Derek Jarman.* London: Afterimage (no. 12), 1985.

O'Pray, Michael, and Simon Field, eds. "On Imaging October, Dr. Dee, and Other Matters: An Interview with Derek Jarman." In (No. 12)—*Derek Jarman.* London: Afterimage, 1985.

Orwell, George. "Writers and Leviathan." In *All Art Is Propaganda: Critical Essays.* Boston: Mariner Books, 2009.

Postma, Laurens, director. *Six into One: The Prisoner File.* Illuminations, Wider Television Access, 1984. 58 mins.

Pound, Ezra. *ABC of Reading.* London: Faber and Faber, 1991.

————. *The Cantos of Ezra Pound.* New York: New Directions, 1993.

————. *Guide to Kulchur.* London: Peter Owen, 1952.

————. *Literary Essays of Ezra Pound.* New York: New Directions, 1968.

————. "The Teacher's Mission." In *Literary Essays of Ezra Pound.* New York: New Directions, 1968.

Prisoner, The. "A Change of Mind." Dec. 31, 1967. Season 1, episode 11, directed by Patrick McGoohan, Everyman/ITC.

————. "Fall Out" Feb. 1, 1968, Season 1, episode 16, directed by Patrick McGoohan, Everyman/ITC.

Rowlandson, Thomas, et al. *The English Dance of Death.* London: Methuen and Co., 1903.

"Sången om Vavtrudner," paragraph 53, page 49. In *Eddan,* Niloe, Stockholm, 1982.

Solomon, David, ed. *LSD: The Consciousness-Expanding Drug.* New York: Putnam Berkley Medallion, 1964.

Spare, Austin Osman. *The Book of Pleasure (Self-Love): The Psychology of Ecstasy.* Quebec City, Canada: 93 Publishing, 1975.

Ström, Folke. *Nordisk Hedendom: Tro och sed i förkristen tid,* Akademiförlaget/ Esselte Studium, Stockholm, 1985.

Tilton, Hereford, ed. *Touch Me Not: A Most Rare Compendium of the Whole Magical Art.* Somerset, UK: Fulgur Press, 2017.

Tuchman, Barbara. *A Distant Mirror: The Calamitous 14th Century.* Harmondsworth, England: Penguin Books, 1978.

Vipond, Dianne L., ed. *Conversations with John Fowles.* Jackson, Mississippi: University Press of Mississippi, 1999.

Voluspa / "Valans Spådom," paragraph 44, page 12. As published in *Eddan,* Niloe, Stockholm, 1982.

Wasson, Gordon, et al. *The Road to Eleusis: Unveiling the Secret of the Mysteries.* Berkeley: North Atlantic Books, 2008.

White, Matthew and Jaffer Ali, eds. *The Official Prisoner Companion.* New York: Warner Books, 1988.

Wilson, Colin. *The Outsider.* London: Picador Pan Macmillan, 1978.

Wilson, Peter Lamborn. "The Green Man: The Trickster Figure in Sufism." *Gnosis* 19. San Francisco, 1991.

Books by
Carl Abrahamsson

INNER TRADITIONS/PARK STREET PRESS

Occulture: The Unseen Forces That Drive Culture Forward (2018)

Anton LaVey and the Church of Satan: Infernal Wisdom from the Devil's Den (2022)

BOOKS PUBLISHED BY OTHERS

Free of the Darkness: 136 Photographs from Russia (2022)

It's Magic Monday Every Day of the Week (with Vanessa Sinclair, 2021)

Genesis P-Orridge: Temporarily Eternal: Photographs 1986–2018 (2021)

Different People: Conversations on Art, Life, and the Creative Process (2021)

The Mega Golem: A Womanual for All Times and Spaces (with Vanessa Sinclair and others, 2021)

In Too Deep (2021)

The Devil's Footprint (2020)

Genesis Breyer P-Orridge: Sacred Intent: Conversations with Carl Abrahamsson 1986–2019 (2020)

Reasonances (2014)

Mother, Have A Safe Trip (2013)

Fanzinera: Photographs 1985–1988 (2012)

The Fenris Wolf (an irregular journal, 1989 to the present day)

Index

Page numbers in *italics* refer to illustrations.